VETERANS

VETERANS

The Last Survivors of the Great War

Richard van Emden

Steve Humphries

Accompanies the major BBC1 documentary

Leo Cooper

First published in 1998,
reprinted 1998, 1999 by
LEO COOPER
an imprint of
Pen & Sword Books Ltd
47 Church Street
Barnsley
South Yorkshire
S70 2AS

A CIP read for this book is available from the British Library

ISBN 0 85052 640 X

CONTENTS

ACKNOWLEDGEMENTS

We would like to thank all the people who have helped us in writing this book, with especial thanks to Michael Jackson, Alan Yentob, Peter Salmon and Sam Organ for supporting the BBC1 programmes on which this book is based.

We are also grateful to other members of the Testimony Films team, particularly Andy Attenburrow and Mary Parsons, for excellent additional research and editorial help. Thanks are also due to Miriam Akhtar, Lucy Swingler, Hilary Jelbert, Madge Reed, Mike Humphries, Steve Hasket and Mike Pharey, the cameramen, and the sound recordist, Jeff John.

We would like to thank Roni Wilkinson for his enthusiastic perseverance in turning around this book in such a short space of time, and Henry Wilson and Charles Hewitt for their support. We would also like to thank Joan and Wolfgang van Emden for their help in editing and proof-reading each chapter of this book – even on holiday!

For their support and advice, we are grateful to Peter Barton, Dennis Goodwin, Jonathan Hupfield and David Bilton.

Lastly, and most importantly, we wish to thank all the contributors to this project, the men and the women whose vivid memories from over eighty years ago have enabled us to write a book which we hope is a fitting tribute to their courage and endeavour. We would also like to make special mention of those veterans who were filmed for the BBC1 documentary, but whose invaluable stories do not appear in this book: Bill Cotgrove, Dick Trafford, William Lunn, Smiler Marshall, Alfred Wood, Jack Davis, Tom Brennan, Alfred Henn, Sydney James, Harold Judd, William Hall, and Allen Short.

PICTURE CREDITS

The authors and publisher would like to acknowledge the following for their permission to reproduce the photographs.

The Imperial War Museum, London

The Taylor Library, Barnsley

The Tank Museum, Bovington

Dedicated to Harry Patch, aged 100,
former private in the 7th Duke of
Cornwall's Light Infantry, and to the
memory of the Lewis Gun team he lost,
22nd September 1917.

Introduction

THE GREAT WAR, one of the most catastrophic and traumatic wars in human history, will very soon be beyond living memory. It is now eighty years since it ended. This book and the BBC television programmes it accompanies were commissioned to commemorate the eightieth anniversary of its ending. It seemed that this was the last chance to tell the story of the First World War through the first person testimony of the men and women who experienced it and whose lives were shaped by it. The aim was to retrieve the memories of the tiny and dwindling band of survivors from the heady days of 1914 and 1915 when two and a half million young men volunteered to serve King and Country. In the following years, they would face the shocking reality of modern, industrial warfare, witnessing the deaths of many close friends and comrades. More than a million servicemen from Britain and her Commonwealth and Empire would die on active service. Two million more would be injured or maimed. How these men, some as young as sixteen or seventeen, coped with this maelstrom and then lived with the memory is, for later generations, a source of abiding fascination and respect.

As well as documenting the men's experiences, we also wanted to record the memories of the women, some of whom served alongside them. They too played an important and often forgotten role in the war. We wanted to hear from the nurses who tended the soldiers' injuries, the canary girls who risked their lives making shells in the munitions factories, the wives and sweethearts who lived in terror of the telegram boy, and the daughters, still in school, who would never see their father again.

How much would these men and women, now in their late nineties and early hundreds, actually remember? Would the historical detail and drama they lived through still be fresh? Would the emotional hurt still remain? How did it feel to look back across eighty years at such a cataclysmic event? How did they cope with the loss and sacrifice suffered by so many? These were just a few of the many questions we asked.

But to start with, there was the daunting challenge of finding the people to talk to. The men and women of the First World War form a kind of lost community. There are probably around 4,000 men still alive who fought, perhaps 200 nurses who worked behind the lines, maybe 1,000 munitions workers. A tiny handful of the most active veterans still attend the Cenotaph each year and return to the Western Front to remember their fallen friends every summer and autumn. These are relatively easy to contact through the ever helpful Veterans Associations, such as the World War One Veterans Association and the Western Front Association, which still organises reunions and activities. However, most veterans have completely lost touch with their old comrades and have no contact with any First World War organisation. This isolation and anonymity is even more pronounced with women who served and worked in the war. A few organisations like the Red Cross and Queen Alexandra's Nursing Sisters have until very recently kept in touch with a handful of elderly nurses, but apart from this nobody knows how many are still alive, where they are or what their stories might be.

In trying to track down the survivors of this ancient, lost community, it has been my enormous good fortune to work with Richard van Emden. When I first met Richard around four years ago, he astounded me by claiming to have been in personal contact with one hundred and twenty First World War veterans. He had been obsessively collecting them, almost like a vanishing species, tape-recording their memories and photographing them for over ten years. A few of these old soldiers have been interviewed again and this time filmed for our project. But a contact book bristling with centenarians can within two or three years dwindle to almost nothing, and sadly before "Veterans" had got under way, many of Richard's veterans had died or were too ill to be interviewed.

We virtually had to start again. Over the last fifteen months we have made a determined last attempt to uncover the men and women of the Great War. We have placed letters in almost every local newspaper in Britain, contacted hundreds of old people's homes, combed through agencies that specialise in working with old people, spoken to a long list of museums and libraries, made appeals on local radio, and pleaded with others working in the field for names and addresses. The response has been generous and overwhelming. Many hundreds of people have helped us with leads on friends, neighbours and relatives, or occasionally with details of veterans they had themselves tape-recorded. We seemed to have tapped into a genuine feeling that the memories of these men and women should not be lost forever.

We have discovered around 120 new veterans in our research. A few died before we even met them. Others, we were told, had only fading memories and were too ill to withstand an interview. The veterans were scattered all over Britain, and with little time to spare we had to be selective about whom we met and whom we filmed. The average age of the twenty-five veterans who feature in this book is 101, and twenty-one are centenarians. The oldest veteran is nearly 105, the youngest just 95 (he was thirteen when he went to France). The interviews were carried out in two stages. Richard first recorded the stories with a tape recorder, and then those with the most pertinent memories would be filmed. Our criteria for this selection were the vividness of their experiences and a range of stories that would enable us to cover a wide spectrum of events and issues throughout the war.

Men who survive into their late nineties and early hundreds are overwhelmingly middle class, and this was reflected in the veterans we spoke to. Many seemed to have been retired accountants, office managers, and headmasters, who had preserved body and mind through lives of quiet professional service. Some, like Tom Dewing and Fred Hodges, had extraordinary memories which we recorded. But we made a special effort to document soldiers who came from a more humble background. In 1914 Britain was a rigid, class-ridden society, rooted in manufacturing industry and three quarters of the men who joined up were working class. Very few have survived to a great age, and because of this, their voices have rarely been heard in previous oral histories of the Great War. However, they form more than a third of the interviewees who appear in this book. Amongst them is Royce McKenzie, a battalion runner on the Western Front and one of the few ex-miners who has survived the ravages of industrial disease to reach one hundred years old.

Once we made contact with a veteran who still had vivid memories, we tried to film him straight away. It was a race against time, a point that was powerfully brought home to us in November 1997 when two veterans whom we were just about to film died within a week. Five of the soldiers featured in this book died shortly after we filmed them. Like all those we interviewed, they were aware that they had little time left to live. This gave an added urgency to the filming – but the interviews were rarely sombre. Most of the men and women were facing death with great courage and humour. If they were frightened, they certainly weren't showing it. Often they would laughingly quip "You'd better hurry up and get on with it. I won't be here for much longer". Many of them, as young men, had expected to die during the war – they felt privileged and often amused to have survived for so long.

We found just over half our interviewees lived, as one might expect, in nursing homes and sheltered accommodation. I was surprised, though, how many were quite independent, living by themselves (or in one or two cases with their wives), despite their frailty and failing eyesight. Often there would be a relative nearby to help cook, clean and look after the garden. In a few extraordinary cases, veterans continue to live like men who have just retired. Most remarkable is Hal Kerridge, now aged 100, who could easily pass for seventy. When we interviewed him in March 1998, he was living a completely independent life, tending his immaculately furnished detached bungalow near Bournemouth and driving round in his Audi.

To meet and talk to people of such a great age, about some of their most intimate memories, is an awesome experience. I have interviewed many people, but these were different. To speak to men and women born in Victorian England, brought up at the height of Empire when wars were still fought on horseback, provides a rare glimpse into a twilight world that has almost passed beyond reach.

Amazingly, though television arrived in their lives only when they were about to draw old age pensions, they were in no way fazed by the lights, the camera and the film crew which invaded their living rooms. When the camera started turning, there was sometimes an initial period of awkwardness and embarrassment, as they got used to being interviewed. But then most blossomed. Even those who were ill and very frail seemed to find a new vitality. They told their stories in the most moving detail, creating an unforgettable picture of their wartime experiences. Relatives and carers told us it was the performance of their lives. Many said afterwards they had wanted to do justice to the memory of their comrades and friends, most of whom died long ago. This was their tribute to a lost generation.

Tom Dewing, aged 102. Tom was a signaller in the Royal Engineers and is one of the last survivors to witness the slaughter on the first day of the Battle of the Somme in July 1916, the worst day in the history of the British Army. A former headmaster, he continues to live a quietly independent life.

The intimacy and emotional power of these interviews is at the heart of what is new about this book. The stories it contains certainly won't make military historians change their interpretation of the major battles of the First World War. Our intention has instead been to focus on the private lives and feelings of the men who fought, and of the women both on the battlefield and back home. For many years, these experiences have been deeply buried, too painful to be recalled. But in the last two decades, veterans have started to talk of the war with an honesty and depth of feeling that was almost impossible before the 1970s. Significantly, most of our interviewees have begun to talk about what happened to them only in the last few years. Now in their nineties and hundreds, they have finally decided to unburden themselves of memories which have haunted them for a lifetime. Their passion to tell how it was, is of real historical significance. There are, of course, a number of well-known diaries and autobiographies which dig deep into wartime angst. But the emotional experience of the men and women who lived and fought through the Great War has remained largely hidden from history.

Each chapter in the book intertwines personal testimony with the bigger military and social themes of the war. Within the book there is also a broad chronology moving forward from 1914 to 1918. It begins with the call to arms, the journey to the front line, working and fighting on the Western Front and contact with home. It continues with the Battle of the Somme in 1916, front line medical care for the dying and the injured, death and the sense of loss and bereavement, the physical and mental damage done by the war, the important role played by women on the home front and the experience of British Prisoners of War. It ends with the road to victory in Europe in 1918, and finally reflections on the war's conclusion and aftermath. Each chapter opens with an introductory overview which sets the background to the personal testimonies that follow.

Time and space have prevented us from documenting the experiences of survivors in every theatre of war. The war at sea, for example, has had to be omitted. Our main focus has been the Western Front – generally acknowledged to have had the greatest impact and significance for British servicemen. Through the testimonies that follow, we have tried to convey something of the courage, dignity, humour, and the humanity of the last survivors of the Great War. We hear the authentic voice of the infantryman, the officer, the prisoner, the signaller, the nurse, the stretcher bearer. Through these stories, we can perhaps better understand what fighting and living through the First World War really meant.

Steve Humphries
September 1998

CHAPTER ONE

Joining Up

THE poster of Kitchener with his hand outstretched, finger pointing, remains to this day one of the most enduring images from the First World War. The face of the Secretary of State for War was plastered on almost every street corner, on pillar boxes and street hordings, and is still commonly referred to by every soldier who joined up in the British army, over eighty years ago. The eyes, looking straight down the gun-barrel arm and pointing finger, appeared to make the poster's appeal personal and inescapable and ensured a guilty conscience for any man not in uniform. Kitchener's unprecedented call to arms in August and September 1914 saw recruiting offices around the country swamped with 750,000 men eager to do their duty.

The cause of the conflict was ostensibly the invasion of Belgium by the Kaiser's forces, in the first stages of a wide sweep that would take them across the poorly-defended border of northern France and onwards towards Paris. Britain declared war because it had guaranteed Belgium's territorial integrity.

In August 1914, war fever swept the country. Here, would-be recruits queue for hours in the rain at Whitehall Recruiting Office. IWM Q.42033

Many men joined up because their mates had enlisted, because work was monotonous, or because war offered an escape from the daily routine. Here new recruits are being sworn in and will receive the traditional shilling. IWM Q.30071

However, for the soldiers who joined up in their tens of thousands, that was scarcely a reason to enlist. The broad fear that if Germany were not stopped, she would attack Britain in due course did provide such a reason. But a more common one was simply the contagion of the war fever which spread nationwide in August 1914. Men joined up because it was the thing to do, because their mates had all joined up, because work was monotonous, because war offered an escape from the daily routine.

The public expectation that the war would be brief was quickly dispelled by the fighting which took place in northern France and Belgium that autumn and winter. The regular and the territorial army had only just been able to hold the Germans at bay. But by the following summer the divisions made up of Kitchener's new army were beginning to arrive. The Battles of Loos and later the Somme gave these erstwhile civilians the chance to prove themselves. The cemeteries which dot the former Western Front are tragic evidence of their steadfast efforts.

The demand for recruits spawned a new style of unit, popularly known as the Pals Battalion. While each conformed to the regulation army size of around a thousand men, containing the usual companies and platoons, uniquely they were made up of men who worked together and socialised together, because they had joined up en masse from their places of work. Born principally in the industrial towns of the midlands and north, such as Accrington, Grimsby, Birmingham and Hull, these men epitomised the enthusiastic spirit of the Kitchener battalions. No one foresaw at that time that when these battalions suffered heavy casualties in action, a town could be devastated.

As these men were recruited together, scant attention was given to whether they complied with the army's regulations on age and health. However, such was the number of volunteers in 1914 that the army could be particular about whom they selected for service. Many were rejected as unfit and found themselves back on the streets along with those who had still to enlist.

So great was the fear of public anger at being seen to be in civilian clothes when others were at the Front, that the Government introduced the Derby scheme early in 1915. This offered men the opportunity to join up but to return home to their jobs until the army specifically required their services. An armband was issued to all men who enrolled in the scheme, thereby reducing the risk of their being accosted by armchair heroes or white-feather-wielding ladies wanting to know why these men were not in khaki.

However, as the casualty figures continued to grow and the public's clamour to fight gradually diminished, fewer young boys were willing to countenance the idea of personal sacrifice in the seemingly endless attacks and counter-attacks at the Front. Only when voluntary recruitment had peaked did the British Government introduce conscription in January 1916. The age of enlistment was expanded from the initial age group of 19-38 to 18-41. The recruits of 1917 and 1918 still included boys eager for action, but they also contained others horrified at the prospect of fighting, who could see no virtue in enlisting. These boys would form the fresh drafts for the Front along with men returning to the fight after convalescence. Alongside them now were men unnecessarily rejected for service in the first months of the war, and increasingly, those physically undernourished and genuinely unfit to fight. Britain was beginning to exhaust its supply of manpower.

Robert Burns
1997

ROBERT BURNS, born 12th November 1895, 7th Queens Own Cameron Highlanders.

If an elixir of life does exist, then Robbie Burns has secretly been sampling it for many years. Aged nearly 103, he stands bolt upright, walks with the assurance of a man thirty years younger, and has a razor-sharp mind that comfortably lends itself to both deft wit and serious discussion. Born near Glasgow in November 1895, he joined up almost as soon as war broke out, inspired by the bagpipes playing beneath the office window where he worked as an "insurance wallah". Sure in the knowledge that the war would last six months, he volunteered for service and fought at the battles of Loos in September 1915 and the Somme in 1916; in the December he was badly wounded.

Robert Burns
1911

New recruits march off behind a brass band to enlist.   IWM Q53279

Propaganda? This picture purports to show how all classes of men are responding to the call to join up.   IWM Q30072

Everywhere you went in Glasgow, there were great big posters of Kitchener with his finger pointing at you, Your King And Country Needs You. No matter where you went, it seemed to be pointing at you personally. I worked in an insurance office, and day after day I would hear a piper coming down the road and the left, right, left, right of feet. I went to the window and I could see probably two or three hundred men, some with bowler hats on and some with what we called "skips", a flat cap, all marching down the road, with the piper playing to arouse enthusiasm.

I thought to myself, I want to do something like this, so I went to a recruiting office and the sergeant asked how old I was. I said that I was eighteen and a bit and he said "Oh you're too young, go back to your mother." A fortnight or so after that, I met a good pal who was trying to join up and I told him what had happened, and he told me to follow him and when we got to the recruiting office to tell a little fib. You had to be nineteen to join up in those days, so it was a little fib because I was only a couple of months off being of age. I told my fib, was given a shilling, and I was in the army. I took my shilling and went with my friend to a restaurant, the MacDonalds of that time, and for ninepence you got a meal, more than you could eat. We'd threepence left so we bought a packet of Woodbine cigarettes and a penny for the matches, and that was the day.

I think it was excitement more than anything that made me join up. I was too young to understand what patriotism really was. I lived in the country and there were not many boys my age, so I thought it would be nice to be with a lot of lads on something of a picnic, because we all thought the war would be over by Christmas. When I told the manager of the insurance company I wanted to join up, he said "Well, it'll be a nice six month holiday for you, yes, you join up". At eighteen and nineteen years of age, one is not very clever. You stop, you look and you listen to other people and you think that if they are doing something, why can't I? My father had been in uniform practically from the day war was declared and I thought, I'll do what my father does. By the end of the war all the family was in uniform, my father, myself, a younger brother and two sisters, which only left my mother at home to run a hotel out in the country.

A few days after enlisting, I received notification to take a train and go to Inverness for training. We reported to the barracks and they gave us a canvas sack, called a palliasse, which we were to take to the stables and stuff with straw and that would be our bed for the night, with just a couple of blankets. My pal and I, having got our beds ready, thought we'd go into town and have a bit of fun, so we got all dressed up and went off for the evening into town about a mile away from the barracks. When we came back, our beds were missing. About twenty miners had arrived and apparently took our beds. We asked them but they just said "We've got them and we're just as much entitled to beds as you are." I couldn't fight a miner – they were too big for me – so there you are, we just had to sleep on the floor.

The next morning, we paraded and the sergeant saw me and said "Ha, Ha, no shave!" I said that I was too young to shave, but he told me I did now and that after the parade I was to go and shave and report back to the orderly room at six o'clock. I went and shaved for the first time with an open razor and left a trademark on both sides of my cheek. I went to the Orderly room with blood running down my face. "Who are you?" asked the sergeant. I said "Private Burns, Sir". "Well, what do you want?" he said. I explained that he'd told me to shave. "Oh", he said, "I didn't recognise you, right, go and see the doctor." That was my first shave in the army.

Over the next few months, we trained at the barracks at Aldershot, which was a military town. The training was very hard, we were youngsters, not hardened soldiers. The miners, they were hardy blokes, the training was nothing to them, but I was a weakling, being an insurance wallah, but others were weaker than I was. It was hard work – early morning runs, square bashing, rifle drill, musketry, bayonet practice and so on. We got fed up with it; "Let's get out there and get on with it," that was the idea.

GEORGE LITTLEFAIR, born 13th May 1896, died 8th July 1998, 1/8th Durham Light Infantry.

Like many young boys in 1914 and 1915, the glamour of joining up for a six month holiday with his pals was too much for George Littlefair. Escaping the drudgery of life on his father's farm, he enlisted with a close friend, Joe Coates. For George, it was the beginning of a three-year nightmare on the Western Front, culminating in Joe being killed by bursting shrapnel, a death that deeply affected George. Finally, in 1997, George went to see Joe's grave, returning to the battlefields he had not seen since his youth. George lived happily with his grand-daughter and great grand-daughter near Bishop Aukland until his death earlier this year, aged 102.

George Littlefair 1915

George Littlefair 1997

My mother died in August 1914 and her last words to me on her death bed was "George," she says "There's a war on now, you know." I say "Aye," she says "Do not join the army." And what did I do? Joined the damned army. I've thought about it many times, aye – whether she had an inkling I would do, I can't tell you, but I did.

I hung out to November, but I thought I would be helping the country. When you are young, all sorts of things go through your head – there's nowt can get through it now, even if I wanted –but I was ignorant, young and daft then. I was having a drink at the Cleaver Hotel in Darlington with two agricultural mates when we decided to join up, myself, Joe Coates from Shildon, and another lad, all of us 18 year-olds. We'd all known each other as children, and then as teenagers and single, we'd all go dancing together. Joe lived next door to the Co-operative store in Shildon and we were especially close mates.

We thought it would be a novelty, you know, none of us had ever been out of England. To see another country, we thought that was a great thing. We were raw country lads who'd never seen nowt. You thought you was something big, you know, you had the impression you'd grown up from being a lad to a man.

We were patriotic. It had been driven into us a bit that Germany wanted

18

England, that's all we knew. We were young, strong lads, and thought we should go and help the old soldiers out. Anyway, when Major Spencer, the recruiting officer, heard that we were agricultural lads he didn't want us, he told us to get out and stop out; we were exempt.

Not for long though; they soon called us up, in 1916, March it was. Then it was six weeks' training in England before we went over the duckpond to Boulogne with the 8th Durham Light Infantry. We didn't have a clue what we were getting into but we damn well soon found out. First time up the line you wondered what it was like. Will I come back? Aye, I'll look after myself and if bloody Jerry comes for me I'll give him the bayonet.

None of the boys liked the treatment we got during training, getting us galloping about here and there. There was one bugger with a waxed moustache, from Birmingham, he turned up yapping and shouting carrying a big whip, cracking it, making us all run around, shouting, "You're not holding on to your mother's apron strings now," and all that tittle tattle. I didn't like army discipline at all. These corporals had stood on civy street without a penny to their name but were made sergeants because they were good at yelling. They thought that they'd got a job now, they were somebody and they knew damn well they wouldn't have to go up the line. It seemed we went into the war to fight to save England and then you had these men shouting and yapping at you, and it upset you.

DICK BARRON, born 19th October 1895, 2nd London Mounted Brigade Field Ambulance.

Dick Barron
1998

It was only when the troop ship was leaving Southampton that Dick Barron realised he might never see the country of his birth again. Having joined up believing war would be fun and games, Dick's naivety was shattered during a three-month spell on Gallipoli. Within weeks of landing, a close friend was killed in action and Dick contracted near-fatal dysentery. Now 103 years old, he recalls his life at the front with passion.

Dick Barron (circled) with his unit before leaving for Egypt and then Gallipoli.

Schools celebrated Empire Day because we had a great empire, a greater empire than the Romans, the greatest empire that had ever existed. As children, we felt that a British man was worth half-a-dozen of any foreigner and the Day was an important celebration of the extent to which the British Empire had spread its wonderful rule and civilisation across the world.

In the morning address at school, the headmaster used to mention any special anniversary of a battle, sometimes calling us to attention. He was a great patriot and would describe recent battles of the Boer War as well as battles further back such as Omdurman, Rorkes Drift, Waterloo; how we had fought at the Crimea and won, and the wonderful charge of the Light Brigade – it was all very romantic. We regarded battles as something very, very heroic you know, the Thin Red Line.

We were all patriotic in those days. I mean most of the colonial wars had been very successful, a third of the whole landmass of the earth belonged to the British Empire. We knew nothing about wars of course, not the sordid side. I'd seen pictures of the Zulu War where we just captured them – after all they were natives and they were fighting with spears. We didn't see the poor buggers that were wounded and lying there, or bodies stripped of anything worthwhile. No, soldiers were glamorous. The war in 1914 was totally justified in our eyes. Everything we did was right and the Germans were a lot of criminals. I think we hated the Germans and the poor German bakers, well, a lot of Germans lived in London as retailers, they were imprisoned when war broke out.

I saw Kitchener's famous poster, Your Country Needs You, but it didn't have a great effect on me because I had already joined up, 1st September 1914. Recruiting sergeants with ribbons across their chests often went around pubs looking for likely lads, trying to get them to take the King's shilling to make them soldiers. When I became a soldier they never gave me a shilling though so they owe me a shilling and interest, a big sum they owe me!

I was in the Boys' Life Brigade and a contingent of us went together because we were inspired to be patriotic. In those days volunteers swarmed up to recruitment offices – you had to queue up to enlist and sometimes they said "We can't take you today, come again". You can't imagine the war fever in those days. Everyone thought we would beat the Germans – the war would be over by Christmas. I wanted to be a soldier – I wanted to fight for England so I went with my friends to the Duke of York's Headquarters in Sloane Square and enlisted.

I loved the training, it was tremendous fun. It was soon discovered that I had had some medical training. I was very good at First Aid, because I wanted to become a medical student and had led a team in the Boys' Brigade, tending accidents and such like, so I was sent to the Field Ambulance, 2nd London Mounted Brigade. I always remember that we had what we called a monkey box which was all first aid. It had pills with numbers on them for different ailments. Number nine was for constipation, and I always remember somebody, he didn't have any number nines left, so he gave this constipated soldier a five and a four!

Tent lines of the 1st London Scottish, with Hal Kerridge front left.

A mixture of clothing on these recruits ranges from full khaki, fatigue overalls to civilian clothes. Response to the call had overwhelmed the Quartermaster Stores. TAYLOR LIBRARY

Jack Rogers outside his father's shoe repair shop in London, 1911. Jack was to enlist in the Sherwood Foresters in the first months of the war.

GEORGE MAHER, born 20th May 1903, 2nd Kings Own Royal Lancaster Regiment.

Intent on filling the army's ranks with fit and enthusiastic volunteers, recruitment sergeants frequently turned a blind eye to the youth of lads who were eager to enlist. Many were allowed to join one or even two years below the required minimum. Few, however, were younger than George Maher. George had run away from home and presented himself to a recruiting sergeant in Lancaster aged just thirteen. He was accepted without question and, still three months short of his fourteenth birthday, he found himself in France. Today George, a youthful ninety-five year old, lives in Australia, his home since 1924.

*George Maher
1998*

I had already tried to join up once at a recruiting office in Preston. I had borrowed a suit of my father's, turning up the trousers, but as I got half-way up the steps to the office somebody cuffed me behind the neck and gave me a kick up the backside. "Go home to your bloody mother," a voice said. I turned and saw a police sergeant, a friend of my father's.

I didn't want to go home, though. I'd run away that morning, packing a small bag once my aunties had gone to work in the local cotton mills and munitions works. You see, after my grandmother died my mother uprooted the family and moved us into the same house as her sisters. My father was an army reservist and had gone to France when war broke out, so moving in meant they could all manage together. I did not get on with my youngest aunt and I was always getting into trouble for nicking food, that sort of thing, so I decided to enlist.

I failed to enlist at Preston, so I sneaked onto a train heading for Lancaster and slept overnight in the cemetery behind the priory. In the morning, I found a tap to have a wash and then joined a queue of men waiting to join up at the town hall. I was always a big lad, for as well as attending school I'd worked half days at the Horrocks Clothing Mill in Preston since I was eleven. I was five foot eight-and-a-half when I was 13 and nicknamed "Hefty", so when I told the recruiting sergeant I was eighteen he believed me, he never asked for any proof at all.

I joined the Kings Own Royal Lancaster Regiment and was sent to Aldershot and then to Salisbury Plain for training. Of course my mother hadn't a clue where I was, although I had told a cousin that I intended to join the army and I knew that he would tell her in due course. As soon as my mother found out, she would inform the military authorities, so to avoid being discovered I had enlisted under her maiden name of Ashton. This worked, for when the army did come looking for me they found no trace of me under my real name, Maher.

A big batch of newly-trained soldiers from different regiments was sent to France in February 1917 and I was among them. I was a bit excited at the time, but little knew what I was going in to – if I had, I wouldn't have gone, you can be sure of that!

*Fred Hodges
1997*

FRED HODGES, born 18th July 1899, 10th Lancashire Fusiliers.

*Fred Hodges
1918*

Fred Hodges and his wife Olive are one of Britain's oldest married couples. Both were born in the last century, their lives first colliding, quite literally, on a frozen lake in 1917 – an incident about which there is still much mutual ribbing. Within months of meeting Olive, Fred enlisted in the army and went off to serve his country in France. His autobiography, Men of 18 in 1918, was published in 1988; using Fred's photographic memory, it charts how the naive young recruits finally brought the conflict to a successful conclusion. Returning to Britain after the Armistice, Fred began to go out with Olive and in 1924 they married. They still live in feisty bliss in Northampton.

We were boys, and war was seen as a kind of super sport. We were used to hard knocks in football, and competition in cricket and running, getting in the first three, well, war was an extension of sport and manliness. And bravery. If the army had put me down as class B at my medical, I should have been ashamed of myself almost, to think I wasn't fit to go.

Of course every boy wanted to be in the army. In 1914, within days of the war breaking out, we'd had 25,000 Welshmen billeted in our town. We had two nice young men of the RAMC in our house and of course I used to try their hats on and their tunics, and fancy myself as a soldier. It was a bit of a dream, I suppose, because nobody in the family had ever been a soldier. However, since the age of thirteen I had been in the school's Cadet Corps, which was affiliated to the 1st Northants Regiment. We had two companies, A and B. A had uniforms and B wore only football kit. I was in B Company, so I went up to my house captain and told him I was disappointed. So he said "Oh, well, if you're keen I'll switch you. Some kids' parents don't want them to go in 'cos they're against war."

I was only fifteen years old in 1914 and couldn't join up then, but I joined up when I was seventeen and a bit. I was due to be called up under the new arrangements at eighteen, into a Young Soldiers Battalion but I didn't want to wait. I discussed with two grammar school friends whether we should apply for a commission, and went to see our local rector who was said to have influence. We sat round a beautiful table in an octagonal room and he said "Yes, I can recommend you for the Inns of Court Officers' Training Corps, but they won't take you until you are eighteen." Well, that was a great stumbling block, oh, we couldn't wait four months.

We joined up in March 1917 at the age of seventeen years and eight months, swearing to defend with our lives King George V and his heirs. We were then sent for a medical examination at Northampton Barracks, where we came before a medical board which was seeing a lot of men who had recovered from wounds to find out if they could go back to France. When we three walked into the room with our chests bare, I heard one of the M.O.s say "Ah, these three look more likely. I'm pleased to see three young chaps raring to go."

The officers and NCOs who trained us were no longer fit for active service, and were very kind to us as well as training us properly. Then on 21st March 1918, the big German attack started and on the 24th our training ceased, cut off, just like that. We were inspected in a big park in Norwich and we marched past the General, column after column. It was a cold frosty morning; our breath was ascending from our mouths as we marched, and then the General got up on his dais and said "You men, of course I know you're not men, you're only boys, but the Germans have broken through our fortifications and you're needed at the Front at once. You've now got to play the part of men."

I wrote to my parents when I knew I was going to France, and they came to Norwich to see me. I was marching down the street when I suddenly saw my mother and father on the pavement, so as soon as I was free, I rushed up to them and got them a billet in a street near where I was. They stayed for about five days while I was getting ready to leave. We had our gas masks tested, that sort of thing. We had been billeted on landladies across Norwich and they really mothered us, but as we marched off that day they lined the streets and they were in tears. As we got near the station, the thicker the crowds got. The pavements were full, mostly of women, we were their boys. Some waved and said "Good Luck", some were crying. We could hear comments: "Poor little buggers," I remember one woman saying, "Fancy sending them out to France to die for us." And it was true. There was nobody left. The army had squandered troops in '15, '16, and '17, and we were all that were left.

My parents were there on the station platform and I remember my mother putting her arms round me and saying something about "If you don't come back...", I don't know what she was going to say but I interrupted her and said "Don't worry, mum, I shall come back." My father stood with her, I think he was shedding a tear. It was a very emotional moment so I broke away from her and got into the queue for the train.

We were aware of the critical situation in France. But we were anxious that the war shouldn't stop before we could get involved and we were genuinely excited as we took the train down to Dover. On the way we passed a train of German prisoners. We looked at them – they were laughing at us – they were safe, going into captivity, we were youngsters who didn't know what we were doing.

George Louth 1915

GEORGE LOUTH, born 27th February 1897, 15th Hampshire Regiment.

Every year on Armistice Day, the nation remembers with sorrow and with gratitude those who died defending their country. For veterans, it is often a time of mixed emotions as they recall the friends who survived and those who did not. For 101-year-old George Louth there are mixed emotions as well, but for probably unique reasons. He too remembers the friends he left on the Battlefield of the Somme, but he also recalls 11th November 1918 as a happy day for, totally coincidentally, it was the day he married. The bells he heard and the bunting he saw as he left the church at 11am that morning could only have

George Louth 1997

been laid on to celebrate his marriage. At that moment he knew nothing of the end of the war.

We were lined up on Southsea Common when the Colonel came round to visit us – to size us up more or less – to see what we'd got. He came round asking questions, how old we were and such like. I said "Nineteen, Sir". He said "Nineteen?", "Yes, Sir", "Right". He went to the next man, spoke to him, then came back to me again. "How old did you say you were?" I said "Nineteen, Sir", and he looked at me straight. Now I was only eighteen and I had put my age on, but he walked away and from then on it was all go.

We did our training at Aldershot, route marching with rifle and pack. We used to do a route march of about thirty miles one day, then perhaps just a few miles the next day. In the mornings we would get up and have a basin of cocoa, then we might have to go for a five-mile run before breakfast, then after breakfast square-bashing at 8 o'clock for four hours, then dinner and back to square-bashing again until five o'clock. We did all this for about six months until we were ready to go overseas.

Before we left, the sergeant came up to me and said "Louth, the Captain wants to know how old you are". I said "Why, sergeant?" He said "'Cos he doesn't believe you." The sergeant said "We're going to France and we don't want you crying when we get over there, saying you are not old enough, because it won't happen, you won't come back, so say it now." "I'm going with the lads," I told him.

During the long months of training, a lot of men built up resentments against sergeants and would say "I'll shoot him when I get to France", that sort of thing. I remember just before the off, an officer getting us all in a ring and he said "Now if you have got any thoughts about what you would do with your sergeant major or your sergeant when you get to France, get it out of your head, 'cos you won't do it when you get over there because you'll be the best of pals, you'll help out, you'll do anything to help one another." It was true. The attitudes of the sergeants and the officers changed when we got overseas, they were just the same as you when you're in a trench, the sergeants didn't shout their orders and the officers were friendlier, less distant. I remember the Company Sergeant Major, before we went into the trenches, he got up on a box and he sang to us in a ring. He had a candle and he was singing "My Little Grey Home In The West." That's how they were, or they would run a game of bingo, they'd do all sorts of things to keep your morale up.

GUY BOTWRIGHT, born 5th November 1897, Army Service Corps.

Unlike most of the young men who joined up to fight, Guy Botwright saw the outbreak of war as an international tragedy which no country could win. A sensitive young man, who loved nature, Guy joined the forces aged 18 in 1916,

Guy Botwright 1998

Guy Botwright 1917

and went to France the following year as an officer in the Army Service Corps. Ten months later, he had returned to England with shellshock. Now aged 101, Guy movingly recalls his recuperation and the fits of depression that made him want to die.

There wasn't any doubt about it, there was going to be a long war and to imagine such a thing was indescribable. I was 17 in 1914 and the world had gone mad. Hitherto I had led such a quiet, idyllic country way of life, everything was superb. I loved nature, I was a keen butterfly collector, and the whole idea of war was inconceivable. To think people could go to war, well, to me it was the end of everything, it was utterly depressing.

I had just begun studying at Brighton College and the first thing I had to do was to join the Officer Training Corps. It was compulsory, and each day I would work in the morning and then go and change into my uniform and parade every blasted afternoon for drill. I never, ever, thought I would go into the army, it never entered my head, but doing my duty was automatic. Now England was in a dire strait, a major war had broken out and I simply had to play the part of a soldier. I couldn't see myself a soldier. I soon could, I soon had to. I felt we had to fight Germany or they would take over our country and dictate English law. The whole of Europe was being corrupted by this one nation. Gosh! there was

An Officer Training Corps unit learns how to sheathe bayonets. A complicated manoeuvre which invariably resulted in recruits dropping rifles and bayonets on the parade ground, and the occasional cut hand. TAYLOR LIBRARY

no question of being a conscientious objector. I did not want to join up, no, I think I can definitely say that, but I was of age so I had to, full stop. However, I loathed the whole thing, I was going to be cannon fodder.

When I landed in France in early 1917, there was nothing doing, it was late winter, it was stalemate and we all knew that until the weather improved, Jerry could do very little. I was fortunate. The casualties I was to see in France, bits of arms, bits of legs, at that tender age you cannot imagine it. When I saw the devastation of the Front, my one thought was to live: can I get through this hell without being killed?

PERCY WILLIAMS, born 15th September 1899, 5th Northumberland Fusiliers.

Percy Williams 1997

Percy Williams 1918

Percy Williams joined the British Army only because he knew he was about to be conscripted anyway. A reluctant soldier, he was one of the growing band of young men sent out to France in 1918 with few illusions about the maelstrom into which they were about to be thrown. Now aged 99, Percy recalls with candour the feelings of helplessness, fear and sheer panic that gripped him as he held a third line trench during the great German offensive of 1918.

I was going to be eighteen on the 15th September 1917 and I was told, whether it was true or not, that if I joined up before I was conscripted I would be able to volunteer just for the duration of the war and no longer. If I waited for my call-up papers, I would be termed a conscript in which case the army could keep me for years. So I took the line of least resistance and went to a recruiting office with a friend about ten days before my birthday and took the King's shilling.

The patriotism of 1914, of Kitchener's men, had evaporated long before 1917. I wasn't patriotic – you may call me a bit of a coward – but I didn't want to join the army. At the beginning of the war it was said that it would be over by Christmas 1914, yet we'd had the whole of 1915, the whole of 1916 and about eight months of 1917. I could see by the casualty lists that so many had died during the battle of the Somme, I could read between the lines of the reports from the Front and I was hoping and hoping that the war would be finished before I was called up.

After joining the army, I was sent home to await further instructions and then on 23rd October 1917, I was called up. I was very apprehensive when I went in my civilian clothes to Whitchurch Barracks in Cardiff for training, forming fours and drilling with dummy rifles. My only hope was, we were told when we joined up that we would not go abroad until we were nineteen, but I was sent to France six months before I should have been, at the end of March 1918. I knew what we were in for and as far as I am concerned, in the short time I was out in France, I hoped, along with others, that I'd get a blighty, a slight wound that would get me back to England.

*Royce McKenzie
1915*

ROYCE McKENZIE, born 7th August 1897, Drake Battalion, 63rd Royal Naval Division.

Royce Mckenzie is 100 years old but looks 30 years younger. Nicknamed "Lucky Jim" by the men he served with on the Somme and at Passchendaele, Royce served as a company runner, dodging the bullets and shells as he carried messages across the exposed battlefield. Today he is as likely to be found having a small flutter on the horses, an abiding passion, as he is to be found at the home he has lived in since the 1930s. Fit, well, and ever "lucky", Royce lives an independent life in Doncaster, his home town.

*Royce McKenzie
1997*

I was working at Bullcroft Colliery, pony driving, when I went to join up. I was only seventeen, and the sergeant looked at me, he says, "You'd better go home". I went home and mother asked me where I'd been and I told her, to join up. She gave me a slap at side of face, she says "That'll learn you not to go and join the army." I waited a year before I tried to join the Naval Division, with one or two more besides, so the sergeant says all right but you're not eighteen now, you're nineteen and you know what you're doing? The date was 21st August 1915 and we were all just young lads; king and country - that were it.

It was patriotism, that's all we joined up for. Old Kaiser Bill, he was aiming to get into this country and we had to stop him. Life was different in those days, you lived for your country and when Kitchener said "I want you", well, that was it, millions joined up, millions of young fellows like myself.

I was sent to the Crystal Palace in London, a beautiful place, all the buildings being named after our colonies as they were then, Canada, Australia, India and South Africa. I was billeted in Australia and kitted out in navy blue. We got into a routine straight away, up at six with the first drill, physical jerks, then we were issued with a mug of cocoa and breakfast. Then it was on parade, all cleaned up, forming fours and other exercises. A couple of days later we were given rifles and learnt rifle drill so we could be put on guard duties, the pinnacle of which was main guard, for local people used to come and watch the guard drilling, a real spectacle. It was about that time when I was having a stroll in the grounds one night. I stood for a minute or two looking up at the sky because the searchlights were looking for something and then they got it. It was a wonderful sight, a German Zeppelin, shaped like a cigar, all illuminated.

Royce McKenzie (circled) training on Imbros Island in 1916 prior to his leaving for the Western Front.

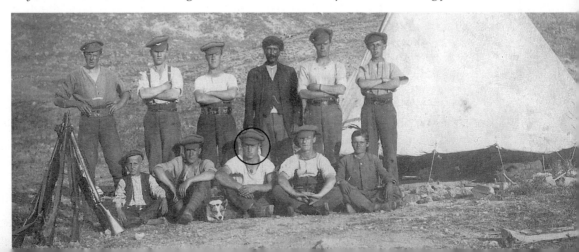

CHAPTER TWO

Leaving For The Front

THE young men who went to France had no conception of what trench life would be like. From early on in the war the Government heavily censored battlefield images that appeared in newspapers, war magazines and cinema reels, giving a sanitised impression of the Front. However, images of smiling, enthusiastic soldiers ready and waiting to advance from a dry and tidy trench rarely reflected reality, while the accompanying newspaper copy or film titles were usually a shrewd concoction of half-truths, lies and propaganda.

Leaving for the Front would be an occasion of general excitement, usually tempered by an anxiety and a realisation that "this was it". Most left at short notice, perhaps with familiar faces to wave to, more often with just a "cheerio" to strangers wishing them "good luck". Some men were given brief leave prior to going overseas; others were able to send notice of their impending embarkation to loved ones who made it to the railway station or coastal port to see them off. Owing to the presence of enemy submarines in the Channel, most soldiers went to war at dead of night, sailing across to one of the Belgian or

Troops embarking for France from a British port on the south coast. The usual sailing time would be after dark and with a destroyer as escort. TAYLOR LIBRARY

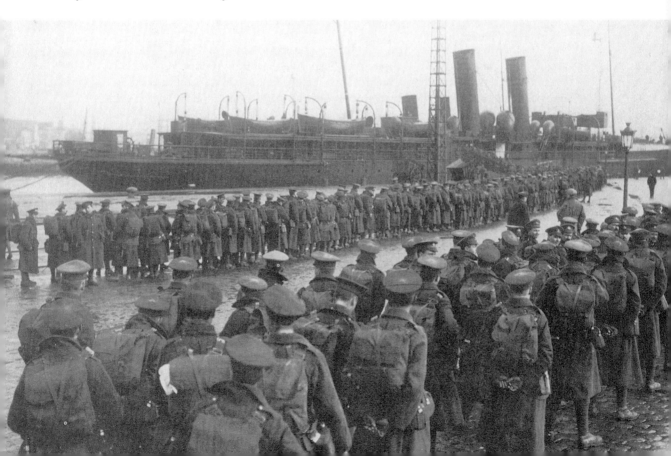

French ports in any old boat commandeered by the Government to transport them. Bigger boats, including commandeered liners such as the *Olympic*, sister ship of the *Titanic*, were used for longer journeys to the Mediterranean, but whether they were liners or cattle steamers, a destroyer escort normally accompanied them.

All lights on the boats were dimmed or extinguished, and all port holes closed. The men were packed in by the hundreds, crammed together below or lying out on deck, under strict orders not to show any light, including the smoking of cigarettes. Many were too seasick to smoke even on the short journey to France, although those who were going further afield to the battlefronts in Africa, Turkey, and the Middle East, usually had a worse time as they sailed through the notoriously unpredictable Bay of Biscay.

The apprehension of arriving on the Western Front gradually heightened with the sound of distant battle. The guns at the Front could be heard on the south coast of England and on occasion as far away as London. This far-off rumble grew as the Channel was crossed and the men began the slow, rambling journey towards the line.

For many, the front line was the focal point of the entire conflict, where a trench as little as fifty yards away contained the enemy. The term "The Front Line" had great emotional significance, as much as the town names it defended, such as Albert, Arras and Ypres, and the villages it stood before, such as Beaumont Hamel, Thiepval, and Passchendaele. These places had been so widely reported in the British press that they had become household names. One veteran recalled the magic of seeing the famous leaning statue of the Madonna hanging over Albert Basilica, as confirming that he was now at the Front. Yet such enthusiasm could be fatal. New men up the line for the first time were vulnerable to enemy fire. "So this is the front line I've heard so much about," one new arrival told Cameron Highlander, Andrew Bowie. He had not been in the trench more than a few minutes before he took a peak at the German line and was instantly killed by a sniper: he was not the first nor the last to die that way.

ANDREW BOWIE, born 3rd October 1897, 1st Queens Own Cameron Highlanders.

A doctor once told Andrew Bowie that if he had not been gassed in the First World War, he would have lived to be 120. He may yet confound the medical experts for he is now aged 101, physically fit and mentally very active. Surviving the German Army's best efforts to kill him during the bloody battles of 1916, 1917 and 1918, he now maintains an independent life in Sydney, Australia, where he has lived for the last 32 years. He remains a Scotsman at heart, however, and remembers with pride his unit, the 1st Cameron Highlanders – the first Battalion, in the first Brigade, of the first Division, of the First Army of the British Expeditionary Force.

*Andrew Bowie
1916*

As soon as I was nineteen, I was sent to France with a draft of 200

*Andrew Bowie
1997*

men because the army was desperate for men at the Front. The troop train was to go through Edinburgh's Waverley Station, so I sent a telegram to my parents telling them I would be passing through. Everybody from Edinburgh had done the same, and their people came to the station. My mother and father came, and my aunt and uncle and sister were there, all to say goodbye. The Red Caps – Military Police – were there and they said that no one could leave the platform; they were afraid of people deserting, I suppose. There were some rough fellows amongst our boys and they said, "We are coming onto the concourse, our friends are there." Two Red Caps still said no, so one or two of the men turned out with bayonets, and said "We're coming out!" and the police stood aside. The old man in charge, Major Howard, appealed to us and said "If you go out, boys, will you come back," because he was responsible for taking us to France. I was able to say goodbye to my relatives, but getting back on the train there were two big Highland boys, and they had nobody and tears were running out of their eyes. They had a foreboding that we were going to face death, I suppose, and these boys were

Andrew Bowie shortly before he left for France and the Battle of the Somme.

really broken up seeing us saying goodbye, and nobody to see them off. Their families were all in the West Highlands somewhere.

Once we got to France we spent about a week at Etaples, at the Bull Ring, a place where a lot of second-rate sergeant majors knocked steam out of you. You were there for fitness training, but it was over-fitness training really. Each morning we got up, had breakfast, and were given a couple of hard biscuits and a piece of cheese that was meant to last us the rest of the day. In the Bull Ring they would have you running round in circles and jumping over obstacles, and all the time these NCOs were roaring at you, swearing all the time. They tried to make you look ridiculous. We had to jump in and out of trenches, and if you didn't get out quick enough they would swear and make you do it again; if you weren't agile or athletic, you were a bit of a target for them. We weren't all built

A Scottish regiment marches towards the front. The pipe band helped to bouy-up anxious soldiers. IWM Q790

Troops exercising on the infamous 'Bull Ring' at Etaples in France. By the time the drill sergeants had finished with them the new arrivals were relieved to be sent on to the Front Line.
TAYLOR LIBRARY

the same way. I played rugby and I was pretty good, but you could tell a lot of the men weren't up to it.

As you left the Bull Ring, if you were out of step or out of line, the instructors lined the road shouting at you, taking names. If you said anything to them, you were in trouble, even if you looked at them, you could be up for dumb insolence. It only took a week in the Bull Ring and you weren't particular where you went, I think that was the idea.

We were in the main street one day at Etaples, and a party of about twelve men marched past me with one man in the middle without any hat on. I can see his face now, he was aged about 25 and was staring straight in front. As they went by, I said to a soldier, "What are they doing there?" And he said, Oh, they are taking that fellow away to be shot." Just like that. I went over the words in my head, "Taking him away to be shot". It looked mighty like it too, the set-up, I mean, they were all round him, twelve of them. The sight was a terrible blow to a young soldier like myself, the first time out in France.

ROBERT BURNS

After nine months training, Robbie's battalion, the 7th Cameron Highlanders, landed in France on 7th July 1915. As part of the 15th Scottish Division, he was to go into action at Loos just ten weeks later.

In July 1915, we sailed for France. On board, a sergeant took me to the bow of the ship and above me was a bell and he said "If you see anything unknown, ring that bell". The ship had set sail and I was looking down into the darkness and I could see a little light and I thought, "Oh, that must be somebody, I'll ring the bell". There was pandemonium throughout the ship, everybody running about, not knowing what to do. I could hear them all round me until an officer said to me "What is it?" I said "There's a submarine down there." I was stood down and afterwards I was told it was the pilot boat taking us out of the dock. So that's the kind of watchman I was!

I was sick all the way across the Channel. Many of us were, just lying down on the deck, vomiting. I felt a bit better when we got into Boulogne. It was four in the morning and just getting light as we walked up the high street, right up the hill to a camp. The pipers of course give you a bit of enthusiasm, you came to when you heard the pipes, and the

Robert Burns snapped prior to leaving for France.

windows of the houses opened, nearly all women and children with their heads out welcoming us. In camp we were put six men to a Bell tent and I got busy chatting to the three or four kids who had followed us up, wanting this and wanting that. Their mothers would come up looking for them and would talk to me as I could speak some French, the other men wanting to know what I was talking about.

I felt a real man being in France and marching behind the pipe. I felt really well, no fear whatsoever. Nobody expected to sleep in a cowshed or eat outside, it was all a novelty, and there's nothing more pleasing than seeing something new. We'd start singing. No, there was no unhappiness at that time because we hadn't been in the front line or even the reserve trenches, and we could only hear a very faint noise of gun fire. It was only when we got nearer that we realised what we were up against.

Going up the line, ah then, we began to shake then, yes, began to shake for a bit. You heard the noise first before you saw anything, a prolonged thundery noise. The closer you get to the line, the more tired you get. You had been going through intact villages, now there started to be badly damaged ones. I remember one village and the inhabitants were still there leading a normal life. We stayed there for two days and got friendly with the people who owned the café or estaminet as they call them. There were girls working behind the bar and half a dozen old men with sticks sitting at a table having their drinks, and I remember saying to these people "Now you ought to get away from this place, you're going to get shelled, take our advice and get away". Two months later we happened to come back through this village and it had been knocked flat. The estaminet was non-existent, but in the cellar there were two bodies, still there, they didn't take our advice.

DICK BARRON

Having joined up as war broke out, Dick could have expected an extended training period in England. Instead, his unit sailed in September 1914 for Egypt, from where he wrote home assuring his parents he was still able to "celebrate the occasion" of his 19th birthday.

We were on field exercises when one night, practically with no warning, we were entrained with all our equipment. We found ourselves next morning in a drizzling autumn rain at Southampton Docks and there looming above us was the *Aragon*, a Royal Mail Steam Packet liner which had been converted to a troop ship. Just before we were about to start something happened which I will never forget. The whole of the ship's company from the top deck right down, including ourselves, suddenly burst into song. "Homeland, homeland, when shall I see you again, land of my birth, dearest place on earth, I'm leaving you, oh it may be for years and it may be forever. Homeland, homeland." Up to then the whole thing had been most enjoyable, but my heart stood still. I suddenly realised that this was warfare – I may not return, you know. It had been a field day up till then, I enjoyed everything, but now we were on our way.

Soon after we left port we were accompanied by two cruisers, one a Russian and the other Japanese. The Russian ship had five funnels and soon became known as the Packet of Woodbines. The boat was overcrowded and the whole company got sea sick, you can't imagine what the ship was like – the smell. Our final destination was Alexandria where we entrained and took over the old cavalry barracks near Cairo, while the New Zealanders and Australians were camped out near the Pyramids – a finer body of men I never saw and they were annihilated at Gallipoli. Our training was all in the desert, a place which had a wonderful fascination for me, at dawn as the light changed, you can't imagine the silence. The air was broken by the cry of the local native temple, with that strange voice. It reminded me of the old poem The Rubaiyat of Omar Khayyam – "awake for morning in the bowl of night has flung the stone that puts stars to flight and lo the hunter of the east has caught the sultan's turret in a noose of light".

A photograph of the **Aragon** *as it set sail 10th September 1914 with Dick Barron aboard.*
IWM Q62926

"Homeland, homeland, when shall I see you again, land of my birth, dearest place on earth, I'm leaving you, oh it may be for years and it may be forever. Homeland, homeland."

GEORGE MAHER

Despite fooling everyone that he was old enough to serve, 13-year-old George was to find France nothing like the land of adventure he had expected. His enthusiasm soon waned when he came face to face with the conditions of life near the line.

We left in darkness on a boat from Sheerness to Ostend and then entrained for the Somme battlefield. The Germans were in the process of retiring to the Hindenburg Line and I was sent to live under canvas just near the town of Amiens. The fighting was miles away but I disliked what I saw.

We were living in Bell tents, sleeping on ground sheets, and ankle-deep in mud. It seemed to rain every day, the ground was heavy and waterlogged and we were lousy and smelly. We did very little except further training, attacking mock trenches, bombing, that sort of thing. There was plenty of gunfire in the distance and I saw a lot of ambulances passing the camp bringing back the wounded. I'd never thought about being killed or wounded, but now, every so often the camp would be attacked by German aircraft dropping bombs. The bloody noise. The explosions shook the floor, and I was frightened, don't worry; and all I could think was that the noise was going to get worse. "What had I done to get myself in here?" I used to ask.

It wasn't the first time I'd burst into tears, but I hadn't let anyone see me other times. I wasn't the only one scared. Men used to mumble in the tent, frightened too, but if they heard me cry they didn't worry, in any case I tried to hide it, crying under the blanket. I mean you've got to try and be brave even if you're not.

I was lying on my ground sheet crying in the tent when this man said "What are you crying for?" Then it all came out, that I was thirteen. He went and reported what I'd said and I was taken to see a major. I can see him now, wringing wet, with rain dripping from his helmet. He swore at me. "You bloody fool, it costs money to get you here and you bloody well cry." He had no option but to have me arrested by the Military Police and to send me home, but I wasn't the only one going back. When I was taken under escort to the railway station, I found I was one of five under-age boys from different regiments being sent back to England, and one of them, as I discovered, was even younger than myself. A little nuggety bloke he was, too! We joked that he could never have seen over the trenches, that they would have had to have lifted him up.

We were locked up together in a train under guard and sent first back to Etaples, then back to England, arriving at Harwich in time to witness a Zeppelin raid. From there we went our separate ways to our depots where I was discharged from the army and was given a new suit of clothing and some money owing. There was no punishment for my actions, in fact, being musical I was offered the chance of rejoining the regiment as a bandsman, which I jumped at. I was given a month's paid leave and then told to return in November on what was known as `boy service'. I was to play the bassoon and cello and, thankfully, no further part in the war!

FRED HODGES

Despite the emotional farewell with his parents in England, Fred landed in France full of enthusiasm. Not discouraged by the sound of shellfire in the distance, he eagerly awaited the train that would take him to the front line, from which he well knew he might not return.

Let me tell you when I realised I was going to die. On the beach at Calais, they'd got us in a long queue and were handing out this and that, a ground sheet, jack knife, and eventually we came to a place where they gave us two hundred rounds of small arms ammunition. There was a boy standing just in

25th March 1918. Fred Hodges and some friends are pictured just prior to leaving for France. The hat decorations had been purchased at Woolworths to celebrate. Wally Beale (top right) was to be killed in action a week before the Armistice.

front of me from Northampton, a lad called Ablethorpe, and he was a refined boy, wouldn't swear, probably a chapel boy. He said to me, "Now they've given us all this ammo, I shall kill as many of the buggers as I can before I'm killed." I said "Yes, d'you know we must have been born for such a time as this. Our lives no longer belong to us, we're called. There's people older than us and people younger who are not here."

We went and got into some cattle trucks, and after a time they started jolting along the coast to an enormous army base. With the excitement of having ammo all to ourselves, some of the boys started firing at passing barns. Other adventuresome kids climbed out and got on the roof and came back with black faces, we'd been through a tunnel and they were laughing. You'd have thought we were going on a picnic. In our truck was a man named Brandon, who wore the medal ribbon of the 1914 Mons Star on his tunic. He was watching our

Troops moving up the line. With the land a quagmire, the only way to the front line for men and transport was along the few passable roads. Carnage often resulted if German gunners got wind of the congestion. IWM Q5794

Within sound of the guns. This section of men is heading across a frozen landscape towards the Front Line. TAYLOR LIBRARY

boyish tricks with some interest when, grinning, he said, "When Jerry sees your lovely pink faces he'll say "Mein Gott!" rat, tat, tat, new troops, rat, tat, tat, tat".

Eventually we got into a siding and there was a Quarter-Master-Sergeant waiting for us. He looked after the stores. Our eyes went straight to his cap, we wanted to know what his cap badge was. He told us we wouldn't be needing one just yet, then he picked up a bundle of sacking and threw it out and said

"Put one of these on your helmet." They had been made to put over your helmet to stop it shining in the dark, in the same way that our bayonets had been dulled.

The battalion was three-quarters boys and one-quarter men. It had had to be re-formed and we waited for our new officers. Four came, one becoming my platoon officer. He was a public school boy, you can tell that in a moment, and he had authority written all over him and I was glad to get into his platoon. We were lined up and I saw a man coming along in a private's uniform, not an officer's, and when he got near I saw he'd got a pip on his shoulder. At last they'd realised that the Germans picked off the officers first because they were so distinctive, with their collars and braided rank. He got to me and said, "Now then, I want some more Lewis Gunners, what about you?" I told him I was training to become a signaller but Jim May, a friend of mine, spoke, saying that while he didn't have his Lewis Gunner's badge he knew how to fire one. "What you mean is you haven't killed anyone yet," said the officer and we all laughed. "You'll have plenty of time, we'll give the buggers a bloody nose."

Shortly afterwards we started to march to the Front and in the distance we could hear a mummummum and we said "Is that the Front?" "Yes." "How far is it?" "Oh, further than you'd want to march today." We stopped at a village called Toutencourt and made for a wood just outside, where we slept. During the night the Germans dropped anti-personnel bombs on the wood and there was a cry for stretcher bearers. We pushed on next day to a village called Forceville which had been badly damaged, where we were dismissed. Some of the lads started writing letters, but I went for a walk with a friend to the edge of the village where we found some artillery, but they were unfriendly and told us they didn't want sightseers round their guns. That evening we moved out. We didn't march as a battalion now but in platoons, so as to minimise the risk of casualties if we were attacked. It was dusk and in the distance we could see the flickering of shellfire and star shells going up. Suddenly, some guns close by fired and there was a terrific roar next to us and a big flash. We walked on until we saw a plane coming towards us, very low. We could see a black outline in the darkish sky and Corporal Hobson, a regular soldier, said "Don't worry, lads, it's one of ours," and then the bombs dropped. We'd just passed an empty trench, so we turned round and scuttled back. Corporal Hobson was annoyed. "I thought I'd brought some men up the line, not a lot of bloody scared kids." That settled us, we never showed fear again.

CHAPTER THREE

Trench Life

L IFE IN THE LINE was hard, brutal, and often short. Around half of all the soldiers who enlisted in the First World War were killed or wounded, a shocking figure that rises to 60% for those who served on the Western Front. It is perhaps surprising, then, that, despite the carnage, there were many peaceful parts of the line, places where there was an appreciable distance between opposing trenches. In summer time, there were no doubt occasions when it was pleasant to doze, sitting on the firestep with the sun beating down. Many soldiers appreciated the poppies growing on the parapet and the larks singing overhead; occasionally men were able to make pets of cats or dogs that strayed into the line from deserted villages nearby. It was to such quiet sectors

Quiet sectors were used to initiate fresh units to the Western Front. Here, members of the 1/5th York and Lancaster Regiment man the trenches at Fleurbaix in 1915. TAYLOR LIBRARY

that new units, fresh out from England, were often sent to get used to the Front. The baptism of fire would come later.

Yet the front line was nothing if not a place of extraordinary contrasts. In winter, in the marshy land around Ypres, it was possible to crouch in a trench which was little more than a collection of shell holes linked together, being plastered by heavy autumn rain and enemy shells, with the cry of "Stretcher bearers!" occasionally penetrating the terrific noise. Water and mud could be ankle deep, possibly knee deep, while panic-stricken rats, with their noses poking above the waterline, would swim past, or scuttle along the parapet. The stench of the rotting dead might have given way to the aroma of cordite fumes, but this in turn could be swamped by a cloud of poison gas. Then gas hoods would be worn, un-comfortable apparatus which made breathing difficult and, as the eye pieces quickly misted, restricted vision.

Any soldier still able to contemplate his condition might well be worrying about his soaking, frozen feet. He might have trench foot, for which he could face a charge of neglect, but then perhaps he was unable to think that far ahead when driven to distraction by body lice which caused him interminable itching. All this might pale into in-significance if he knew he was due to go over the top into a muddy morass the following dawn. Before then he would, of course,

Passing up a communication trench into the front line. Despite the mud these men are having little difficulty getting along. Chaos ensued, however, if a heavily laden battalion was coming the other way. IWM Q10612

need to survive being blown to pieces or buried alive by a shell burst, but if he did, he would then leave what remained of the trench to take part in an uphill attack under the noses of German machine gunners ensconced in their concrete pillboxes.

Whether in a mud-filled or a dry trench, there were some constants to life in the line. In particular, the lice which lived in the seams of a soldier's underclothes and amongst body hair were a bane, no matter what time of year it was. Most soldiers went weeks or even months between baths and changes of clothes, and even then, within hours the lice grew and the men were just as lousy as before. Sanitation was primitive, generally a small sap dug into the recess of a trench, with often a pole across on which men sat; toilet paper was anything to hand. However, it was not unusual for a man to be seen relieving

Constant companions of soldiers on both sides were the lice. Hunting them and their eggs was known as 'chatting' – a pastime indulged in during quiet periods, and one being practised by the men below. IWM CO 1463

himself on an entrenching tool and throwing the result over the top. All clean water had to be carried up by fatigue parties and was reserved for drinking, not sanitation. Any spare water was used and reused – the dregs from a dixie of tea could be used to shave with – but on the whole, men remained encrusted with dirt until they could leave the trenches for rest, well behind the line.

The men spent approximately ten days in the line, rotating between the reserve, close support and front line trenches. They would get ready at dawn for Stand-to, when the enemy was most likely to attack, and similarly for Stand-down at night. During the day men dozed, read letters from home, and kept periodic watch, but it was at night, when the hours of darkness gave cover, that most trench duties took place. Rations were brought up to the line, with fatigue parties detailed to carry up everything that might be needed, from duck boards to boxes of ammunition, from barbed wire to dixies of stew. Trench repairs were undertaken and men went out to check the wire in front of the trench. New trenches or saps might be dug from the front line out towards the Germans, and a sniper's post built and concealed. Communications with Brigade Headquarters would be maintained, with signallers periodically checking the telephone wires for breaks. Runners were always on hand to take messages back, either through the communication trenches or by taking a risk and jumping over the top. Forward of the trench, listening posts were manned in No Man's Land, and patrols sent out to find out what, if anything, the Germans might be doing. Occasionally a raiding party might be sent to the opposing trenches, principally to grab a prisoner for interrogation. Yet possibly the most testing of all front line duty was to be involved in a general attack. For those in so-called "Shock Divisions", going over the top was an all too frequent trial of endurance. Each battalion in the division was known for its aggressive traditions in warfare, and was expected to perform well in close combat. For other men, in less renowned regiments, the stress of going over the top, even in support of crack regiments, was enough to last a lifetime, short as that time too often was.

JACK ROGERS, born 21st March 1894, 1/7th Sherwood Foresters, later 2/7th Sherwood Foresters.

At 104 years old, Jack Rogers is Britain's oldest columnist. Writing for the Lincolnshire Echo, Jack recalls the past, utilising his phenomenal memory of 100 years of British social life. Born in 1894, Jack effortlessly recalls the time Queen Victoria waved at him from her cortège during the Diamond Jubilee celebrations of 1897, and the occasion when the soldiers returned from the Boer War. He also vividly remembers his own war, the First World War, when he worked as both a sniper and a concert party entertainer, took part in trench raids, and was eventually captured at the point of a bayonet.

When we went up it was pouring with rain, I remember, raining hard. We had no idea what we were going into, we were just on foot, marching, laden

*Jack Rogers
1915*

*Jack Rogers
1997*

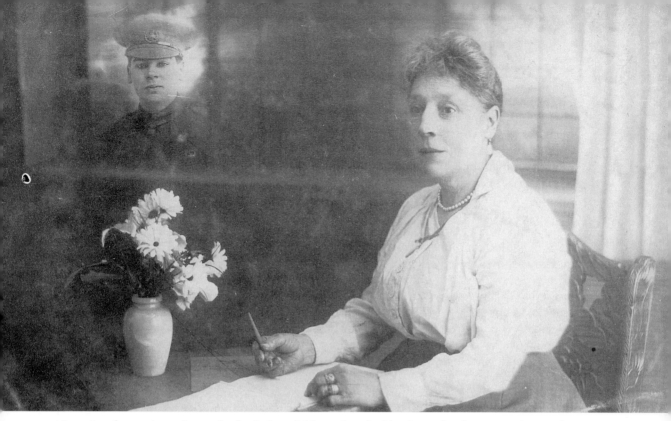

A postcard meant as a keepsake for Jack and his mother. Jack's picture has been superimposed in the window, a slightly ghostly effect.

with all our equipment, all you could carry, and suddenly you begin to see the sky lighting up, flashing, flashing, flashing, and you begin to hear the noise of the guns. You know you are getting near. We stopped overnight in one of the little villages, just sleeping as we were, if you could go to sleep that is, and then in the morning they brought us a ration of tea and some biscuits. You can't help the butterflies in your stomach. I was not what you would call a brave man, I was always fearful, and here you were with this enormous illumination ahead of you that you have got to face. It was a terrible thought, really, especially for a young man.

We were up to our necks in the mud once we got in the trench. Well, I had trained as a sniper so I teamed up with another sniper, a lad called Ginotti. He suggested that we dug a hole under the parapet, just enough to make room for us both to get in to make a seat, so we could sit there out of the rain. So we kept digging away, digging away, throwing dirt everywhere until eventually we were able to get in and dump our bags. All of a sudden the Germans, they must have anticipated our arrival or seen some movement along the trench, because they opened up shelling and one big shell dropped right on the parapet above us. There was a terrific bang, the earth and dirt suddenly collapsed right in on top of Ginotti and myself. We were completely buried. Now further along in the trench, our other pals had seen what had happened. They knew just where we were so they apparently hurried along and dug and dug until they came on Ginotti's boot. They knew he must be somewhere close behind so they kept on shifting and shifting until they began to get hold of a hand, and an arm, and then they were able to pull him right out of the earth. He was apparently in a bit of a state but he was able to tell them I was next to him, so they started to dig away for me.

I was buried for a long time but luckily I was wearing my steel helmet. This was pulled down in front of my nose by all the falling earth, but saved my life because it kept the dirt from going into my face, and gave me a tiny space in which to breathe. I can't recall much except for the terrible experience of sitting there and struggling to breathe. I couldn't move a hand or a foot, although I recall I could just move my toes in my boots, and move my eyes, I can just remember moving my eyes. I was absolutely covered, I just remember breathing, struggling, fighting hard to get my breath, keep breathing, keep breathing, struggling, I've got to keep going – in my mind. My eyes were shut but eventually I began to feel my foot being pulled and then the other and then it came to pulling me right out. I was breathing terribly quickly, ah, ah, ah, gasping, trying to get air. How I survived for that length of time amazes me now, it must have been that little space within my helmet, I can't think of any other way I could have lived.

I know when they eventually pulled me free I did not quite know where I was. I had to have a little first aid and they kept me there for a bit until I was able to get up and move about and recover. How long was I buried? I don't think I had any sense of time. It can't have been long. It might have been a quarter of an hour, I've no idea, it might have been much longer.

I was very anxious after that experience. On several other occasions, I was in a similar position in trenches full of water, nearly over the tops of my boots, the sides of the trench all muddy and slippery. With no shelter, you felt once again

"Funk holes", dug into the side of the trench gave men the opportunity to get under cover and get some sleep. They became potential death traps if a shell landed on the parapet above, as Jack Rogers and his friend discovered. IWM Q4389

like digging a little hole, somewhere to get in. Then I thought of the previous experience. Could it happen again? So I put up with the mud, pulling my mackintosh cape over the top of my head and staying with it in the rain. I didn't become claustrophobic, but I still don't like to be enclosed too tightly so that I touch all the walls.

ROBERT BURNS

After all the enthusiasm of training, the stark reality of trench life hit many soldiers hard. Robbie Burns quickly had to learn the rules for survival in the front line, and was expected to pass on what little experience he had to even less experienced troops just out from Britain.

Our battalion was in the 15th Scottish Division when we went to France. We weren't in the trenches very long before the 16th Irish Division came along. Command said we had to break them in – well, the Irish Division were new to trench warfare so we had to tell them this and that. They thought it rather funny when the rum ration came round about four or five in the morning – a young officer and a sergeant with a jar of rum with the initials SRD on the side. They'd tell you to bring your dixie out, that's your little tin can with a lid on it, and they pour a small amount of rum in. I said that I was sorry but I did not drink rum, and my pal said the same, but we were ordered to have it just the same. After the officer had gone further along the trench, one of the Irish soldiers said "You don't like rum? Well, give it to me". So we gave him the rum and he rather liked it; it went to his head rather than his stomach, I think, because after two or three minutes he said "Oh, I'll show you how to kill those Germans, I'll show you how to kill them, what are you staying here for?" He jumped up on the parapet with his rifle and he looked over the top and he came back with a bullet in his head, just like that, and that's what rum did to him. So I never had rum in my life after that. Every time anyone mentions rum, I think of the poor Irishman who met his death through drinking my rum.

The food, well, we had something called iron rations. They were hard biscuits, very hard biscuits which you ate in the front line. If you were lucky, you might have some little flat candles and if you could put your waterproof sheet out on top of the trench and get some water, and keep it clean, then you could put sufficient in your dixie to make a little brew. You made a hole in the side of the parapet to hold the candle, and heated the water, making sure no light was showing. Hot drinks might be brought into the line but it depended on the shelling. If the shelling was heavy, the chaps who made the tea or the food – probably a mile back – couldn't get up the trench because it was being knocked to bits and they'd probably be knocked to bits too. So we didn't get food every day, and there was no question of breakfast at nine, lunch at one and dinner at seven, you just didn't know when you were going to get a meal.

It was a surprise, and very disappointing, that we should be in the front line for all these weeks and months, getting nowhere. "What are we fighting for?"

we asked. Weeks in one place without making any progress whatsoever, just a waste of time, living like rats, living with rats. You could throw a biscuit down and see half a dozen rats coming out and having a fight for it. It was fun watching them, two or three holding on to the same biscuit. They had plenty to eat, they had a lot of dead bodies to get on with, you could come across a dead soldier somewhere in the open and find a couple of rats running away as you got near it. By the same token, you could sit in a trench when all was quiet and watch the larks up above you singing, and enjoying themselves – having a lark! Watching the birds and watching the mice, yes, and the rats.

We were filthy most of the time because we lived like rats. You couldn't wash unless you could collect some rainwater in your waterproof sheet, but if there was no rain for a fortnight you didn't wash. When you came out into reserve, you might go to a school in which there were probably sixty to a hundred barrels, ordinary barrels cut in two and filled with water, and the RAMC would come along with some disinfectant that turned the water white. There might be a hundred men having baths in the water, which burned you because it was there to kill the lice that stuck to your body. The lice were terrible, making you itch as they ate you. The kilts we wore were pleated and the lice got into the pleats, hundreds of them. I don't know who thought of the idea, but when the chance arose you dug a hole in the ground about two inches deep, put the soil to one side, put the kilt in the hole and covered it over with the soil. If you left it for a couple of hours, came back and removed the soil, you'd find nearly all the lice had gone. The other insects had eaten the lice.

If there was no shellfire, you would sleep, but if there was shellfire, you couldn't. You'd sleep more or less sitting up on the firestep, or you'd doze. You wore a heavy greatcoat which kept you as warm as possible but you felt very tired at times. There was always somebody on duty looking over the parapet, and if you were picked for guard duty you would have to take over from him to do a stint, well, you could be frightfully tired. I know of one or two soldiers, they were so tired that to keep awake they stood with their bayonet attached to their rifle under their chin. If they began to nod off they would feel the bayonet in there, under the chin. Sleeping on duty, you could get sentenced for neglect of duty, you could even get shot.

The strain took its toll at the Front, but you became hardened to it all. Oh yes, no doubt about it, you get hardened, and you wonder all the time when it's going to finish. You are hoping for a blighty one, a wound that's not serious, in the arm or wrist, that would get you back home. I hoped to get a blighty and I know those who looked for one, but getting one in the right place was difficult. At the Battle of Loos, the chappie sitting next to me was lying down with his legs in the air. I said "Keep your legs down." "Why?" I said "You'll get shot." He said, "I want to get shot in the leg. I want a blighty one, then I won't have to go on any further. I don't want to stand up and get shot in the stomach." Then another chap next to us said "Good idea that" and he did the same.

'We were filthy most of the time because we lived like rats.' Using water from the River Ancre these soldiers make an attempt to clean their rifles and other items of equipment and clothing. TAYLOR LIBRARY

DICK BARRON

After military training in the shadow of Egypt's great national monuments, Dick Barron was shipped across to the rugged and unforgiving landscape of the Gallipoli peninsula in August 1915. His stay in the line was both emotionally harrowing and physically daunting.

Dick Barron
1914

There had already been a landing on Gallipoli at Cape Hellas, the Lancashire Landing. We were to make a new landing at Suvla Bay, made easier because the Australians had made a diversionary attack. Well, we knew nothing, the army tells you nothing, we just arrived off the coast on the ship *Caledonia* and transferred to lighters pulled by a naval pinnace. We turned into the bay and landed easily with just a little desultory fire.

Conditions on Gallipoli were terrible. During the day when the rations came up, the flies swarmed. They were almost cloud-like and anything sweet or edible, they used to descend on it, it was fly telepathy I suppose! You could hardly get a mouthful of bully beef to your mouth before it was covered in flies. You waved your hand over them or lit a cigarette and blew the smoke onto the food to chase the flies away. The heat was another problem. It was blistering hot during the day but within half an hour of sunset, it was damn cold. All the flies then seemed to disappear, where they went to at night I don't know, but within an hour of sunrise they came back again and caused as many casualties through disease as the enemy action, particularly dysentery.

I caught dysentery soon after, but didn't report it for ages. If I'd been wounded I'd have been down the first aid station at the head of the queue but I thought it was in-for-a-dig to report sick. I carried on too long, I thought I could out-last it, shake it off, silly kid really. Dysentery is very lowering, your guts are terrible the whole time and you pass blood, you always want to be in the field loo. One morning I found I couldn't stand up. I was taken down to a hospital ship in the bay and then over to Malta. There were so many men like me suffering dysentery at various stages. I don't think there is a cure for it really. I was dangerously ill and I thought and I hoped I was going to die. If the pearly gates haven't opened for you, you have no idea, but I was in such a state that I just wanted to give in. The medical officer, I am sure, never thought I would recover until one morning when he said to me "Barron, when you're a bit stronger we're going to send you back to England". Well, that sparked something in me. England meant something, to see mum and dad and all the family.

I hadn't been long in warfare but it had lost all its romanticism. There is nothing *Boys Own* about warfare. Warfare was a grim, unsatisfactory, bloody silly business. I found out that I wasn't one of those heroes that warfare made of some men. I was not prepared to do anything spectacular. I just did my duty. I did come to one conclusion: the person who won the war was the ordinary Tommy who was always cheerful, not a brilliant intellect but always had a story

50

On Gallipoli men were as likely to be carried out of the line suffering from dysentry as from a wound suffered in action. Some 251,000 men were to become casualties during the eight month campaign. IWM Q13325

to tell, and whatever the bloody awful conditions carries on right through. Mind you, I don't take any fame from the chap who in a moment of aberration crawls out and drops a bomb in an enemy machine gun post and obliterates it. He's brave, he gets the VC, sometimes the DCM. But the bloke who is always cheerful, who'll carry your pack for you, he's the bloke that won the war.

ANDREW BOWIE

As a signaller in the front line, Andrew Bowie received some of the more inane messages sent from Divisional Headquarters. It gave Andrew the lasting impression that some high-ranking officers behind the lines did not always keep the men's best interests at heart.

We were in the trenches on iron rations, and were due to leave the line, when some bright spark at Divisional Headquarters said "Oh, keep the men on iron rations when they come out on rest." And why was that? Oh, it was to "Make the men hardy, don't you know." Now this was winter, November, well, the men didn't like this at all and they stuck a notice up when they came out of the line and it said "No hot rations, no F...ing fight." This got back to Headquarters and we were put straight back on hot rations. There had been some unrest at the training base at Etaples, so I think they were afraid of problems spreading to the

Andrew Bowie (third from left standing) with the battalion signallers. The equipment, signalling lamp, heliograph and semaphore flags, was impractical for conveying messages on the Western Front. Use of these means would have brought instant death or wounding to the operator.

front line.

These officers at Headquarters who'd come out of Sandhurst had no idea what hot rations meant to the lads. It was something you looked forward to when you came out, a nice hot dish of stew, a piece of bacon, or if you didn't get bacon, some fat in which to dip your bread.

When you went into action you always had emergency iron rations, a tin of pork and beans or bully beef. We also had Huntley and Palmer No 6 biscuits, army biscuits, and you needed very good teeth to get through, otherwise you just sucked them until you could get your teeth into them. They were about six inches by three, and some of the boys used to make picture frames out of them, cutting an edge right round, leaving about a quarter inch, paint them with boot polish and stick a girl's photograph in there.

The latrines in the line were just a hole and a pole stretched across, and you just sat on the pole. And the sad thing was that all you had for toilet paper was your love letters from your dear folk at home. And that was where they ended, nearly all the letters ended up in the latrine. You would see men sitting on the spar reading the letter and you knew the fate of it. It was humorous but it was sad to say you had nothing to wipe your bottom with but a letter. It was a tough life.

FREDERICK HODGES

The fighting into which nineteen-year-old Fred Hodges was sent in April 1918, was some of the most concentrated and costly of the whole war. Fred was quickly made a full corporal and Battalion Gas NCO, so taking on great responsibility for the welfare of others, under the most trying conditions. Men in the trenches were now subjected to attack by every weapon devised and refined over the previous three years, and life could be very short. However, as Fred discovered, nature still found room to thrive.

We had only been there a few hours when we were subjected to a very fierce bombardment. Captain Drummond came along and said "Now do what I'm doing," and he sat on the firestep and he pulled his feet up so his heels were touching his backside and he put his arms around his head and shoulders and said, "Now you've covered your vital parts, so there's nothing more you can do. If you're going to die, if you do stop some shrapnel, what better place to die than in the front line in defence of your king and country?"

Death could come quickly. If you heard a 5.9 shell coming, there was first an intensifying roar which hurt the ear drums and then its whoosh just before it exploded. You had time to dodge one way or another, but with whizz bangs there was little chance to escape. The only way I can compare their arrival is to sitting on an express train near the window and another express train passes in the other direction. It sort of shocks you for a moment, and that's just about the amount of time you have to get away. You're dead or you're not dead.

The first three men we lost were not killed by a shell but by the blast of a trench mortar, a Minenwerfer, as they were called. I was told that the big bangs we could hear were trench mortars. I was assured the men feared mortars more than the shells because they were devastating when accurate, and because it was so difficult to predict where they would fall. They began their travels with a barely audible bang behind the German line after which, at night, we might see a small red spark like a cigarette end moving across the sky. During the day you might just see a black dot, which got bigger very quickly before it exploded with hot deadly shrapnel flying everywhere. I remember some of our own Stokes mortars landing short, not far from our trench. One whooshed over and burst about forty yards away with several pieces whirring back over my head. They would have easily decapitated me had I been in the way.

Everybody put on a bold front and shut off feeling. You wouldn't face reality, you were there and you could be killed at any minute, it's no use dwelling on it. I always went to look at bodies to see if I knew people. Twice I saw a dead officer and I picked up the corner of the ground sheet and I thought "Your parents don't know you're dead". Aren't those queer thoughts? I knew what his own people at home didn't know.

Legitimate searching of the dead for identity disks, paybooks, and personal effects for return to next of kin. TAYLOR LIBRARY

I was leading a party of men when we came across a lot of dead – our own men – nine of them hit by one shell. They were just all funny shapes, and as I glanced round I saw one of my party taking a badge off an arm. It was a Lewis Gun badge, L.G. in brass with a wreath around it, a pretty badge and he wanted it. I told him to leave it alone, and he sullenly put it down. "I won't have any looting." I was strict and stern and I shouted at them. An NCO has to be a bit of an actor to get a point across, but looting was totally against my beliefs.

When you passed a body of dead men, the pockets were always empty, hanging out. I've met men with four wrist watches taken off dead officers, two on each wrist. On another occasion, I discovered that two London boys in the Regiment had been looting graves, getting rings off corpses. That shocked me. It didn't matter whether they were British or German, if they were dead and there was money, they'd take it. Oh, it was quite callous. I had a policeman under my command and on one occasion he was wounded in the backside. I slit his trousers open with a jack knife and told him he'd got a nice blighty wound and I would sent for a stretcher. But what he was most concerned with was what was in his two breast pockets. He'd got the very best quality German cut-throat razors, he'd made a collection of them and he was most anxious that they should accompany him on his way home.

Although I lived amongst the carnage of war and its many dead bodies, I also became very aware of nature. At night when I was all alone, I imagined I might be the only man in the world. The rest of the Company are close by, but you and a mate are the only two sentries awake, and you look around and nothing is going on. You notice the stars, and I tried to remember what some of them were named. On a still day, you'd see white clouds lazily drifting over the battlefront, larks singing above your head; nature was going on just the same, yet all round men were dying. You were struck by the contrast between the horror that we men had created over four years and nature that was proceeding in its quiet,

Souvenir collecting after an attack. These men have a cache which includes bayonets, pipes, helmets and at least one Luger pistol. Exausted men would put on a display of enthusiasm for the official photographer and be fast asleep moments later. TAYLOR LIBRARY

beautiful way. Whatever the scene, nature grows, bulbs will come out and flower, and the birds sing – it doesn't stop and say "Well, I'd better not sing here, it's rather a sad place". Stars, birds, flowers, especially poppies, they were scattered everywhere. You'd see a bank of poppies half as wide as a street, just sheer red, or you'd see them clustered on the trench you were in, growing. One of my officers came along one day and gave me a cup to fit on my rifle from which to fire a rifle grenade. I removed my bayonet and placed it back in its sheath and fitted the cup onto the rifle barrel, then I picked a bunch of poppies and put them in the cup, like you would a vase. I kept them there for a few minutes, but I knew if my officer came back he'd tick me off, so I pulled them out again.

ROYCE McKENZIE

Before the war, Royce had worked down the coal mines, and every trick he had ever learnt dodging hazards underground was used in his new job as a battalion runner. His ability and speed over the battlefield were admired by his comrades; his survival was against all odds.

There were ten runners on the Headquarters Section, ten men running messages back and forwards between the companies in the line and command, wherever it happened to be. Well, I was picked for the job and the lads said "Tha's got a good job now, Mac". I said "Ah, we'll wait and see." The lads felt I'd got a cushy job but I found it different, six runners had been killed or wounded out of the ten they'd had, because snipers used to pop off the runners all the time. Of course they had to get one or two more out of the companies to build up again. Aye, I found out it were a bloody sight worse than being in trench.

I wasn't picked because I was a fast runner or because I was fit, I mean I used to play battalion football, and before that I used to play football for pit, for the colliery team, but it made no difference, we were all remarkably fit then.

A lot of the runners kept to trench but I didn't, I used to get out and away from it, if I could. The Adjutant, Lieutenant Clark, once asked me how I got all these messages through and I says that I worked down pit and you learn a few tricks when you're down there, and I said I'd been using them up here. We worked in twos because so many runners were hit. My mate was a Scotch lad, and we got on very well together, Bill Nielson, he worked down pit just the same in Scotland, and we used that knowledge to get through all these shellings, knowing how to take different roads. When you're down pit, say you're pit pony driving, well, you go up what they called a road, a slit road, with yer pony pulling tubs, and you were dashing about getting out of way, this way and t'other, and that's what kept us going as runners, getting out of the way quickly, avoiding danger, not getting panicky. Lads who'd joined up as clerks didn't know any different, they'd just go and take a message, but lads who worked down pit, they were more canny.

56

A Company Runner awaits a reply from this trench Orderly Room of the Royal Fusiliers. The job of Company Runner was a dangerous one as German snipers were always on the lookout for movement in the lines opposite. TAYLOR LIBRARY

We were going down to D Company and I said to this mate of mine, "Come on, Bill, we'll get out on top, you never know who you are going to meet in these trenches, you know," because Jerry used to raid ours same as we used to raid theirs. So we got out on top and we were walking, dodging this way and that to avoid the shells, when I saw this yellow light coming. I watched it coming through sky and I watched it dip down. "Look at that light, Bill," and all of a sudden it come down and I said "Run like hell, Bill, it's coming right for us!" Anyway it come straight down and plunged into ground only a few yards at back of us, but it didn't go off. It was a dud shell but it threw a lot of dirt up and a piece hit me between the shoulders and knocked me for six and when I picked myself up I couldn't see Bill at all, he'd been buried with muck that shell had knocked up, so I went and scratched him out, spluttering but all right. I said "You didn't run fast enough, Bill!" "I will next time," he says. If it had gone off, we'd have been no more.

Headquarters was always at back of line. There was a front line and the support lines and the Headquarters was usually in back of support. You had to go from there either way to A Company, B Company, C Company, and D Company. Runners were the only means of relaying anything to the companies,

57

otherwise the company officers wouldn't know what to do. You couldn't stop, you had to keep going through the shellfire. The message might be urgent, ten minutes longer than necessary might cost lives. Of course the message was sealed, you wasn't allowed to read the messages, you just popped it in your top pocket. The Adjutant told me, "If you get in any difficulties, get shut of the messages you're carrying." I was to swallow them, that was orders. No, you didn't dare read them, you could be court martialled for anything like that, you know. The army didn't mess about with blokes then, if you did anything wrong, bang.

I expected to be hit at any time. The shrapnel flying about, you were lucky if you got through it all right, and I were lucky. I was the luckiest man in France. Nothing seemed to go wrong. I always seemed to come through somehow, me and my mate Bill. If a message came, well, C.O. says to me "You again, McKenzie?" Messages often were taken over very short distances, the shorter they were the more dangerous, often. The C.O. gave me an urgent message for D Company which was cut off, had been for a couple of days, with no food or water. I'd got sixty yards to cross and when I got to end of B Company the lads there said "Are you going across there, Mac?" I said "Aye, got to" and they said "By God, you got summat to do." I says to Bill, "If I don't get across, wait till everything's died down and then dash across." Anyway I got across and Lieutenant Whitaker says "You again, McKenzie?" I says "Yes Sir, I'm getting

A Company Headquarters, housed in a captured German dugout in the Ypres Salient, with a Runner setting off with a message. TAYLOR LIBRARY

quite used to you." He asked me how I was. "You're not too tired, are you?" I said no, he said "Well I've got a message to take back." He was real droll, one of the nicest blokes I ever come across.

When we went up into the mud at Passchendaele, we were told that we would not get into the front line without losing somebody, that means someone falling off the duck boards and into the mud. You couldn't walk on the ground, there were shell holes twenty foot deep, full of water and mud, a devilish place, wicked. I told the Adjutant what I'd heard and he issued every four men with little bits of rope, just held in the hand so if anyone slipped off you had a chance of saving him, and we did get into the line without losing a man.

There wasn't a trench or owt like that, there were just shell holes which you tried to dig out, empty out the water. Taking messages was almost impossible because you didn't know where you were. Bill and I had to try and find D Company. We kept pushing on and we didn't see anybody. I was getting a bit nervous but we went on a bit further when all at once a Véry light went up, a German Véry light, and we were only fifty yards from their front line, we'd walked right through our line of shell holes and almost into the Germans'. We'd got back about thirty yards when a voice said "Who are you?" I say "It's Mac" and he says "You're bloody lucky, it's a wonder I didn't shoot you. What are you doing out there?" It was a mate of mine, Bill Shrewsbury, so I told him if it hadn't been for the Jerry light we'd have been in their trenches. Anyway, he says "This is B Company. Come in. Follow these 'ere shell holes and you'll see two or three blokes in each one, follow 'em down and you'll come to D Company." Lieutenant Whitaker was there. "You again?" he says. I say "Aye, bit friendly aren't we sir?" He was always ready for a joke, nice fellow that.

JACK ROGERS

Most men slept during the day and worked in carrying parties at night. For snipers like Jack, work was a daytime job, observing the enemy and taking pot shots at careless Germans who appeared above or behind the trench line.

The Royal Engineers would come up into the front line and dig a post for you and they'd cut a hole in the middle and put in a steel plate which you could use to fire through. The post was also good for observation because we always carried binoculars and a telescope, reporting on anything seen. We worked in twos, and would man that post all day, taking up a haversack of rations, a runner coming up from Headquarters to take our messages. If there was a lot of activity, Headquarters might send one of us out into No Man's Land to watch, all camouflaged of course. You would choose a point, anywhere, perhaps on a little bit of a rise where you could just see, and it was left to you entirely whether you thought it was worth having a pot or two, but targets seldom appeared, I can assure you of that.

I didn't take any great pleasure in sniping, and I shouldn't like to think that I'd killed anyone, but then you would rarely know if you shot anyone anyway.

Sniping was not like having close combat, it was something in the distance. To prevent them killing us, that was the idea, but not to kill unless someone was specifically trying to kill us, then of course we would want to get rid of him.

There was a German sniper working, having a go at our communication trench, and occasionally I think he had scored a couple of hits. Whether he had killed anybody I don't know, but the order came down that we were to find out where this sniper was. We set up three posts along the line, both scouts and observers, the idea being that at all three posts the observers concentrated on the German line and when they saw the sniper fire, they were to take a compass bearing on exactly where it came from. Now we were to keep watch all day and sure enough a shot came from a position on top of this German trench. We all took bearings and when we met at Headquarters in the evening, we compared our results. We looked at a map and drew a line according to each bearing, and where they met on the trench all we could see, the next morning, was a big old bucket that seemed to have no bottom to it.

This was where the German was firing from, so we trained our sights on that bucket, all three riflemen ready, and if there was a shot we were all to fire simultaneously. Well, a bullet was fired and we all fired back, not one shot but as many as we could into that bucket. Of course the bucket seemed to spin round so whatever face or head was behind that I wouldn't like to think.

If your target is close and still enough that you've got the time to think of where to shoot, I should probably shoot for the head – that is where someone would wear a steel helmet, so perhaps it would not kill them. My purpose, in my opinion, was not to kill, rather to stop too much activity going on through the enemy's communication trenches linking the front and second lines. There was always traffic there, Germans moving up and down with impunity, you might say not worried about the enemy being over there, so you had to remind them, as it were.

Charlie Shaw and I were on the observation post one morning, Charlie looking with the telescope and I using the binoculars. There was quite a stretch of country between us and the German front line which was up on a bit of a crest. All of a sudden, Charlie said "Look!" and over the top, out over the German lines, two men appeared and they walked down the slope a little bit, both of them carrying shovels. They hadn't got down a long way before they started digging quite a large hole. They dug and dug and got a load of earth on the side. They then went and got a big box with a hole in it and pushed it down into the recess they'd dug. Apparently they were making a latrine, just this wooden box stuck in the ground for anybody to sit on. Charlie said to me, "They haven't got the cheek to build a toilet there, surely, I mean nobody's going to use it, are they?" I said I didn't know but we should wait and see. It wasn't so very long afterwards before another soldier appeared over the top. He came walking down to that toilet and began to pull his trousers down, sat on the toilet and had the nerve to pull out a newspaper and sit there reading it. "Are we going to put up with that?" Charlie said. "Not if I can help it, what about you, Charlie, about how far, do you think?" He said "I think it's best part of a mile, wouldn't you?

60

Right, are you going to shoot or am I?" I replied that he'd better shoot and I would observe, so Charlie loaded up his rifle, got it poised and the man was still sitting there reading. "Ready?" I said "Yes." "Right," said Charlie, "watch out", and he fired. I don't know how near he was to the German but that man never stopped to pull his trousers up. He just got up and tore away as best he could, over the top of the hill out of sight.

We had heard from one or two prisoners we had captured in previous trench raids of a place called Malakoff Farm, just on the other side of the German trenches. But it wasn't known if it was part of the second line defences and if so, how strongly it was defended. Command was wondering whether there was a big machine gun post there or not, and whether it was going to cause us a terrible blow if we had to advance. So they asked Robinson, one of our officers,

A British sniper team at work with one looking for targets through a periscope and the other sighting up for a shot.   TAYLOR LIBRARY

A British sniper's post indicating three Germans sniped; empty cartridge cases pressed into the earth spelling 'III Huns'.   TAYLOR LIBRARY

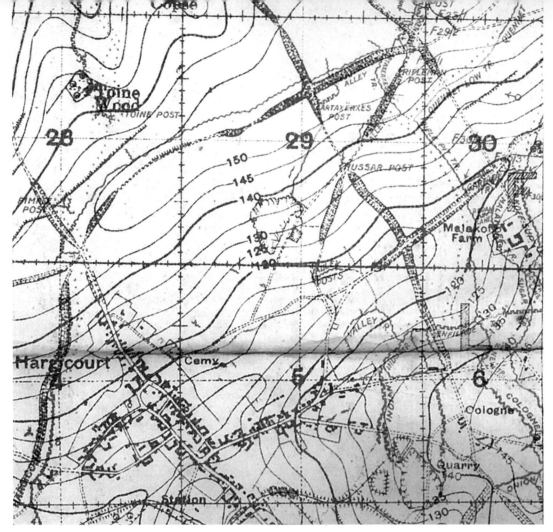

The above is reproduced from an original map and shows the trenches and positions around Malakoff Farm. Jack Rogers was detailed as part of a four man patrol to check out the farm to determine the strength of the German presence.

if he'd pick out two or three men to go with him, to make a raid and see if they could get near to Malakoff Farm to see what the position was.

Charlie Shaw, Frank Richards, and myself were picked to go with Lieutenant Robinson that night. All traces of identification were removed and we put some black on our faces. The only unfortunate part was that Mr Robinson wore glasses so we had to be careful with him. Anyway, we started out from a post so they knew when we were going and when we would be coming back, and we were given a password to identify ourselves in the dark. Then, using a prismatic compass to get our bearing, we set off in the direction of Malakoff Farm.

There was a lot of loose German wire in front of us, so we used a pair of wire cutters, bending the wire back before we jumped down into their first line trench without any trouble. There was nobody there and it was quiet. Walking a little way, we found there was a place where there was a low climb over the parados – the back of the trench – and on we went again in the open towards their second line. Charlie was in front, Frank and Robinson and I brought up the rear as we dropped into the second trench, which seemed hardly manned at all. Continuing on near to where Malakoff Farm was, we stopped and my goodness, what you could hear there, you could hear all sorts of going on, people talking, any number moving about. This proved the farm was strongly held and was all the information we needed. Then all of a sudden someone must have heard a noise, or spotted us from somewhere, because there was a hell of a wind up. A German Véry light went off in the air, bathing the ground in light, then another light and we could hear shouting. Robinson says "Get back as quick as you can, hurry, anyway you like," so we had to run back up this trench, across the open and into the big trench but then we had to stop. Lieutenant Robinson had lost both his hat and his glasses, they'd fallen off and he could hardly see. He was in the trench, helpless, scrambling about. It was a nightmare and I shall never forget it. Charlie and I grabbed hold of Mr Robinson and followed Frank, going along as fast as we could. We found the place where we could climb up and we helped each other over the top, but Richards was missing. We waited for a moment, then all of a sudden we heard Richards coming up, he'd gone the wrong way. He shouted and we called him over and helped him out of the trench before passing through the hole in the wire we had cut, that was one particular bit of luck to find that. We then tore across No Man's Land, dropping half way for a breather and to find our bearing. It was important to find the post we'd first passed through, because shadowy figures coming through the dark, well, the sentry is likely to have a pot at you. We gave the password and got into the trench puffed and beaten. Oh, what a relief! You think, thank God I'm still here today, how wonderful, and the only sad thing is the second thought, it isn't all over for you yet, there's more to come; will it be like this or could it be worse? You've got it all still to face and you often wondered how much more of this you could stand.

Robinson was given the Military Cross, so we thought we were going to get the Military Medal, but we only got a high commendation from the Colonel. Later, there was a proper parade when Lieutenant Robinson was awarded his MC and he asked that mention be made of us and we were awarded some francs and a day's leave to Amiens by train.

ANDREW BOWIE

Of all the duties undertaken in the line, trench raids or general attacks were the most dangerous and harrowing. Whether the Germans anticipated an attack or not, many men were likely to be killed or seriously wounded within minutes of zero hour.

I felt more nervous before an attack, when you see fellows writing letters, and you are told to clean up all your equipment. The bombers had to get their grenades primed, the Lewis gun people had to get the panniers clean: you knew you were going over the top. They didn't actually say you were going over, but that was what it amounted to. The fellows would start writing letters, giving

them to someone else to post just in case they were killed. There was this feeling in the air that something was going to happen. You were numb and you knew that it would be the end for somebody. You Stand-to the next morning, and you were nervous then because the Germans very often knew you were coming. They seemed to shell before you got off the mark.

At Passchendaele it was somewhat different. Prior to the attack, about a week or so beforehand, they talked to us about taking this Passchendaele Ridge. It was all done in model form, showing us the terrain. We were supposed to be shock troops and we were to rehearse the attack. We knew the contours of the land to a certain degree, but it all looked different when we got there. The Battalion was to attack on 12th October and, as a signaller, I was supposed to accompany the Captain over the top, then act as a runner taking messages back. The Lieutenants went forward with the platoons but the Captain was a little bit behind, perhaps fifty yards. I carried a rifle but if you put it down, it became jammed with mud.

About an hour before the attack started, my Captain came along in the dark. MacDonald and I were together, and the Captain shouted "Who's there?" and I said "Cameron Highlanders". He came towards us. "Can I sit down anywhere?" I told him we'd dug a little hole. "That's all we have, but you can have it and we'll sit outside." He said "Oh no, boys, I'll go on. I've been laying out the tapes and I'm dead beat, but I'll go on." You see there were no trenches at Passchendaele, just shell holes linked together, so tapes had to be laid out for us

Two remarkable photographs of an action near Hooge in June 1915. These pictures show British troops taking cover behind the German front line, a flag indicating that the trench has just been taken. Both pictures were snapped by Private F. A. Fyle, 1/10 Kings Liverpool, a press photographer in civilian life. IWM Q49751 & Q49750

to line up on before we went forward. Anyway, that was what the Captain had been doing, but I did not see him again. He was killed in the attack.

There were three of us together and when the attack started, one was hit straight away. "Andrew, Andrew, I'm hit!" He was hit in the shoulder and blood was gushing out. I took his equipment off and put a field bandage on. "What do I do now?" He was excited, the boy; I said, "You get back to the duckboards and go down there to the artillery lines, they'll look after you." He was just a new boy to us and it was his only chance, as he would bleed to death otherwise. I don't know what happened to him to this day.

We didn't get fifty yards. I couldn't measure time but I would think the whole attack was finished in half-an-hour. The Germans were above us and that made it easy for them, and with their machine guns rattling, we were just targets. There just seemed to be a blast of fire straight away, there was no battle, we were just knocked over. I saw men dropping down, but they were dropping down for safety as well, because you can't imagine how intense the fire was, with red hot metal flying around.

I was on the extreme right of the battalion and I fixed on a big shell hole where there was a sergeant of the Seaforth Highlanders and two of his men. We sat in mud, heads down, otherwise they would have been knocked off by a

65

Two men, one wounded, receiving a helping hand. "We came out, the two of us, the only two left of the battalion as far as we were concerned."   IWM Q4210

machine gun. We could hear the machine guns still playing occasionally and I could also hear the wounded crying out for water. I was getting desperate because my pal, MacDonald, had been out east and had had malaria and he was having shivering bouts, and was in a terrible state. When it got dark, he said "Oh Andrew, try and find a way out," but I told him that in the dark I didn't know north from south and that we could walk into the German lines. We sat there for a long time when the sergeant said, "Well, there is one way you can try to get out. Put your two rifles together and put your two ground sheets over the top and pretend you are stretcher bearers."

We did what he said and we came out, the two of us, the only two left of the battalion as far as we were concerned.

GEORGE LITTLEFAIR

After ignoring his mother's plea not to join the army, George found himself in the front line as his battalion was due to go over the top. George might have answered his country's call to serve, but unnecessary heroics were not the order of the day. He would use his head to survive.

All our officers were local to home, good 'uns who were men, mucked in with us. But we had one, a bloody college boy, he didn't, not him, he was an officer boy, a bloody doll dressed up, that's all he was. We were muck where he was concerned and he knew we didn't like him. "I've been to college, you've been scraping for a living," thought he was much better than anybody else, but when it comes to bullets the buggers are all alike. He was always picking at one little Irish lad we had, every chance he got. He was real Irish, I mean we had difficulty understanding him but we got on with him all right, he was damn good, he'd do owt for anybody, help any lad out. Paddy called all us lads "Durham". He says to me, "I'll tell you, Durham, when we go over the top," he says, "that bugger'll not come back". Well, we went over the top and this officer got a bullet in him. Might have been from the German side, might have been ours.

You didn't do anything daft going over the top, you went quietly over, keeping as low as possible, and where there was a bit of shelter you took it, aye, you learnt to be very canny. I didn't go rushing over "I'll get a bloody German" style, because if you tried to go full steam ahead when everything was going hammer and tongs you knew you didn't stand a cat in hell's chance. A lot of lads dropped on purpose 'till it got less rough, and then advanced. I'd see lads going down, lads getting wounded, going back or calling for help, but there wasn't time to help. The sergeant would shout "Get down, get down!" You'd get down, you'd get in the back of a bloody thistle for shelter, if you could. I remember reaching the German trenches but the Germans had gone, empty they were and the lads were sitting, lying, moaning and groaning.

The rest of us went further along the line where we thought the fighting was, but the Germans were already up with their hands. They were told to get out, to get rid of their guns. They thought we were going to shoot them, but we would

German survivors of an attack submit to searches before being marched off carrying some British wounded. One prisoner is being made to carry a captured Maxim 08/15 (over). TAYLOR LIBRARY

tell them different as long as they kept their hands in the air. The Germans used to say "It's not us that's keeping the war going, it's not us, we didn't want to fight you", You'd be surprised at the English they could speak, aye, and they'd ask for a cigarette too. There were some grand lads among the Germans. It was the Kaiser and his gang that caused the trouble, they didn't want to kill us. To think you'd shot a man, you know, and he'd done nothing to you, that was how I used to look at it and then again I'd think, well, if I don't get him, he'll get me and my life is worth a hell of a lot to me! There was little close fighting, though. I'll tell you something about bayonet fighting, there's more lads put bullets into the enemy instead of their bayonet. When you got a German there you put a bullet in him instead of the bayonet, 'cos he was standing solid when you are on the move, aye, just pull the trigger and down he would go.

CHAPTER FOUR

Dreams of Home

URING the First World War, the sending and receiving of letters to and from home played a crucial role in maintaining morale amongst the front line troops. As the soldiers of the regular army were killed and wounded in France, so a new army of civilian soldiers was sent out to replace them. Unlike the regulars, many of whom had served in far-off corners of the empire, the new civilian soldiers were unused to leaving their homes and communities for any length of time. The knowledge that loved ones were thinking about them, that "normal life" continued at home, was of central and immeasurable importance.

Military-controlled Field Post Offices had been directing parcels and letters to the troops practically from the moment the British Expeditionary Force set foot in France in 1914. The army had long recognised the importance of home contact to the men's well-being and had channelled all mail through the FPOs, keeping

Somewhere in France – sorting out the incoming mail. IWM Q53349

Sheer delight in receiving parcels from home is written all over this artilleryman's face. He is collecting mail for his battery near Aveluy, September 1916. TAYLOR LIBRARY

Writing home knowing that his words will be subject to censorship. Many were to develop codes so that their loved ones would know where they were.   IWM Q2308

up an efficient delivery to every war zone at considerable cost in manpower and resources. Indeed, such was the emphasis given to communication from home that the death penalty hung over anyone caught stealing mail meant for the men at the Front.

Letters received at the Front were commonly read and re-read by soldiers, not just to themselves but to others in the trench craving news from home. But while these letters were a source of comfort to fighting men, they could equally bring bad news. For ordinary ranks who received precious little home leave during the war, news of a wife's infidelity, or the illness or death of a relative, could prove devastating. Compassionate leave was given infrequently, and many soldiers were left to sort out marital difficulties by letter, or to attend family funerals in spirit only.

In theory, there was no restriction on the number of letters home, although the practicalities of trench life and duty ensured that most letters were written behind the line. Even then, fatigues meant that many letters home were a quick scrawl, the promise of a longer letter soon. Those who did write had to submit the letter to censorship by an officer, invariably a young Lieutenant, who was likely to be the writer's platoon officer.

The army was anxious to restrict the flow of potentially dangerous information from falling into enemy hands. Such secrecy forbade soldiers to

I am quite well.

I have been admitted into hospital

$\begin{cases} sick \\ wounded \end{cases}$ *and am going on well.*
and hope to be discharged soon.

I am being sent down to the base.

I have received your $\begin{cases} letter\ dated\_\_\_\_\ \_\_\_\_ \\ telegram\ ,,\_\_\_\_ \\ parcel\ ,,\_\_\_\_ \end{cases}$

Letter follows at first opportunity.

I have received no letter from you

$\begin{cases} lately. \\ for\ a\ long\ time. \end{cases}$

Signature $\begin{cases} \\ \end{cases}$
   only

*Date*_____

(94890)   Wt. W1566-R1619   14,000m.   6/17.   J.J.K. & Co., Ltd.

This card allowed only the very briefest of information to be conveyed to Blighty. Nevertheless the news that a loved one was still alive was very important to those at home.

reveal anything other than casual generalities, "it is cold", "we've had a rough time". Indication of location or recent activities was immediately removed from an offending letter. This led to some soldiers inventing their own code, a capital Y in the word "Yes" would indicate he was at Ypres, two or three kisses at the end of a letter was a "yes" or "no" to an equally disguised question. For anyone hoping to sort out difficulties at home, the knowledge that their own officer would read and become au fait with private and intimate details was anathema to many men. The sole opportunity to write home privately came in the form of a green envelope, given to the men on condition that they revealed nothing untoward. The men signed the envelope to this effect and, while a sample was read at the base to deter abuse, most reached home unopened. Sadly, most men report been given no more than one green envelope a month.

The chance to return home came fleetingly to most soldiers. A three or five day pass was not untypical, beginning from the moment a soldier stepped off the leave boat at Dover and ending as he re-boarded. Such brevity of leave was troublesome enough to those who lived close to the channel ports, but for those who lived in Scotland, home leave was a virtual impossibility. No allowance was made for the distance a soldier had to travel, and it was not unknown for a soldier to arrive home hours before he had to leave again.

The frequency of leave also varied wildly. It was possible for a soldier to serve on the Western Front continuously for four years and to receive just two short bouts of leave, while another soldier might receive the same amount of leave in little over a year's service. Nevertheless, getting back to Blighty was a treasured aim for the men, as it was for the families who awaited their return: the wives who had been left to cope on their own, and the children who missed their father's re-assuring presence. Even so, leave was often a time of conflicting emotions, of relief and anxiety, happiness and distress.

While the frequency and length of leave was a major problem for soldiers, there was another, often unforeseen, problem. Many soldiers suffered a strong sense of dislocation from those at home, who had no conception at all of war's brutal reality. Taken aback by the continuance of everyday life, angered by seemingly petty civilian disputes, a few could not wait to return to the fold of the regiment back in France. Most simply felt uncomfortable at being paraded by proud parents to well-meaning neighbours. Even sleeping once again in warm comfortable beds, eating well, washing at will, could make some soldiers feel strangers in their own country. They were separated from the lifestyle they had once known and accepted, and for a few the separation was permanent.

HAL KERRIDGE, born 21st September 1898, 1/14th London Regiment (1st London Scottish), later 1st Gordon Highlanders.

Whenever Hal Kerridge sees the flickering black and white footage of the First World War, he can barely believe he "was in that lot". A remarkably forward-looking centenarian, he feels 100 years old only when someone else happens to mention the fact. Living in his own home near Bournemouth, Hal still drives his Audi to all the local amenities. He cooks, hoovers and gardens, takes holidays: a modern man who nevertheless fought on the Somme and at Passchendaele.

Hal Kerridge 1915

Hal Kerridge 1998

I had volunteered to exist in terrible conditions for weeks, months, years, and it became a way of living. Home was another world entirely, but home news was treated like gold dust. Getting mail was the joy of the day if you got any. It was the one link you had with home, your one and only link with sanity, hearing how everyone was in England. Writing home was very restricted. We had printed postcards to say "I'm well, I am wounded, I have received your parcel", and so on, but you couldn't tell your family where you were, who you were with, what you were doing or where you were going. In letters we would write only about personal things, what we'd had for dinner, asking how the dog was, is the sun shining? The only thing you would get past the censor perhaps was that you were resting, that perhaps you'd had a bath. You could give a vague description of what trenches were like, but then that was hardly a secret from the Germans. Every letter was censored by officers and anything untoward that was said was blue-pencilled straight away. There had to be no indication at all as to where you were or what you were doing. We quickly got used to writing letters in a very innocuous style. You didn't want to make your parents any more miserable than they were already, so you kept quiet about conditions as much as you could; as far as they were concerned you were getting on all right.

Hal Kerridge, (legs crossed) snapped as he left France for two weeks' leave in England. The photograph gives some indication of the numbers of troops crowded onto the leave ships crossing the Channel.

It must have been nearly two years before I got to go home, two weeks' leave. To think you were going to get out of the line for a little time away from the misery, well, you felt absolutely sky high, everyone felt the same, even the wounded. I caught the boat home from Boulogne and it was crammed, jammed tight and someone took a picture of me, I've no idea who it was.

You have to remember we'd been with men, men only for years. Good pals as they might be, you were sick and tired of seeing the same men, eating with men, sleeping with men, living in the mud with men. It was a joy to get away from it and see a bit of civilisation, if you like, we were youngsters and keen to see the girls. We would have much preferred to have been left alone to go and take a girl to the pictures or a dance, to relax, but, I suppose, I, together with others who had a duty towards their parents, never got the chance. We just went out with our parents, kept them company, and they took us round to our aunts and uncles and God knows who, and made an exhibition of us, and none of us wanted to be an exhibition – we just wanted to be left alone.

You just accepted it. You were home with your parents and it was their joy and you were out to please them. They did everything for you, so I suppose, unconsciously, you did what you could for them. Father in particular was immensely proud of me and took me everywhere. I didn't enjoy it, not one bit. Of course relatives asked what conditions were like but you didn't want to scare them any more than you wanted to scare your parents, you didn't tell them about the dangers. I mean, I wasn't going to tell my father the misery I was living in the mud there. All I could say to him was, "Oh we manage, we get along". You'd never talk of the darker side, you minimised what you told them for their sake.

My father came with me to the station. He said "Cheerio, son, look after yourself, I'll be glad to see you back again," and that was that. My father was a great scout. He was a gentleman, a very gentle man, yet he'd got nerves of steel. He'd never show his emotions, it would upset me, so at the station we shook hands. He would never show me that he was scared and I hoped I would never show him that I was scared either. It was no good standing on the station crying your eyes out because your son's getting in the train to go back to France. That doesn't help him, it doesn't help me. No, you treat it in a man's way. It was the way we behaved in those days. I mean, our people at home had a duty to do – the same as we had – and their duty was not to make our lives harder than they were already. I knew it could be the last time I saw him and he knew that as well. I said goodbye to my mother at home, she could not bear to come. Many mothers were crying, in floods of tears, hanging on to their husbands' arms. It was usual at any station, some signs of hysteria and all that. You saw it every time you got a crowd going back to the Front.

ROBERT BURNS

Not long after the 7th Cameron Highlanders had been badly cut up at the battle of Loos, Robbie received permission to go home on leave. He returned to Scotland, to a world far removed from the misery of the Front.

I had two leaves during the war. The first time, I got on a train full of civilians, and I was the only soldier in the compartment, but by the second time, there were special leave trains laid on for soldiers to take them home. When I got home it was 9.30am and my mother said "You'd better go and see your brother". He was at school, so I went and looked through the school door and I could see him sitting in the class. We lived in a small village so there was only one room in the school, and one teacher, so I opened the door and put my head in. The schoolmaster saw me and said "Come in, come in". I'd a German helmet and a gas mask which I took and gave to the school as a souvenir. The headmaster said "What did you say – you want a holiday? Right, who wants a holiday?" All the hands went up, so a holiday it was for everyone for that one day. The kids went home and told their parents and within half an hour the village knew that I was back from the Front, being the first man in the village to join up.

I had women coming to see me and old men wanting to know what the war was like. I was treated like a hero. I didn't tell them anything, of course, about what it was like. I was man enough to know it wasn't a nice subject to talk about, especially to kids. I didn't think I would get into trouble from the authorities, I just thought it was the wrong thing to tell them about the horrors of the trenches,

Arriving home on leave. This image, obviously posed, is intended to convey the moment of meeting after months of grave danger for the young soldier and intense worry for his mother. Despite their desire to get home, many soldiers were to feel a profound sense of dislocation from the world they once knew. IWM Q30402 people lying there with their heads blown off, it was not the right thing to speak about and they couldn't possibly understand.

I enjoyed myself. I went to the cinema in Glasgow nearly every night and walked the four miles back from the station at night. I played billiards nearly every day, as my uncle owned one of the biggest saloons in Glasgow, watched football matches, oh yes, I kept myself fully occupied until my leave was up.

I didn't want to go back but I knew I had to, it was my duty. When you leave home, you say cheerio, I might see you again, that's all you've got to say – might see you again, 'cos we all knew what we were going in for. Of course I wrote home. You put any letter in an envelope which was collected by the NCO and given to your officer to read. He closes the envelope and signs it and it is then taken to the FPO, the Field Post Office. About once a month we were given a "green" envelope in which you can say anything you want because it is not opened by your officer, although a random selection was opened further down the line. In some of the French villages, I used to post letters through the French Post Office, which was forbidden, but I knew I could write more in those letters. If you told the truth about what was going on, you would get into trouble. I was one of those types who was afraid of getting into trouble because in the army you suffered for it.

GUY BOTWRIGHT

There were many burdens placed on the shoulders of young Second Lieutenants, but one of the most irksome was the endless censoring of letters. New to the Front, Guy found it a difficult and depressing task reading his own men's private correspondence.

It was the officer's job to censor the letters the men sent home from the Front. It was never a job I enjoyed doing. If things were peaceful, you could bet the men were writing letters home, there was going to be quite a pile. All the letters had to be brought to the officers whose job it was to read them, and we would have to make sure the men had not said anything compromising such as where they were, or where they had been. One had to be very, very careful, you dare not let things go, for if anything ever happened I would be for it in the true sense of the word. Afterwards I had to seal the envelope and initial it in a certain place certifying that I had read the letter.

Censoring letters was a difficult job to do and very distressing at times. I might get thirty a day to read and I got into the habit of being able to gloss over the letter trying not to read the contents. We were losing men all the while, so it was perfectly possible I might have been reading a letter from a man who might already have been killed. The letters were so personal, but you couldn't help picking up details. A lad might be asking why his loved one had not written earlier or the wife had obviously gone off with another man and this soldier was writing back to ask how she could be so faithless. It was depressing, the breaking up of families.

The men did not talk of conditions in France. They might say that it had been jolly wet, or we've been a bit hectic lately but because it was raining it had all stopped. I never read a letter, as far as I can remember, that said "It's hell's delight", or "You wouldn't believe how bad it is here". They were very good at not worrying those at home, they wouldn't say that they had been heavily shelled or anything like that, they might say "We had a bit of a flare up but it's all settled now". Of course I wouldn't have censored that, but he'd never like to worry her more than she was worried already. More often he just said that he wished he could see her, or talked of something in their past together.

JACK ROGERS

If it was difficult for officers to censor letters, it was even harder for men like Jack to write them in the knowledge that his personal words were not private. It placed Jack in an invidious position when he heard that his girlfriend might have been unfaithful.

I had a girlfriend called Elsie Carter who I was fond of. She worked as a nanny for a family, looking after a little child. However, soon after I left for France she went to work in a munitions factory at Shepherds Bush. The authorities were urging people to go and join the local factories to do war work, so Elsie did the patriotic thing. My mum knew Elsie quite well, 'cos I used to take her home to meet the family, so when she heard Elsie was working nearby she asked her if she would like to come and live in a spare bedroom.

I used to keep writing to her from France and she wrote back to me sometimes. She told me about working in the factory and about living with my mother. But the letters dropped off and then she didn't write at all. Well, there was a sad ending to all that, for the simple reason that my sisters and mother had seen her out many times with other men, staying out at night and that sort of thing. My mother used to go on at her about her behaviour until eventually she left the room and never came home at all, she went elsewhere.

You don't realise the position you are in, you don't know what to do, you don't know if the stories you are hearing are true. Of course, the stories were coming from my people telling me just what was happening, and I could only believe them because Elsie was not writing to tell me anything different. So I wrote to her in desperation asking her about what was going on. I wrote saying I hoped she would stay at my parents and I'd try and get home and we'd get engaged to be married, but I never heard from her, she never answered it, so I never wrote again. It was a betrayal, it wasn't fair, but of course a lot of this sort of thing went on behind the soldiers' backs. I wasn't the only one.

In or out of the line, there were always one or two soldiers you could talk to about your family life. I had one particular friend, Charlie Shaw, who became quite a close chum. He was a gypsy from Lincolnshire who used to travel around the county in one of those old gypsy vans. We used to chat and I was able to talk to him about most things, including Elsie, and he would tell me about his family and what was going on back home in the countryside. It all helped. I was upset, but the feelings wore off and I gradually began to forget about Elsie.

One day, this was after the war when I was living back in Hammersmith, there was a knock on the front door and I found Winnie Carter, Elsie's sister, standing there. She said that Elsie was standing just a few yards round the street corner and would I like to see her. I said "No, thank you, I don't want to see her again," and she went off. I knew what she'd been up to and the sort of life she'd been living. She hadn't even written or answered my last letter, she finished with me, so now of course I finished with her. I've never seen her again from that day to this.

NORMAN COLLINS, born 16th April 1897, died 2nd February 1998, 4th Seaforth Highlanders.

Of the casualties suffered amongst the ranks during the First World War, it was the young subalterns like Lieutenant Norman Collins who bore the greatest losses. If these officers were not killed, they were almost invariably wounded, and Norman was no exception: he was badly wounded on two separate occasions. He suffered pain from his injuries throughout his life, but remained ever charming and a friend to all who met him. His memory of the war was wonderfully detailed, and covered its entire duration from the bombardment of Hartlepool in 1914 to his very personal feelings on Armistice Day. He died on 2nd February 1998, aged nearly 101.

Norman Collins
1997

Norman Collins
1916

It was the closest bond because we were both living in the same world. It's extraordinary really, because the association between officers and men as a rule was very short. Neither lived very long but during that period it became the most intense feeling. Your affection for the men under you – there's no doubt about that. We used to write to their mothers when they were killed, and mothers used to reply asking for some sort of memento of

Norman Collins, left, recuperating from wounds near Le Touquet.

their dear son which you could never send, of course, because when you had to write these letters, sometimes there were about sixty letters to write, and you didn't even know who you were writing about. We always tried to write a nice letter to the mother or father because we felt for them, we understood what they were feeling. "Dear Mr and Mrs so and so, I'm sorry to have to tell you that as you no doubt have already heard by telegram, your dear son was killed on such and such a date. He was a fine chap and I was very fond of him and he was a good soldier and you, I'm sure, are very proud of him" and so on and so forth. As much as you could do, you made her feel that her son was a hero and that's about all. There was quite a bit of hype, there's no disguising it. There must have been quite a bit of hypocrisy in it, but it was kindly hypocrisy, you were doing it to comfort the mother. By the time you got to the stage of writing fifty or sixty letters, you couldn't remember who they were, too many. But at the time when they were killed you certainly felt, you felt for them very much, very much.

CHAPTER FIVE

The Battle of the Somme

THE BATTLE OF THE SOMME has come to typify most graphically the awful carnage of the First World War. Yet the beauty of the Somme's rolling downlands belies the history it has now almost hidden, principally the terrible casualties suffered on the first day, 1st July 1916. The weather conditions were perfect for the attack that morning. Early mists gave way to blazing summer sunshine, but at the end of the first day's battle, some 20,000 British troops were dead and 40,000 wounded.

The aim of the Big Push, as the attack became known, was decisively to breach the German defences. British troops would storm the enemy's trenches in the first of a series of prolonged strikes that would shove the Germans out of northern France and onwards, back towards the Rhine. The troops chosen to make this attack were overwhelmingly the young men who had joined up in the wave of enthusiasm which followed Kitchener's appeal in August 1914. Most had been training for over a year, although a few had seen action the previous summer at the Battle of Loos. However, for almost every one, this would be the first occasion when they would go over the top in a general attack.

The preparations were seemingly meticulous. As ten new Army divisions made their way to the Somme battlefront, a devastating seven-day bombardment would begin, smashing the enemy trenches and cutting the barbed wire in front. The popular belief was that the shelling would be so overwhelming that there would not be a rat alive in the German lines when British troops went over the top at 7.30 in the morning. As if the eager British troops required any further help – or reassurance – five huge mines, dug beneath strongpoints in the German line, would be blown, not only killing those in nearby trenches, but so demoralising anyone left alive that British troops could simply enter the trenches and round them up. Such was the confidence of the British High Command, that British troops would be ordered to walk towards the enemy lines, not run.

This order was one of the major reasons why so many died, for British troops were to find not only that much of the German wire was left uncut, but that the trenches behind, while superficially damaged, still supported the majority of German troops, who had simply taken refuge below in dugouts forty feet underground. On the lifting of the barrage that morning, the German machine gunners were able to climb into the trenches and open up with a withering fire, mowing down the British troops as they made slow progress across No Man's Land. It has been estimated that the ratio of British to German casualties was in the region of 12:1.

Although the Battle of the Somme is remembered for its tragic first day, it was a battle that was to last some four-and-a-half months. After the initial shock of widespread failure along three-quarters of the front line, the High Command began a series of further attacks that would continue throughout the rest of the summer and autumn. The results were generally mixed, although the Germans were gradually pushed back, field by field, wood by wood. In September, in a further attempt to break open the front line, the British launched their new secret weapon, the tank, with strategically limited but visually stunning results. One small village after another fell to the Allied forces, but by winter the offensive ground to a halt. The last attacks were made in early and mid November, when the notable village of Beaumont Hamel fell, in truth notable only for the reason that it had been a first day objective all those months before.

TOM DEWING, born 21st April 1896, 34th Division Signals Company, Royal Engineers.

Tom Dewing is still haunted by the visions of destruction he witnessed on the first day of the Battle of the Somme. As a signaller manning an observation post behind No Man's Land, he watched as his brigade launched its ill-fated attack. In the confusion of the fight, Tom little realised he had a bird's-eye view of what was to become the worst day in history for the British Army. Tom, a quiet but immensely personable man, lives alone in his well-kept home in Saffron Walden. Now aged 102, he recalls with emotion the day when any remaining innocence about war was lost.

We had no doubt, we were all convinced that this was the push, the big push that was to end the war. We quite thought that when the attack came, we should just go through their lines but it didn't work

*Tom Dewing
1915*

*Tom Dewing
1998*

Setting fuses on six inch shells for the Battle of the Somme. TAYLOR LIBRARY

18 pounder gun position on the Somme. IWM Q4065

out that way. The bombardment started all at once and we certainly were very impressed; the thunder of the guns was terrific. It went on and on, gradually increasing in volume. You could, if you were practised, pick out the field guns from the heavy artillery but I should say it was thunder, thunder, thunder. We got so used to it we really didn't take a great deal of notice. On 30th June we were sent to Smiths Redoubt which was dug into the side of a hill looking towards our brigade's objectives, the village of Fricourt and, beyond, Contalmaison. A camouflaged curtain was pulled in front of our position so the Germans would not see us, and equipment was set up to send and receive messages.

I remember the La Boisselle mine going up, one of several mines blown under the German lines to help the attack that day. We had been told beforehand it was going up and there was a terrific explosion. I don't remember what it looked like, but I do remember there was a vast hole, a vast crater after the explosion and I know that it was several seconds before we felt the explosion, the whole ground heaved and shook.

The La Boisselle mine crater, the biggest mine exploded on the Western Front. Blown with 60,000 lb of gun cotton, this crater is now a permanent memorial to the dead of the Somme Battle. The small figure of the man on the far side gives an impression of just how big the crater is.

IWM Q3999

In the first place there was a certain amount of mist and then when you add to that the enormous amount of smoke from the barrage, a great deal was hidden, so for a time we didn't see anything. Then when the mist and smoke cleared, we were able to see the infantry going forward in open formation as if on parade ground. We could see a group going forward and lying down, another group following, but there was so much smoke and disruption I can picture little bits but only certain little bits. In many cases the men didn't get very far, they were just wiped out. One of the officers in our dugout had a telescope and some field glasses which he allowed us to use from time to time, and looking into the crater we could sometimes see a German getting up, raising his rifle and firing. Those on our left had been stopped from the start, as soon as they got out of the trenches they were mown down by machine gun fire. For a long time we knew nothing and then presently a heliograph flashed our call sign, ZJA. We were delighted. Evidently some of our troops had got to their objective of Contalmaison. We waited, but no further message was sent. The Germans had spotted the signal and had turned their machine guns onto them. It was the last we heard.

We didn't realise what had happened until afterwards. We didn't realise until the next church parade. At Brigade Headquarters we had regular church parades and on this occasion, instead of the troops coming along as they usually did, there was just a handful out of each battalion. We felt sick. The colonels were sitting in front of what was left of their men, sobbing. The service was

British shells exploding on the German lines at La Boisselle just prior to the assault by 34th Division, 1 July 1916.   IWM Q23

Men of the 34th Division Tyneside Irish advance from their trenches on 1st July. Once over the rise they were cut down by German machine gun fire. IWM Q53

taken by Padre Black and how he managed to take that service I don't know. His text was "I will restore unto you the years that the locusts have eaten". There were so few, so few men left. How can you describe a mere handful of men where you used to see about a battalion? I know that church parade was a very, very emotional time. Did I shed any tears? Probably, probably and often since.

FREDERICK FRANCIS, born 20th January 1894, 11th Border Regiment.

Eighty-two years after receiving the last rites in the aftermath of the Battle of the Somme, Frederick Francis is still awaiting the final roll call. Still remarkably fit and aged 104, Fred has outlived the medical orderly and the priest who gave him twenty minutes to live, and has now outlived every comrade in his unit, the 11th Border (the Lonsdale) Regiment. He continues to bear the scars he received soon after going over the top, and owns a jam jar containing the metal taken from his body on 1st July 1916, a day which remains vivid in his mind.

Frederick Francis 1998

Frederick Francis 1916

"On the 1st of July the Lonsdale Battalion was slaughtered, wiped out. On the 1st of July the Lonsdale Battalion ceased to exist. The remnants were posted to the 12th Battalion, some of them back to Carlisle, but the Lonsdale Battalion, as a Battalion, finished that day in 1916, and I am one of the only survivors."

The officers and NCOs, such as myself, had seen a model of the terrain we would attack, and we did actually think we had nothing to do but walk over. For six days before we went, we'd assembled all the artillery we could get and pounded and pounded the Germans' line. But the Germans had deep dugouts and just kept a lookout and of course when we went over they were sitting waiting.

We had heard of the Leipzig Redoubt, we knew it was a real hot spot, but we

85

were determined to break the line. After all the training and practising digging dugouts and one damn thing after another, we were going into the real thing. Funny, in Carlisle, camped on the racecourse, we were all afraid that the war would be over before we got out. In barracks, the lads had been full of themselves, I'm a bomber, I'm a machine gunner, and all of this, but by God they were silent when we got out to France.

We sheltered in Authuille wood all night on 30th June, including my company, B Company, 7th Platoon. There was a lot of foliage and the German shells were not getting down. Most of the men were dozing or asleep when a shell came over, and two of my section woke up shaking and I thought "Oh my God, two with shellshock already". I couldn't take them into battle so I sent them out of the line. At zero hour, we filed out of the wood to find the Germans waiting for us. The 15th, 16th and 17th Highland Light Infantry had already gone over to bleed the enemy, you might call it, and we were going to follow to relieve them and take our objective, Mouquet Farm, which we were supposed to take by 11 o'clock. As we filed out, the colonel, Colonel Matchell, patted me on the back and said "The best of luck, son". Before the battle he had said that if we met with stiff opposition he would come and lead the men himself. We met with stiff opposition so he came out. Bullet in the head. Finish.

The Germans just mowed us down like grass in a hay field, enfilading fire, not just from the front. We only had about three hundred yards to cross, but truthfully my thoughts were "I wonder how long it will be before I get hit". Anyone who was not hit that day must have had angels on their back. I'd only gone a little way, stepping over the barbed wire, when I got a bullet through my water bottle, and through my hip and I dropped on my face. I put my steel

Mouquet Farm (Mucky Farm to Tommy). The planners had given the Lonsdale Pals three and a half hours to reach this objective on the morning of the Big Push. They did not reach further than the German defences at Leipzig Redoubt. TAYLOR LIBRARY

Frederick Francis "Somewhere in France" in early 1915.

helmet on the back of my head and I could hear the shrapnel dropping all round. I went to crawl under our own barbed wire but the shelling was terrible and I was being buffeted about like a piece of paper on a windy day. I hate to think about it. It was hellish there, the barbs on the wire would stick into your clothes. I just said to myself "This is the last of the Battalion, there'll be no Battalion left after this", and there wasn't, they were lying dead and wounded all over.

It wasn't so much the hot summer's day as the blood I had lost that made me thirsty, and when I could stand the thirst no longer I started to crawl about as best I could, dragging my wounded foot. I'd lost so much blood and I had no water in my bottle, so I crawled until I fell into a shell hole at the bottom of which was our Sergeant Major. I'd known him, in civvie life he was a well-known cyclist in Carlisle. Now he was lying dead, so I said to myself "You won't need your water bottle, I'll take it". So I took it and to my amazement and disgust it was full of rum and it made me violently sick and I seemed to lose consciousness altogether.

I lay out there all through the day and night, but I never remember hearing anybody else. I seemed to be a lone bird. I lay there and kept shouting "Will anybody come and get me in?" and a voice said "If I volunteer to come out can you climb on my shoulder?" I said "I'm sorry but I can't, my foot's hanging off and my left shoulder is all shattered with shrapnel." I could feel the blood on my shoulder. "I'll try and get somebody to come out with me and get you onto my back," he said. I then heard "We're coming now" and I saw a stretcher thrown over the parapet. They rushed out and put me onto the stretcher before lifting me over the parapet and into the trench, the Germans turning their machine guns onto us all the while but luckily they didn't hit us.

They lowered me in our own front trench and our medical officer got a big bottle of iodine and wherever he saw blood he poured it all over me and then he said "Take him out of the wood and hand him over to the RAMC". They took me to the edge of the wood and they told the RAMC to come and get me but they said "No, bring him a bit further", they were thinking about their own skins.

I was taken back to this aid post, a tent, where we were lying around in a ring, wounded Germans as well, and the medical orderlies kept walking round and saying "Ah, he won't live much longer". I can see them now, stealing my watch, a government watch, sychronised for the attack. Very feebly I put my hand up to say "Look, it's a Government watch", but he just pushed my hand aside. The RAMC had a reputation for pinching anything they could and they were going

A dressing station 1st July 1916. Some lightly wounded men have already arrived and received treatment. IWM Q57

around assessing who wouldn't live, "He won't live long...and he won't live long", nicking our things. RAMC, Rob All My Comrades, and that was the truth, the whole truth and nothing but the truth.

I was sent down the line on an Ambulance Train, lying in a luggage rack. I kept trying to ease myself up as I was in terrible pain and kept hitting my head on the top of the coach. I eventually arrived at a Base Hospital where two Sisters came and got some scissors and just cut my uniform off and they could see my wounds, my shoulder, my stomach, my bladder, my foot hanging off.

I had no expectation of living, but every morning a voice used to say, "The following are for Blighty today" and they would call the names out, but never mine. I asked a nurse to ask the voice to come and see me and I recognised him as a man from my home town, Carlisle, Fred Stubbs. "Well," I said, "why don't you call my name out for Blighty?" He said I was too badly wounded, I was a cot case, and that I would not be safe in a Hospital Ship, but I insisted and insisted. Eventually they sent me back to England, Sheffield, where the first thing they said was "We're going to send for your mother". I was wounded from head to foot and said "No, I don't want my mother to see me like this". The Bishop of Sheffield was in the hospital and when he saw me I heard him say to a nurse, "Wheel him down into the corner and draw the curtains, I'll go and put my regalia on and come back and give him the last rites. Then you can lay him down and he'll be dead in twenty minutes". I heard him say that and I thought "Aye, that's what you think".

I had two surgeons for the top half of me and two for the bottom half. The bullet wound was the most serious. Going through my water bottle, the bullet had lost its point and had been turned into a dum dum. They told me the bullet was 3cm deep and clinging onto the wall of my bladder, although it didn't pierce the bladder otherwise I would have been incontinent. I also had a blood clot in my right leg where my foot was hanging off and they were going to amputate. Luckily the clot moved. And here I am today, as fit as a fiddle.

It was a year before they'd got me patched up at Sheffield enough so that I could go home. I'd only been at home a day when the recruiting officer came down and he asked me would I like to do something for the war effort. I sarcastically said he must be joking, I'd only just come home and he said, "Well, we need everybody for the war effort". I asked him what I could do.

Thomas Gay
1997

THOMAS GAY, born 25th April 1898, 2nd Royal Scots Fusiliers.

Thomas Gay
1915

Full of patriotism, sixteen-year-old Tommy Gay enlisted on a whim while crossing Tower Bridge on his way to work in 1914. Choosing to join his uncle's regiment, then in barracks in Scotland, Tommy enjoyed the train ride north from his home in Peckham, the beginning of what he felt sure would be a great adventure. After training for the best part of a year, he was sent to France at the start of 1916 to join the 2nd Royal Scots Fusiliers, only to find that his was one of the few regular units chosen to attack on the 1st July alongside the new Kitchener battalions. Undaunted, he left the trenches in what was to be one of the only successful attacks of that otherwise disastrous day.

We'd had a tot of rum that morning, on 1st July, to help liven us up. They'd give you a good old dose, knowing what you had to do, because a man with his booze, he don't care what he does, it makes you feel like you could fight anything. We knew what we were doing because we'd trained hard for the Big Push in the months before, going over mock battlefields, that sort of thing. I mean, we had landed in France six months before, and this was our first big attack.

Before the attack, we were given a sheet of tin to put between the straps on the back of our pack. One side was painted white and the other was shiny. If it was sunny, we was to turn the tin plate with the shiny side upwards, but if it was a dull morning we put the painted side up so the artillery half a mile back could see us and fire over our heads.

We were attacking a village called Montauban which had been shelled for more than a week by our guns. I'd been made a lance corporal in the few months I'd been there, because my uncle saw to it that I'd done everything as it should be done, that I was properly trained. So, of course, I was one of the first to get up and over the top in my Regiment "Come on, boys, here we go" and we went forward with fixed bayonets. It was brilliant sunshine.

We were not in the front line for the attack but were held back to support the men of the Manchester Regiment, and so we didn't go forward until about 9 o'clock. There was a lot of firing going on, rifle fire and a lot of sniping. The bullets actually whizzed by my ears at one point, you know, ping, ping, ping. I thought how marvellous that they've missed me, I couldn't understand it. We just had to get along up a small slope. A few men had been hit and you'd hear a man saying "Oh, give us a fag", but that's the most you could hear, but we weren't long before we got on the German lines, because No Man's Land was no distance at all. The village was further back and when we got there it was just a lot of rubble, flattened by our artillery. The Germans had mostly gone, they'd pulled well back and only left a bit of resistance. Later, when it was quiet, we were able to have a look around and we saw marvellous German dugouts, with three flights of stairs, forty feet deep with beds at the bottom.

In the evening, I was detailed to bury some of the dead. There were a lot of bodies around and we had to gather them in, take their identification discs off

The village of Montauban after its capture on 1st July the one success of that disastrous day when men of 30th Division, Liverpool and Manchester Pals, took all their objectives, driving the Germans back. TAYLOR LIBRARY

and just put three or four men into a shell hole and cover them over a bit with a few shovels of dirt. We'd been very happy with our success, but burying those men, that was a terrible thing that was, but there you are, you had to do it.

ARTHUR WAGSTAFF, born 12th May 1897, 2/4th London Regiment, later 1/4th London Regiment.

As no German was supposed to have survived the bombardment of the enemy trenches, the British troops who went over the top on 1st July 1916 were told to walk. Most, like 101-year-old Arthur Wagstaff, believed the attack would be literally a walk-over, but as he left the trenches, Arthur saw the bodies of two inseparable brothers lying on the parapet, and realised the hell he was about to meet.

We were sent up to the reserve line and put into dugouts and instructed as to how we were to act the next day. We were told that we should go up to the front line and into deep dugouts just for the night, so that at the right time we would be called out to go forward. We were told "First thing in the morning the whistles will blow and then you jump up into the trench and then over the top and attack the German front line, but remember, you must remember do not run, you must walk." Previously, in attacks, the fellows would jump over the top and run like hell into the German lines, but in spite of that we were told not to run, "You'll run into your own bombardment, just walk". We realised they had dugouts just as we had, and they would be called up as soon as they saw that our attack would be made. But of course our bombardment would be knocking out those Germans in the front line, so hopefully when we got there, there wouldn't be many left.

We had joined the army willingly and we knew that we would have to go forward to kill the Germans and in the process, of course, we stood a rough chance of being killed ourselves. Duty, that was the key word. It was my duty to do this and I must take my chance like everyone else.

I expected to be wounded, but even so I had a terrible awakening because as I left the dugout I saw those who had gone ahead killed and wounded. I saw two of our chaps – they were brothers – lying dead in our own trench, killed before they had even got going. I remember, too, our own Company Sergeant Major sitting on the front of the trench and shouting "Forward, forward. Over the top, boys, over the top, over the top" and then "but don't run, don't run." So that's the way we went.

It was hot, the bombardment so bad, terrific noise of course, the rattle of machine guns, what I would call total gunfire. There were shells going over the back of us, German shells going over, and I suppose our artillery was still firing on the German lines. We looked along the line and we realised there were very few of us left. Some were left in the trench, dead, some were dead on the way over. We got half-way there and three or four of us dropped into a large shell hole. Looking about, we could see that most of our chaps had been killed while

Arthur Wagstaff 1998

Arthur Wagstaff 1913

a few were still walking across.

There were four companies to a battalion and our company was on its own. There were two or three companies left or right of us, but we couldn't see how they were doing except that there seemed to be very few about, very few making the attack. It was a disaster, really. We had been there a short time when a Captain of the 11th Londons fell in on top of us and he said "Who are you?" We said "4th City of London" and he said "Well, stay here. My company is over in the German lines – they've either been killed, wounded or taken prisoner". So it was our order from the Captain to stay there until we were recalled at night.

There was a lull later, quite a bit of a lull because our artillery realised that some of our chaps were over in the German lines and it would be wrong to fire on the German trenches now, but of course there was plenty of German–held territory behind the front line which they could fire their guns onto.

Arthur Wagstaff's brother had been wounded the night before the 1st July attack and so missed the carnage.

That night we were ordered back into our own front line. We dropped into our trenches and then we were instructed to go down the communication trench to a tiny village, I forget the name of it now. I was worried because my brother was in the 11th Londons, in the company this Captain was speaking about, and on the way back down the communication trench I saw one of their men, a friend of my brother's. I asked him how my brother was and he said, "Oh, he was taken away wounded last night. He has been sitting in an ambulance in a village behind the line". So he'd never been in the attack at all! We sat and talked about it of course, three or four of us, thankful that we had survived. We missed our friends, so many friends were missing, killed or wounded, but I was alive. All right,

This battalion is on its way to the rear and has stopped to rest and clean up. The men look weary and, unusually, have little time for the photographer. TAYLOR LIBRARY

tomorrow there would be another battle and again I would run the risk of being killed or wounded, and of course in the end, at the finish of the Somme battle, I was wounded.

Perhaps some of our generals had made mistakes, I don't know. It's just the luck of war – there have to be winners, there have to be losers.

GEORGE LOUTH

After the disaster on 1st July, the Somme battle settled down to a long series of attritional attacks that gradually pushed the Germans back towards the town of Bapaume. On 15th September, however, the British High Command introduced a secret weapon to the fray – the tank. With supporting infantry attacks, this new weapon would break the stalemate, starting with the small village of Flers. George Louth was one of those who went into action that day.

We were in the front line waiting to go over the top in the morning and I was talking with one of the lads I had originally joined up with, Stokes, he was called. He was just finishing his stint of two hours on guard, standing on the firestep. It was getting dusk and he got down for a kip in this little place he'd cut into the side of the trench. Now I began to talk to another bloke when all of a sudden this shell dropped in the trench, right in this funk hole. It blew Stokes to pieces, there was no flesh on him at all, he was just bones, while the man facing me had his right arm blown off, or nearly off, it was just hanging by a thread. The man said to me, "George, my arm is gone, isn't it, can you see anything?" I said "God, Arthur, you'd better go on down to the Aid Post right away." So he went down and I never saw him again. He had shielded me from the blast and I was uninjured. I was left alone in that part of the trench, about to go over the top in the morning.

The bombardment began and went on for hours on end and it was deafening. I was in the trench with a cigarette, my last cigarette, in my fingers and I was shaking like a leaf, I don't mind telling you. It was the worst part, waiting to go, like facing the hangman, I would guess. Just before we attacked there was a strange noise, I didn't know what it was but I could hear it; it turned out to be a tank, the first attack the tanks had ever made.

At half past seven, the whistle sounded and we had to go. At that moment I lost all feeling, I wasn't nervous at all. We got over and laid down. I looked down our trench and I could see mates lying where they had dropped, dead on the trench floor. I thought to myself, they must have been there before. It seemed, I don't know, it seemed funny to me at the time, that they were all down there and I thought they were killed some time before, a few days or a few weeks ago, but they were killed there and then, a few minutes ago. I got up and ran forward, but I could hear the whistle of the bullets going so I lay down again and aimed my gun towards the firing line some thirty yards away. A group of Germans suddenly appeared up on top of the trench, they were brave, you have to admit that, to stand up and be fired at. Anyway, I started firing, then I saw

The village of Flers – the fighting over. George Louth walked up this street alone on 15th September IWM Q4270

two Germans throw their guns down and run down towards our lines, then down our communication trench. After a short while it went quiet, so I got up and looked around but everyone was missing. I looked towards the German line again and I saw a line of German helmets on the skyline. I thought to myself, "Christ, they're coming towards me," but they weren't, they were going away.

I began walking and I went into Delville Wood. It was all quiet, nobody at all. All dead, both sides of me. Six or seven men ran up and an officer came running out from somewhere waving his revolver and he said, "Lads, this way. I'll shoot the first bastard that goes the other way." I tried to catch up with them but I lost them, so I went out of the wood and started walking across the fields and on the way I saw this tank. I looked at it but I didn't take much notice of it. Whether it had broken down I don't know but I couldn't see anybody.

I walked on into the village of Flers, but as I approached a fork in the road I saw a rat run down one side of the road, as big as a Jack Russell. I decided that I wasn't going to go down there. Instead I walked down the other fork, but as I went forward I began to feel apprehensive, so I turned back. Where I had seen the rat, I met up with six or seven men coming up and they joined me in a trench, and we stopped there the rest of the day until we were relieved.

ARCHIBALD RICHARDS, born 7th January 1897, died 10th February 1998, A Company Tank Corps.

Archie Richards has a claim to fame: he served in one of the first tanks to go into action. The date was September 1916, and the lumbering machines attacked at a racy three miles an hour. Inside, the crews fainted and were sick as the heat and smell of diesel oil took their toll. Most tanks broke down or were ditched, yet when Archie's tank was finally knocked out, it was one of only a couple to reach the objective – the tiny village of Flers. Eighty years later, Archie was to be found living quietly with his daughter and son–in–law near Maidenhead. His abiding passion was the garden, which he tended with all the Archibald Richards *care and attention he once lavished on the 6lb gun which armed his tank. He* 1921 *died in February 1998 aged 101.*

Archibald Richards
1997

The secret weapon that was to break through the German lines and bring an end to the stalemate on the Western Front. TAYLOR LIBRARY

95

A Mk1 makes its way towards the firing line for the attack. IWM Q5575

We were lined up and they said "Here you are, here's the tanks and you people are going to crew them". We didn't know what they were at first. "Well, what's this, they've got tracks and guns pointing out. They must have an engine so they must crawl around." That was how we sized them up. We had been at Bisley, training on Hotchkiss machine guns, when we had been sent to Thetford to this new secret weapon, what I called at the time "armoured crawlers". When we got inside and saw the armaments we said, "Well, this is really it", we were very impressed. Eight men were picked out for each crew, a Second Lieutenant was in charge of the tank and each had an experienced driver. I was made a 6lb gunner, and we trained every day for about three or four months, getting acquainted with the tank and our guns. We did no physical training, we lived a totally different life from the rest of the army. I didn't even learn to fire a rifle.

Everything was secret for the trip to France. As we left the station, the tanks were covered with hessian, each side, so people couldn't see anything and the tanks were put on flat cars and covered up, as we boarded the train. We were sorted out, and off we went from Southampton, the tanks going separately from us.

In France, we were taken up by train towards Amiens, where we started to move up towards the line, always travelling in the dark, so many hours at night, pulling under trees in the daytime. It took us two or three days to get up, through Albert, to the line, where we put the noses of our tanks under a steep embankment for shelter from the shells. It was while we were waiting to go into action on the Somme that Jerry started to shell the ground behind the embankment, where the artillery was. The gunners had come up for the attack and they had had to wait, same as we had to wait, for the order to move up. The shells were going over the top of us and dropping amongst the tethered horses, killing and wounding any number. We all carried hand guns, and an officer came to me and said, "Richards, let's go out and see what we can do about these horses". It was a terrible sight, horses with their legs off, squirming and screaming, so we had to put them out of their misery. I remember that quite vividly. It was my first taste of carnage.

On 17th September, all hell broke loose. At about six o'clock in the morning, our barrage opened up, you couldn't hear yourself speak, shells flying everywhere, and the Germans were retaliating. We were scared, really scared, but we just resigned ourselves to putting up with it. We had orders to move out down to a village and on to the first main road, a hard cobble road. The Germans had not shelled it because they had brought up supplies on it previously, and we did not want to shell it now because we were using it for the same reason, so the road had remained quite sound, just a shell hole here and there. We attacked Delville and High Woods, two German strongpoints, then we pushed on to our objective, the village of Flers.

Inside the tank, the atmosphere was sickening. When you are in action and all

Tanks in action. Infantrymen usually crowded in behind advancing tanks to take advantage of any protection they could find from enemy machine gun fire. TANK MUSEUM 4153/A4

the traps are down, the fumes are hardly bearable. There is a thick haze of petrol and gas fumes and the cordite fumes, oh terrible, terrible, I think we had to have breathing apparatus, I can't quite remember. It was hot, I mean September was hot that year, very hot and with the engine running it was incredibly stuffy, it was a wonder anyone could live in it. The engine was in the centre of the tank and there was a little passage to step around it, but we were very cramped, and you had to watch your head. The noise was deafening, with our guns going, the German guns firing and the engine running, we had to make pre-determined signals with our hands and fingers. It was impossible to speak to anybody. I had a good stomach, but others were sick, spewing up all over the place and passing out. You can imagine what it was like, eight men cooped up in a tank with no air for five hours or more, the smell was awful.

Your nerves get worn, the noise and everything, it gradually gets to you. If you're a nervous person or if your nerves are in any way bad, then it's going to affect you. We had two men in the tank in the attack on Flers and their nerves gave out and they went funny in the head. They had a kind of glazed look in their eyes; the smells were affecting their minds, they didn't know what they were doing and they were unsteady on their feet. It was hard. We were all on the verge of collapsing sometimes, your eyesight could be upset by the fumes and we all went a bit fuzzy in the head, your mind didn't seem quite as clear as it would be if you were outside.

Our officer sat at the front with the driver and signalled what he wanted, and the tank would swing round to face the target. The tank would turn on its own in a wide circle, but with the two gear changers you could turn the tank in its own length. The engine was quite powerful and vibrated the machine somewhat, but it was the movement that was worst, up and down, this way and that. I had a job sometimes to set on my target, to shoot. I'd just get set on the target and ready to fire and bang, the tank would lurch somewhere, throw me right off. When the tank was going over shell holes, holes fifteen feet deep, it used to get on the edge and drop, drop right in, the nose would go right down. It would shake us up, of course, a sudden drop was sickening. You had to hold on or be thrown forwards. We were full of bruises.

My gun sight could traverse about half the tank's width and with a telescopic sight on the gun, I could look at the target. Each gunner had a loader, well, the gear changers were the loaders, they did two jobs, gear changed and loaded the shells which were in cases on the inside of the tank. All the loader had to do was draw the shell out of a case and shove it in the bore, tap me on the shoulder and I was ready to fire. I would fire direct at the target, like shooting a rifle, and very accurate it was, too. I could reckon to hit a target ten feet square at 1,000 yards if the conditions were right.

The targets were the trenches, anywhere we thought there'd be machine gun posts. The Germans would have strong points every so often, and in between it'd be manned by infantry, but the strong points had two or three machine guns. The Germans turned these guns on us, particularly on the trap doors, and the bullets smacked against the tank, causing the metal to splinter inside. Tiny flakes

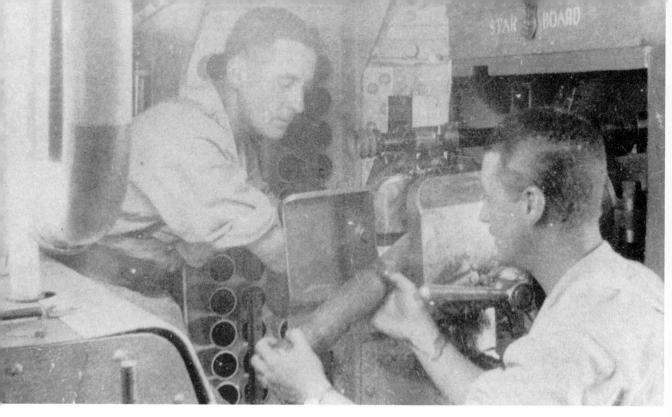

Two rare photographs taken inside a Mk1 tank. The men are loading a 6 lb gun as fired by Archie Richards during his fighting around the village of Flers.   TANK MUSEUM 4615/E3 33/H3

would fly about and cut you all over; our faces often bled so we wore goggles to stop ourselves being blinded.

All feelings of humanity leave you when you're in action, when you're firing. You say to yourself, "It's either him or me, so I've got to get in first." You've got no feelings of humanity then; afterwards, perhaps, but at the time, no, I'm killing and if I don't kill them they'll kill me and I didn't want to die just then, I was too young. You get into a situation like that, that you can't back out of, and you've got to put up with it, you don't give up, you say "To heck with it", and go forward.

There was no choice but to drive over the dead, lying about, you couldn't pick your way through. If they fell in your way you had to go over them, we never deviated the tanks for anything, only for action, no, no obstacles deviated the tanks. Going into action, the infantry kept tucked in, clustered behind our tanks for a bit of shelter, then as soon as we took a trench they took over, going along the line ferreting the Germans out. I only saw Germans when we got right on the trench, with our guns laid on each side. They had never seen anything like it before and when they saw we were armed with small guns and machine guns, they gave up straight away. We hardly had time to get on top of their trench before they were out with their arms up. A few of their machine gunners had got away and we could see them silhouetted against the sky with the machine guns on their shoulders, going like hell back to the third lines.

We had entered the village, on the main Flers road, when a shell dropped just in front of our tank and smashed one of our tracks, so we were out of action, that was our lot. We had carried on two men short, but now we got them out of the tank and splashed some water on them and with the fresh air they recovered quickly. Our officer got us together and said, "Now look, it's not wise for me to keep all the crew up here in danger, you can't do any good. I need a couple of you to volunteer to stay with the tank until the engineers come up in the morning to fix the tank and get it out of range." Two of us volunteered. We were right in the middle of the village and there was a house, just a pile of rubble, but there was a hole going down into the cellar so we agreed it was safer down there than in the tank, which would remain a target for the German artillery. There were two wicker chairs down there, so we sat and waited until it was dark. Jerry began shelling the village again and one landed right on the rubble. Choking dust flew everywhere. I'd been smoking, and the cigarette was cut right off in my fingers and my front teeth knocked out, the other man wasn't injured, but we hopped back into the tank to spend the rest of the night.

They all praised us after we came out of the action. We did a job that the infantry had been trying to do for months and lost thousands trying, and we did it in an hour. There was a pride of something well done and a great thing achieved. We thought it was a privilege to be under cover with half-inch metal plating, for when the infantry came face to face with a machine gun then there was no chance at all. Then there were other times when the fumes were bad and we used to say, "Oh, I wish I was outside", but we couldn't have it both ways. We had other things to put up with, but we had cover from machine gun bullets.

FLERS

An aerial photograph of the battlefield near the village of Flers a few days before the attack. The ground appears heavily shell-pocked, although the village looks reasonably intact. **Inset:** *a tank apparently crashes down on a German gun crew.* TANK MUSEUM 452/B2 4963/A5

In action, our officer would make his own decision as to when our action could be broken off. He'd say, "That's it, we've done enough, we'll turn and go back." As soon as we were out of action, we could open the tank traps, oh you would never believe the relief. You took long breaths of lovely fresh air again, you gulped it in. Freedom – freedom all round. Freedom of limbs, freedom of arms, freedom of breath, freedom of mind, freedom of everything.

You lost friends, we saw other tanks burnt out, but it didn't affect you at the time, you were so full up emotionally. Afterwards, yes, after it was all over you felt the loss, when they ought to be in camp and they weren't. You looked around and you'd see all the vacant places and you talked to your mates who were alive, saying poor old so and so had it and poor old so and so, he's gone. I think being cooped up in a small area brought us closer. We were together all day long, all night long. When you are out of action, you're working on the tanks so you're closely associated all the time and when you're in action, it's closer than ever, like brothers. Our officer used to treat us as a friend, talking to us like he would talk to his own ranks. He would call me Arch, he used all our Christian names. I'm sure he thought we might all go up together so we'll be pally, we'll be pally to the end. Of course when we were out, that would be a different story, he would have to change his attitude. He had to carry his rank then. Would we die for one another? Now that's saying something. I can't vouch for that, I can't say, probably, probably we would.

I thought that if my number was up it's up, it'll come, and I resigned myself. For that reason I could sleep well, and all round my nerves seemed pretty good at that time. We were still on the Somme when for some reason I had to go up into the front line trenches. To this day I don't know why, but I was sheltering with some infantrymen in a hole dug in the side of the trench. The Germans were shelling unmercifully, every size of shell you could mention was dropping all around. Every time a big shell crashed down, I cringed up, I felt terrible in myself, cowering, which I had never done before. I was shellshocked at that time, oh yes, there was no doubt about that – I was shellshocked. I wasn't in my right senses, I shook, my hands shook, I shook all over. And the infantrymen were looking at me as if to say "What's wrong with him?" They didn't seem to take any notice of being shelled, I seemed to be the only one affected. Every time Jerry shelled nearby, I hid, I covered myself, hoping, hoping he wouldn't drop one right on the shelter. I remember thinking, "Have I survived the tanks to get killed like this?" Then I would say to myself "No, my luck'll hold out, I'll be all right, yeah."

I spoke to the other men. "I've come from a different regiment, I'm not in the infantry. You are here under shellfire all day and all night for weeks, I'm not, the only time I'm under fire is when I'm in action." I mean, when we were in action all thoughts of fear or anything else goes. I had to justify myself, I felt after I'd gone they'd think I was a coward or something like that, see, so I explained I wasn't used to living under shellfire like that. Shellshock is really fright, fright that can't be coped with.

I couldn't believe what had happened to me at the time. I thought my nerves would carry me, but no, the shelling broke my nerve. Later, when the shells stopped, the fright and the shock seemed to go and next day I was ordinary, just like before, only the memories, only the memory of it.

NORMAN COLLINS

The tanks did not bring the hoped-for break-through, and the Battle of the Somme petered out in November when the last tactical attacks were made. Beaumont Hamel, a heavily defended village, was finally seized by the 51st Highland Division, in a daring attack on 13th November. Norman Collins was one of the officers who took part.

I had been commissioned into the Seaforth Highlanders from Lichfield Cadet Corps and when I was nineteen, was posted to France to the 51st Highland

Norman Collins aged 19.

"Gefallene Englander"–"Fallen English" says the postcard, however, these Scotsmen are beyond caring. TAYLOR LIBRARY

Division, a division held back for battles. That might sound silly, but some regiments did a lot of work in the trenches but did not take part in great battles. The Highland Division – the Gordons, Black Watch, Seaforths, Camerons – were trained for special attacks, all trained together behind the lines and then when we were ready we entered the trenches and were told the order of battle.

I went to France in 1916 and took part in an attack at a place called Beaumont Hamel, a village on the Somme battlefield. This village had been an objective on 1st July but the attack had failed and so four months later we were sent forward to take it. It was a cold November morning, foggy. The night before, my batman came to see me and asked if I could provide him with the means of buying a small bottle of whiskey – quite illegal of course, but I gave him the money to do it. He would be going over the top with me and he was likely to be killed, as I thought I would be. I thought my chances of coming back were very small, but it doesn't deter you because you have no choice, no alternative. We were told that we would go over the top at six o'clock, so our watches were synchronised and we waited for the creeping barrage which was to cover our advance.

You're looking at your watch to see the hour, and then you're looking in front to see when the barrage will open, and then you look and see that your men – the men you're standing to go over the top with – are equipped and ready to go, and that nobody's turned around and gone back. Then you encourage them, right and left, to go with you, all go together and you keep looking as they drop occasionally.

The guns opened up simultaneously and the Germans were taken entirely by surprise. The main German defensive position was known as Y Ravine, a place with deep dugouts, and the Germans had to get their machine guns up to defend themselves as we moved forward under a canopy of steel. I suppose I might have blown a whistle but it didn't mean anything, I went out and saw men dropping right and left, I've a vision of a Gordon Highlander pitching forward with his rifle onto his hands and knees, stone dead, his kilt raised showing his backside. You're working in a very small area, the rest of the Front is nothing. You quickly look to see if a man who has dropped is dead or not or if there was anything you could do for him, but you hadn't time to stop, so you sort of shepherded the men over. You are very aware of the example you are setting the men; if they saw you funking it – showing fear – they wouldn't think much of you. They looked to me for encouragement, and you made jokes if you could, you made little jokes. I remember once in an attack, a Captain Harris waved for me to come on and I ran forward and flopped on the ground beside him. We were being heavily shelled at the time and I did a very silly thing. I took my tin helmet and I rolled it like Charlie Chaplin used to do with his bowler hat, and put it back on again. That's the way I reported for duty, little jokes like that.

We took the German front line with very few losses, although farther back the Germans managed to get their machine guns up and they opened fire on the second wave. You couldn't avoid the bullets or the shells, it was sheer chance. When machine guns are firing, it's like a solid wall of lead. You can smell the gunpowder, well, I suppose nitrates, the high explosives, you could smell the high explosives. I had a .45 revolver and Mills bombs, so I was not defenceless, and I fought when the opportunity came. My role was to get into Y Ravine and throw Mills bombs down into the dugouts where the Germans were, I suppose killing quite a number. You throw the bombs down and say "Share that amongst you", that's what you said as a rule and all the time I've no doubt whatever that I was as frightened as anything and hoping, a faint hope, that I would survive.

After any battle, you always had men lying out in No Man's Land probably with their testicles blown off and crying in agony and lying out there all night long in the dark, in the rain. You couldn't get them in and in any case they would never have survived. But you had a choice. They could die in agony or you could shoot them. You were shown how to do the thing very cleanly, you put your .45 revolver muzzle against the back of his head and pulled the trigger and immediately the whole of the front skull came away and exposed the brain, just blown off. A lead bullet hit the inside of the skull, and they were dead instantly. There was no pain about it, but I can honestly say this, that I never had the courage – because that's what it took – I never had the courage myself to shoot a wounded soldier. I carried out the operation many times afterwards on animals. I could kill a pet dog far better than a vet could, but I was never able to shoot a wounded soldier. I probably should have. I had an officer friend, Murray Dickson, quite a close friend, and he was wounded in the stomach. He was in great agony from what I was told. The kindest thing would have been to have shot him on the battlefield. Instead of that, they took him back to hospital and he died six days later. It's a tremendous thing to shoot a friend, even though he's in agony, and I just didn't have the courage to do it. Most of them died overnight but of course they didn't thank you for it, I'm sure.

CHAPTER SIX

Saving The Wounded

THE AFTERMATH of every major battle was human carnage on an unimaginable scale. One of the most demanding and heartbreaking jobs on the Western Front was that of giving medical help to the wounded and dying. In the worst fighting, there could be more than 10,000 British casualties in a single day. The stretcher bearers, medical orderlies, nurses and doctors who had to try to save the lives of the injured did a remarkable job – but they were often overwhelmed by the scale of the tragedy they had to deal with.

The British army had prided itself on the quality of its medical services in the front line ever since the days of Florence Nightingale, who had campaigned for better treatment of wounded soldiers during the Crimean War. The trained personnel of the Royal Army Medical Corps, and the Queen Alexandra's Imperial Military Nursing Service, were helped by medical orderlies from the Red Cross and the Order of St John. Between them, wounded men were evacuated from the battlefield through an infrastructure of Advanced Dressing Stations, Casualty Clearing Stations and Base Hospitals. Convoys of Field

A team of stretcher bearers on their way up the line.   IWM Q1214

Ambulances, Ambulance Trains, and even barges, ferried the wounded along the chain of medical command, all the way back to Britain and the many war hospitals around the country. Despite the careful integration of medical services, nobody could have predicted the vast number of casualties or the appalling nature of the wounds, in what was the first war of the modern industrial era. Shrapnel and machine gun fire tore apart the bodies of the countless thousands who advanced through No Man's Land.

Depending on the terrain, a minimum of two, but often four, men were needed to carry a stretcher. Yet, with only 32 stretcher bearers per 1,000 men, it is easy to see that if 60% of men became casualties in battle, the stretcher bearers would be hopelessly understaffed. In the terrible mud of Passchendaele, many stretcher bearers could manage only two trips to pick up the wounded before total exhaustion.

The worst possible conditions for transporting a critically injured man – the cloying mud of the Ypres Salient. Here, seven men to a stretcher make slow progress, near Boesinghe, August 1917
IWM Q5935

An Advanced Dressing Station on the Somme. All that was available here was First Aid of a rudimentary kind, given by the RAMC.   TAYLOR LIBRARY

While riflemen and machine gunners could distinguish between the combatant and non-combatant, artillerymen could not. Shrapnel was responsible for a large proportion of the 4,039 RAMC officers and men who were killed in the war, and for three times as many wounded. It meant stretcher bearers joined the long trail of injured men making their own way back for treatment, leaving even fewer men to help the wounded. As most battlefield wounds became septic within six hours, many men either died or had to have limbs amputated simply because their evacuation and treatment was too slow.

After each battle, the walking wounded and the stretcher bearers would converge on Advanced Dressing Stations near the trenches. All that was available here was first aid of the most rudimentary kind, given by the RAMC. The wounded were then loaded onto ambulances and transported to Casualty Clearing Stations, a few miles behind the front line. Here emergency operations, including amputations, would be undertaken. The wounded were then sent on down the line to better-equipped Base Hospitals near the coast. There were over sixty military hospitals for British troops in Belgium and France, many of them organised around the main medical bases such as Etaples, Rouen and Calais. At every stage of this gigantic rescue operation, the professional medical staff found themselves hampered by dreadful conditions and a lack of facilities. Furthermore, despite a near eight-fold increase in the number of military nurses during the war, there remained a severe shortage of nursing help at the Front.

With the formation of the Voluntary Aid Detachments (VADs) in 1910, the medical services had 47,000 partially-trained women ready for work when war broke out. The VADs were intended for home duty only, but such was the urgent need for volunteers to work at the Front that many more women answered the call. By 1918, there were over 80,000 VADs, of whom around 8,000 were given the opportunity to serve abroad. They were unpaid, and as a result most were recruited from middle and upper class families. The minimum age to join was nineteen, and to go to France a woman was meant to be twenty three. But many younger teenagers tricked their way in and were readily accepted by the authorities, such was the enormous demand for their labour. By 1917, it was not uncommon for seventeen and eighteen year olds, fresh from school or college, to be nursing in Casualty Clearing Stations just behind the front line, and in Base Hospitals.

Nothing could have prepared these young nurses for the life and death struggles they had to face in the makeshift wards and medical outposts to which they were hastily posted. With a sheltered middle class upbringing behind them and only a basic training in first aid, they suddenly had to work around the

A Casualty Clearing Station just behind the lines, the next stage after the ADS for a wounded soldier. Some operations were carried out here, including amputations, and then the men were transported to one of sixty Military Hospitals. TAYLOR LIBRARY

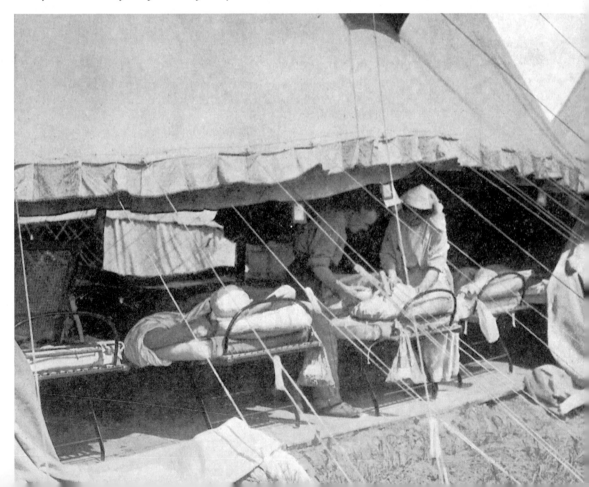

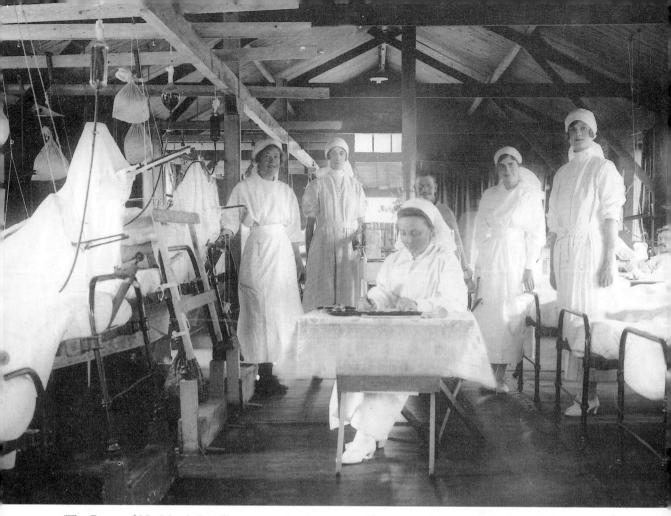

'The Roses of No Man's Land': young volunteers, unpaid nurses who earned for themselves a reputation for displaying unstinting dedication and compassion. Above is a Ward of the Duchess of Sutherland's Hospital, Calais, July 1917. TAYLOR LIBRARY

clock, nursing and comforting men close to death. They had to deal with horrendous physical injuries and to dispose of amputated limbs. The care, skill and courage these inexperienced young volunteers displayed was legendary. They became known as "The Roses of No Man's Land", named after the popular wartime song that celebrated their heroism and compassion.

WILLIAM EASTON, born 15th October 1898, 2/2 East Anglian Field Ambulance, later transferred to the 77th Field Ambulance, Royal Army Medical Corps.

The Royal Army Medical Corps stretcher bearer had one of the toughest jobs at the Front. Roving amongst the dead and wounded, he criss-crossed the exposed battlefield trying to recover appallingly injured men, or carried the latest trench

William Easton 1998

William Easton 1916

casualty perhaps a mile or more to the nearest Aid Post. For William Easton, just 19 at the time, the job was onerous in the extreme, but one which he carried out with great self-assurance, saving friend and foe alike. It was to win him the respect of both the British Tommy and the German Jerry. Now 100 years old, Bill recalls the time when heroism and stoicism had to come in equal amounts.

When carrying a stretcher, it was important to get a good team together. Some of the bearers were hopeless, not very efficient carriers because they would be frightened all the time. At Ypres we lost no end of RAMC men, and replacements had to be found among the men of the Service Corps at the Base. These chaps had only ever dealt with supplies and had never carried a stretcher. They'd turn up for one trip and start moaning like the devil, then you'd perhaps have a day off and they wouldn't be back, they'd go sick. I was lucky, I teamed up with a northern lad called Tom Barrass. He was a rough diamond and swore like a trooper, but he was an absolute inspiration to me. I don't know how many shells would be coming over, but Tom would walk through them, he seemed to take no notice. He told me, "If you're going to get hit by one of these shells, you'll be hit, and that's all you need to know."

The first time we went up to the trenches, Tom put together his new team, saying to me, "You're the lightest of us. Left-handed, aren't you? Right, you'll be on the right side of the stretcher because your left hand will be stronger than your right." Of course he was correct, I couldn't carry a stretcher with my right hand, I couldn't even bear anything on my right shoulder. Then he said, "You are going up the line tonight, first time. Now when we go in just hang close behind me. You'll probably be a bit frightened, but never show it, fear is infectious, just get along." He'd talk on the way, and I don't know what he was saying half the time, but he kept me going so that I got to rely on him. Our Field Ambulance unit lost any number of men, half of whom we hardly knew, but Tom just seemed to go on and on.

As stretcher bearers, we had precious little medical training, and were hardly allowed to touch the wounds. If they had a bad open wound you'd just cover it up and get them out of it, that was the most important thing. But some of the men were so badly wounded, you'd practically pick them up in pieces. If they were still alive, you had to cart them away, and you knew jolly well that they'd die at any time. If a man died on the journey, we weren't allowed to put the bodies down, or tip them off the stretcher, once they were on board we had to carry them out. We didn't think anything of struggling for perhaps two or three hours down to a Dressing Station and on arrival found the man had died. It made you hardened to the sights, it had to. I lost all feeling once I got into the line. My one object was to get the people out and be done with it. Some of the other men thought I was heartless, but it was the only way to survive.

The only time I really got upset was during the Battle of Messines. Tanks were used, and one was hit by a new type of armour-piercing shell, containing mustard gas. Four or five men were brought out alive but there was nothing anyone could do for them. They were just taken to the Dressing Station and laid out in the open on a bank. I was at the Dressing Station at the time and we

110

A badly wounded sergeant receives first aid from a stretcher bearer in a trench near Polygon Wood, September 1917. IWM Q6003

weren't allowed to go near these men, but you could see these little bubbles of mustard gas coming from their mouths. It took two or three days for them to die and I shall never forget that! One of them was kicking up an awful row. I said they should have given them an injection, or shot them, anything. But they kept them lying there, and the men didn't like it. Officially, we didn't know that injections were given to help a badly-wounded man die, and the powers that be were careful you didn't see anything controversial, but it went on because you knew jolly well that some of the wounded you brought in were never going to live.

If a man was shot and fell in an attack, the practice, in our Division, was to stick his rifle and bayonet upside down in the ground, so the stretcher bearers could see where the wounded man was. However, most of the wounded we picked up were going up to or back down from the front line. Most of the wounds were caused by shellfire and unfortunately most of those were pretty hefty wounds, you'd reckon they wouldn't last the journey. We couldn't bandage the wounded, the job was to get them on the stretcher and if there was anything obvious you could tie up, we would, but we rarely had anything other than simple shell dressings, and they were poor affairs really. Of course you couldn't help but get blood on your hands and it was awful feeling them all sticky, slowly drying, gluing your fingers together. It was a horrible sensation,

A lightly wounded soldier clearly in pain receives a temporary dressing prior to his removal to a Casualty Clearing Station. IWM Q6966

and if we could, we would try and stop at a shell hole to wash our hands.

Up at Ypres, we used to go up the line and we'd be waist deep in mud. We were carrying the wounded down near a place called Hooge, where there had been a terrific amount of fighting. We had taken the village but the Germans had retreated to the next height. The only way down was to get across the muddy field to a little rise that was a bit drier, then we could walk down to a place called Birr Crossroads, on the Menin Road. There was a Dressing Station there, nicknamed the Elephant Dugout because it was about forty foot deep, steel-lined, and was supposed to be strong enough to stand any shell. It was no easy job, either, to carry the wounded down into the station or to bring them back up for the ambulances which took them to Ypres at night. The trees along the Menin Road were all shattered, so canvas was hung across the trees to stop the Germans observing who was coming or going. But the first thing they would do was blaze away with shrapnel at these trees to knock the canvas down, so that by 9am, they could see again.

Every now and again, the Germans would lob some high explosive or shrapnel over, perhaps four or five shells. The crossroads was a place the Germans targeted at regular intervals, and we could count the shots and then rush by and get under cover. There was a little shelter built close to the crossroads, where we could stop until we were ready to run to the Dressing Station. You'd got perhaps twenty yards to run, but if you hesitated you could run into the next salvo. One night, the Germans fired some very heavy shells and one penetrated the Elephant Dugout and killed everyone inside. Unfortunately, the dead included a lot of ambulance men having a well-needed rest and a cup of tea, and the casualties were fearful. The dugout was a mess and some of the dead were cut to pieces and had to be removed in sandbags.

You couldn't carry a man down in the mud at Ypres, it was almost impossible; one trip down a trench in those conditions and you would be all in – exhausted. If you got two or three wounded men down in a day, that was all you could expect to do. We had to carry men in fours there, and we had to be very careful because you could do more damage to a man than the shell if you jolted him too much or he fell off the stretcher.

Most of the wounded looked like a heap of rags, and simply trying to get them out of the firing line put finish to quite a lot of them. If we could have carried them out straight away it wouldn't have been so bad, but often we had to wait until darkness. The wounded rarely had clean bullet wounds, most were injured by shrapnel and the shock meant they were beyond talking, beyond words. Now and again, you'd get one who'd ask how long it would be before they went to Blighty. Some would ask which hospital they were going to, but of course we hadn't got a clue. They wanted to know impossible things, we hardly knew where we were, let alone anything else. We never saw a hospital, we only went to the Dressing Stations and then ambulances would take over. Tom was always as cheerful as anything, and used to tell them all sorts of tales, because he was at the head end of the stretcher, but most wounded soldiers didn't worry. They just lay on the stretcher and took the chance of having a rest.

Some of the wounded would groan and kick up an awful row, which was rather nerve-pulling. To make carrying easier, we had slings which we put round our shoulders and over the stretcher's handles, so if anybody was too restless we used the slings to tie them on. It was mostly the older married men that were a bit of trouble sometimes. Some of them would worry about what was going to happen, if they were going to lose a hand or anything like that. Tom would say, "You never know – wonderful what they can do now." Then he'd tell them about something he'd done at home. He was a jolly good chap for that job. Still, some of the wounded were very emotional and would look on the black side. They'd start up and it would be infectious and some of the stretcher bearers would get emotional, too; they were frightened of being frightened, that was the truth of it.

DICK BARRON

In a general attack at Gallipoli, Dick Barron would follow the troops forward into action, quickly tending to the casualties he came across, and evacuating as many wounded as he could from the exposed battlefield. It was a highly dangerous job that did not spare the men of the RAMC, as Dick was to discover.

There was a place called Chocolate Hill and in front of it was a salt plain across which we were ordered to attack. I was attached to the medical officer so I was to more or less follow the fighting troops to deal with casualties. As we crossed the plain in waves we were attacked by bursting shrapnel, flying all over the place and casualties began to fall.

I wasn't in a normal state of mind, I staggered forward. It's difficult to describe the state you are in, you weren't cool and collected, saying to yourself I must do that and look out for such and such. My feelings were of bewilderment more than anything else, I didn't know what was going to happen. I was numb. I knew the direction and I just went that way. I could see the dismounted cavalrymen going forward when my pal Gally was killed next to me. We didn't have steel helmets then and Gally was hit in the head. He fell down and I looked at him, his brains were sticking out. He was unconscious and I knew he'd had it but I stopped. You can't imagine seeing your pal like that. It sounds gruesome but all I could do was to push the brain, which had exuded through the wound, back into the cranium, and then put a bandage – a field dressing – on his head, no good of course, but you don't behave normally in those conditions.

That evening the dry shrub on the salt lake caught fire. The shellfire set it alight and there were wounded out there, so a lot of rescuing had to be done. It's bloody awful trying to carry a chap on a stretcher – I felt my arms were coming out of their sockets. A chap gets very heavy, you know. You have straps over your shoulder, but I was only a lad and when you go over rough terrain where it's all bumpy, it's very exhausting. We had some medical equipment, we had a field dressing under our tunic. This was in case you were wounded, you applied it to yourself if you knew pressure points for bleeding, but many died from loss of blood anyway. Our job was to try and stop the bleeding. A lot of wounds didn't haemorrhage a lot, it depends where it was. On the extremes, toes for example, there wasn't much blood but anywhere near the aorta, the blood was flowing. If blood was pulsing from a wound you knew he'd had it, all you could do was put a dressing on the wound and send him back. You have got to remember, we weren't in an operating theatre, we were in a field, but we had to do something. Was it a primitive instinct? Of course it is, but you don't get rid of a primitive instinct, it's one of those natural things which manifests itself on these occasions.

*Helen
Gordon-Dean
1917*

HELEN GORDON-DEAN née McNEIL, born 28th May 1899, died 8th January 1998, VAD, Order of St John.

Although the intention had been that VADs would work only in hospitals at home, the catastrophic fighting overseas soon ensured that thousands of young volunteers were given the chance to serve near the Front. Helen Gordon-Dean had only first aid training and a rudimentary medical knowledge when she found herself at a Casualty Clearing Station ministering to the wounded. Carrying out duties she would never have been allowed to perform in Britain, she comforted the dying soldiers, some no older than her own slender eighteen years. Helen lived close to her daughter at Drumnadrochit, on the shores of Loch Ness, where she died earlier this year.

*Helen Gordon-Dean
1997*

I told them I was nineteen, but I was a year younger. I got away with it; telling fibs is a gift, but you've got to be convinced yourself. I wanted to go to France very badly but I had to get past this board of eight people quizzing me. One lady was very sceptical about my answers. "What age are you? What year were you born?" I resented the questioning because of all the things I could have chosen to do, it was nursing that inspired me. It is such an intimate job and I just loved it, really, really, really, loved it.

Dad had to pay for everything when I joined up, but then I could always get round him. I could make the job sound frightfully important. There wasn't much glamour about it, it was the idea of nursing pure and simple, seeing somebody improve because of what you had done, that was very creative and exciting. Patriotism? I don't think we thought much about that. There was a war on and we had to win it, I knew that. It was exciting really; at home we were on the fringe of doing things, in France we would see things other people would never know. I suppose there was a curiosity. I don't know if I was a good nurse, I hope I was, but the job had an extraordinary fascination for me.

It was very primitive over in France. There was a tent as a rule, outside which men were often laid on the ground, waiting surgery, while others were put in dirty beds that were lice-ridden. For a girl of seventeen or eighteen the work was so tiring, but I was young and eager. I wanted to see what life was all about.

You heard the shelling and sometimes it seemed very close and noisy, but I never remember fear, naked fear. I was conscious of the shells, but I thought, well, a shell could kill anyone and if it is me, then so be it. But there was so much

Patients at a Base Hospital. IWM Q10667

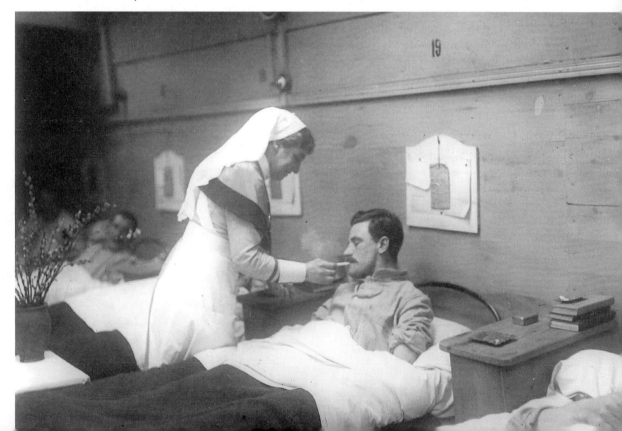

to do, there wasn't time to stand back and think. Ambulances were always arriving, generally in convoys, and you would go out and help those who could walk or limp along, and the rest would be carried in for treatment. Those who weren't too badly injured sometimes asked me for a cigarette.

The wounds were smelly. I think very often the smell was the worst. Every wound was treated with a swab doused with lysol, a red solution. The lysol was in a dish and you held the swab with forceps, dipped it in and applied it to the wound quite brutally to clean this nasty place up. These wounds were so dirty, sometimes full of maggots, and on one occasion I saw lice in the wound too.

Bad wounds were quite horrific, shocking beyond belief. They were filthy really, and you didn't want to believe what you were seeing, the horror of what people, responsible people, were doing to each other. I remember the first amputation. They said "Go on, nurse, you can help, this is a quite simple one," and they shoved me into the room with the others and it suddenly struck me how simple and ordinary it was to deliberately cut a hand off. I felt it was a terrible thing to have to do, and with big amputations I couldn't look, I couldn't bear it. Even though an amputation was very often necessary, somehow you felt they could do it another way, but in the end you saw so many, you sort of tried to make it seem ordinary to yourself, and not the terrible thing it really was. I stood next to the doctor and would lift the amputated arm or hand with forceps and put it where it was out of the way. I knew it had to be done and my job was to do it, not nice.

It's funny how quite strong men that you looked up to, would be wanting to hold your hand during these moments. It was a very real expression of what I believed in very, very firmly, the physical contact with other life. It generally came from them, they wanted to hold your hand and you wanted to hold theirs. It was a horrible feeling to know that somebody is going right into eternity that moment, and you have held their hand, maybe patting it to give them courage. So often, so often these young men would look at you and say, "You remind me of my mother", who would be three times my age. It was something that happened and always the same words, "You remind me of my mother"; I felt pride, privileged.

ALFRED PEARSON, born 11th July 1898, Red Cross Medical Orderly

Rejected by a kindly recruiting sergeant as being under-age to enlist in the army, sixteen-year-old Alfred Pearson sought out an alternative route by which to serve. He offered his services to the British Red Cross and was quickly made a medical orderly. After working at a convalescent hospital in Staffordshire, Alfred was sent to Boulogne just before his eighteenth birthday, to help evacuate the wounded from the Ambulance Trains to the hospital ships destined for England. Now 100 years old, Alf lives quietly in a residential home in Bridlington.

On the 24th of June 1916, I was sent to France in preparation for the forthcoming Battle of the Somme. I went on a hospital ship with a large group

*Alfred Pearson
1997*

116

of doctors and nurses and a cargo of medical supplies. We landed at Boulogne. My job as an orderly was to work as a stretcher bearer, unloading the trains that brought the wounded back from the Front.

In the week before the battle began, everything was very quiet. Any Ambulance Trains were apparently going to Calais, so I was told to hang about as there was no work to do. I was billeted at the Hotel Bristol, where I slept on the floor with a lot of other medical orderlies. The hotel was on the sea front, and every day I looked out and in the distance I could see the coast of England, and I wished I could get there. I watched the ships come into Boulogne and was interested to see them turn round, stern first, before they entered, because the harbour was so small.

Everything changed on 1st July, of course. After that day I helped unload Ambulance Trains day after day, right through until November. Only with winter, when the countryside became too churned up with gunfire so that nothing could move, did things quieten again. The RAMC would evacuate the wounded to the trains at Amiens, where medical orderlies took over some of the work. Occasionally I went up on the train to Amiens to help out, and I remember you could almost put your hand out of the train and touch the magnificent cathedral there. The army had built a new railhead below, in a field, where our trains used to go.

The trains were divided into three sections, British wounded, German wounded, and I've got the idea that any men who died on the way were taken

A Hospital Train arrives at the Port of Calais and stretcher cases are taken to waiting hospital ships for transport to Blighty. German prisoners help with the transfer of wounded. IWM Q23578

down to the third portion of the train. At least, whoever was in there was always the last to be taken off. The nurses who looked after the men coming down the line had a very trying job, the carriages were packed so that even where the luggage rack would normally be, there was a bed. The trains were a tremendous length with two enormous French engines on the front of every one, and when they arrived at the station in Boulogne they took up the whole length of the platform. There was no waste of room inside or outside the train.

The work was very hard, as Ambulance Trains ran back and forwards. As soon as one was empty, off it would trundle again, very often with a new train ready to come in. They arrived well into the night, and as the train approached the station, the nurses prepared the men for moving. I used to help carry the wounded on stretchers to the end of the train, where two doctors used to look at each man, and they would indicate either the harbour or St Martin's Camp, a large hospital which was right above the town. The wounded were very eager to get back to Blighty, and disappointment was often written across the faces of those who were not fortunate enough to be pointed in the direction of the harbour; you couldn't help but feel sorry for them because, in a way, they were so close to getting home.

Many of the wounded were in a frightful state. Some were wounded in the head, or the face, and were swathed in bloody bandages. Worst of all were those who'd been gassed. I saw on one occasion a line of gas victims, one behind the other, with their hands on the shoulders of the man in front, and it looked like a procession – of animals almost – most distressing. They were all blind, most of them temporarily, but whether they all recovered I just don't know.

The work of the nurses was in some ways the most impressive thing I saw. My first job had been at a stately home in the Midlands, called Sandon Hall. This had been turned into a convalescent hospital with volunteer nurses from the social élite, you know, society ladies. These people had mucked in like everyone else, and after my initial surprise, it was nothing to see a titled lady sweeping the ashes from the fire, or scrubbing the floor. But it was their response to injuries that was remarkable. These ladies, and the nurses I met in France, had lived closeted lives, and it was a complete surprise for them to find men who had been so badly wounded. The sights they would see would be very upsetting at first, although they tried not to show it, of course. They got used to the sights like everybody else, I suppose, because we were all thrown in at the deep end in the war.

ALICE McKINNON née BLOOD, born 23rd June 1894, Special Military Probationer, Queen Alexandra's Imperial Military Nursing Service Reserve, No 24 General Hospital, Etaples.

Alice McKinnon 1917

Finding a nurse from the First World War is difficult enough; finding one who served on the Western Front is nearly impossible today. Less than 10% of all nurses who served in the war, served abroad and, of those who went, all were supposed to be

Alice McKinnon 1997

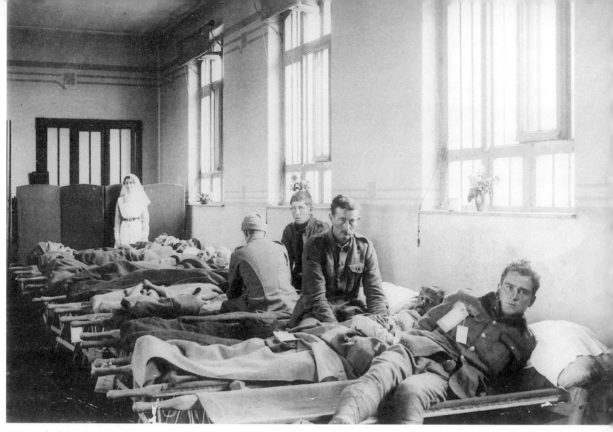

Wounded in transit: details of their wounds, medication and treatment, and personal details are contained on labels attached to the clothing of those being moved. IWM CO428

twenty-three years old or over. Alice was just such an age when she sailed for France in 1917 to serve at Number 24 General Hospital at Etaples, one of the main Base Hospitals during the war. Now 104 years old, she recalls the days when German bombs were not just reserved for the front line.

I felt I had to do something for the war effort, and nurses were needed so badly, and I suppose that was all I felt I could do in a way. I had always had an interest in caring; as a child we had fussed over dolls, hoping they were all right, and tucking them up in beds. I can't say that we pretended to be nurses as such, more to be good mothers, to take care of them nicely. Growing up, I would always take an interest if anyone was ill or had a bad leg, so I took some training in First Aid and learnt quite a bit about bandaging and that sort of thing, taking exams to chart my progress. Then in 1915 the world heard about Edith Cavell, the nurse executed by the Germans. We heard about her good works, and I thought it was wonderful that a woman could do all that. Perhaps I might be as good as that some day. Well, I felt that her death was a terrible crime and we should all do our best, really. After the war, I was in London when her funeral took place. I remember sitting on my little suitcase and waiting for her body to pass. There wasn't a sound, and as the cortège came along I put my head down and I cried and cried. I thought she was wonderful, an example.

I knew that young nurses were needed, and I was told to report to St Barts hospital in London. I remember I took a bunch of flowers, beautiful flowers from my garden, and I gave them to the Matron. I was the only one who did that, well, of course the Matron talked to me. She asked me quite a few personal questions and said afterwards that she would take me on and help me have the war training I needed. I remember I was given a test to see if I was any good, and that was to hold a man's leg as it was amputated. The leg was wrapped up and I held it as they cut through the skin and bone, and didn't cave in or anything. I was pleased I stood the test.

A friend of mine had volunteered to serve overseas, in the east somewhere, and would I like to go too? I phoned my mother but she forbade me going such a long way by ship, but I could go to France if I wished. I heard later that my friend's ship was torpedoed and sunk. She had survived but lost all her belongings. So I was to go to France. I went home to say goodbye to my parents and they gave me a packet of biscuits for the trip and off I went.

As I was leaving on the boat, I saw a Zeppelin in the night sky, and I watched it. This Zeppelin wasn't bombing. It would fly into a cove and then come out again and go into another cove. I heard afterwards that the Germans were examining every possible landing place for an invasion of England. This fitted with what we had heard before the war, and that was that the Germans had been buying up properties all round the coast of England, so that when they came everything would be ready.

When we landed, several of us were taken to a hotel and the first thing someone did was to switch on the light. Well, the manager came rushing in, "Lumière, lumière!" He turned the light out; that was my first experience in France.

The convoys from the Front to the hospital and from the hospital back to England came at all times, we never knew when they might arrive. A convoy of wounded might be taken away and we would leave the hut tidy and go off for the night, and we'd come back in the morning and every bed would be full, so we'd start all over again, looking after them, finding out what the matter was. Of course, the men would have so many lice on them, their clothes had to be fumigated and the men cleaned up. They suffered terribly with lice, I don't know how they lived with them. I heard that they tried taking their underwear off and turning them inside out just to give themselves a few minutes' peace before the lice buried their way underneath again.

Each hut at Etaples was like an army hut and had ten patients along each side of the ward. We had no curtains or anything like that. Because we had no light, I just carried a little oil lantern and I'd walk up and down, up and down.

One night the German bombers came and bombed the hospital. We didn't know that, earlier in the evening, some horses had evidently been tethered outside our hut, and one of the bombs, which I suppose was meant for us, hit these horses instead. The noise was something terrible. I never knew a horse could scream, scream all over. I kept walking up and down the hut as fast as I could, because I always thought if I walked up and down perhaps the bomb would drop the one end while I was at the other. Everything would shake if a bomb dropped close by, and I would just hold myself tightly, it was an awful

During 1918 several indiscriminate bombing raids were on the Base Hospital at Etaples, several nurses being killed.   IWM Q 11539

feeling, though. I always tried to keep a brave face. I thought in my own mind that it was very important that I didn't show any fear, to try and help the men, to keep them all calm, because some had only just come out of the trenches and could not bear the thought of anything happening now they were out. Of course I'd talk to the men to reassure them, but some were more nervous than we were and tried to climb out of their beds to get underneath for protection.

The worst nights were when there was a full moon because that shone everything up. Then, if we were off duty, we took our blankets and we went to where there were trees on a little rise and we took shelter there. We were hidden by the trees and we lay down and tried to sleep. There was a Chinese camp nearby, the Chinese Labour Contingent. They used to dig trenches around our hospital and sometimes, if we thought we would be safer, we would sleep in those trenches, although I always found them pretty damp really. Anyway, one bad night when we were huddled under the trees, the Chinese were so scared they climbed over the barbed wire fence that surrounded their camp, and ran right by us in panic, one grabbing at my blanket, which I clung onto. We were safer under the trees, but several nurses were killed at the camp when bombs hit the huts. I couldn't ever understand why they bombed the hospital, as all the huts had big red crosses painted on the roofs. There was a big cemetery at Etaples and the nurses who were killed were buried there alongside the soldiers.

We were all exhausted from the strain of work. There were no drugs or anything to combat disease, so many would come down with dysentery, and there were never enough things to keep the men clean. Then another illness like flu would come along, and would knock out yet more men. If anyone was ill with constipation, he could have a number nine pill, and if that didn't work he

121

had to have a dose of castor oil, that's all we had. We had so few vegetables and I don't remember any fruit, no wonder everybody was constipated, including the nurses. I was constipated and given castor oil by the Matron and I went out of her office and threw it all up. The food was so poor, I remember a fish dinner being kept for me as I was working late and when I finally ate it, it was just a mouthful of fish and host of bones, but you couldn't say anything. The doctor on our ward looked so haggard and tired, so tired, he asked me not to disturb him unless absolutely necessary. The bombing wore his nerves down too, and on the occasion the bomb hit the horses he came onto the ward and tried to climb under one of the beds to escape the bombs, just like some of the wounded men.

I remember one boy with flu, oh he'd been so ill. He was crying for his mummy, crying for his mummy. "Oh," I said "I'll be your mummy tonight" and I gave him such a hug and he went to sleep quite quietly. The next night the convoy came to take so many back to England, and they'd just take them, nothing to do with me. I mean, they'd know who they had to take and they had one place they hadn't filled, and they looked around and said they'd take that boy. "Oh," I said "he's not strong enough, give him two more days, he'll be all right then." Well, no, the convoy had to go full, so he went, and via the grapevine I heard that he saw his mummy and then he died, and I still feel sad about that in some way. It was kind of unnecessary.

When we could, we tried to entertain the soldiers on the wards. I remember we had some screens you could put round the men when necessary, just wooden screens with thin red cotton covers on them. Some of us got together and wrapped ourselves in these covers to look a bit christmassy and we sang Christmas carols. We were so tired, I don't know how we managed to squeak, much less sing, but we tried anyway, we did our best and the men appreciated it and tried to join in.

I did miss home when I was in France. I remember quite plainly we had a cold spell, and I used to put little dishes of water out on the ward windowsill to see if they had frozen into ice. As a child, I had taken great pleasure in skating on the frozen park lakes in London. I knew if there was good ice, there would be ice in that park in London. Isn't it funny that I had to find out if there was ice back home, in the park?

Nurses attend to wounded soldiers in one of the huts at Etaples.   IWM E4623

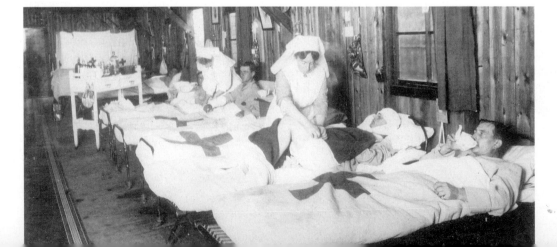

CHAPTER SEVEN

Death, Bereavement and Loss

A DEAD BODY WAS JUST THAT, A DEAD BODY, AND YOU WERE JUST GLAD IT WASN'T YOU. Apparent indifference by men to the fate of fellow soldiers should not be surprising. It is one of the commonest reactions a veteran of the First World War will give, when recalling the sight of bodies on the battlefield. Men quickly hardened to death because there was no opportunity to react differently. Such was the limited area in which battles on the Western Front were fought (it is possible to walk the entire breadth of the Somme Battlefield in little over an hour), that to see a body was of little or no consequence unless there was something peculiar or unusual about it. One soldier remembered three dead men sitting upright apparently asleep together, another recalled the sight of two soldiers who had simultaneously bayonetted each other.

Some men chose to ignore the sight of bodies whenever possible; others happily looked over the dead for souvenirs. One man, searching a mutilated body, was shocked to find the photograph of a girl he knew in England. The body was that of her father, a man he had known well by sight back home. Another recalled how, to obtain one keepsake, he removed a dismembered hand

Dead bodies rarely received a second glance from soldiers accustomed to scenes of all-out war, and all too aware that they could be next. IWM Q23942

still clutching a Véry light pistol, while another remembered how he'd searched the body of a dead German officer simply because he was bored.

The death of a close friend was entirely different. With the advent of hostilities, many men joined up together in twos and threes, choosing, as was their right as volunteers, to serve in the same regiment. Similarly, in the Pals Battalions, whole groups of workmates from cotton mills, mines, and foundries enlisted and fought together. The bonds between these men were naturally extremely strong. Even if men were strangers to each other on joining a regiment, six months, or a year's training in Britain soon brought them close together. The loss of one or more of these friends would be a severe blow. Burying these dead, irrespective of whether death came in the destruction of a battalion in battle or the arbitrary explosion of a shell in the trench, was a traumatic experience and often haunted survivors.

There were, of course, a myriad reactions to the death of friends. Some men became fighting mad, bent on revenge against the enemy at the next possible opportunity; others became depressed, and cared little what happened to them personally. Many would find solace in the corner of a trench and have a weep before reappearing shortly afterwards to resume duties, apparently in a normal frame of mind. They carried on because there was no option, although most remained quiet and touchy for a couple of days afterwards.

The sense that everyone was in the same boat occasionally engendered sympathy for German soldiers occupying the trench opposite. Death was arbitrary, and often de-personalised – the majority of injuries were caused by exploding shrapnel, less than 1% from bayonet wounds – so that it was something inflicted upon, rather than done to, each other. Given the uniformity of risk, many men were fatalistic, accepting survival as mere chance and therefore death as simple ill luck; if your number was up, if your name was on the bullet, then there was nothing anyone could do. Not all soldiers accepted that life or death was pre-ordained, but the idea did help many men to come to terms with the sight and imminence of death.

Lists of casualties printed daily in the newspapers left no one at home in any doubt as to the numbers being lost at the Front. For the families in Britain, waiting for news of loved ones, the appearance of an official letter on the doormat struck dread into the heart. The letters, printed in their millions, would regret to inform the recipient that "a report has this day been received from the War Office to the effect that…" the following number, rank and name was dead, wounded, or a prisoner of war.

News of death and injury was not always accurate. Two interviewees were officially reported dead, when mistakes with their names were made. Errors apart, the army usually preferred to report a man missing until further news was received of his whereabouts. It gave families hope that a son might have been taken prisoner of war and that his name had yet to be released by the Germans to the Red Cross. One interviewee, unofficially reported killed in action in a letter by his platoon officer to his parents, in fact turned out to be a prisoner. But the joy at discovering a son was alive was rare. More often there was disappointment and heartbreak. Many other families clung vainly to the hope that a father, son or husband might one day turn up, when they had actually been killed.

For those left to cope with the loss, there was neighbourly sympathy and a meagre war pension, but little else. The death of the main bread-winner often haunted those who remained, forcing many older children to assume the role of a parent to other siblings while the mother went to work. Many families were too impoverished to visit the grave, if there was a grave. Many soldiers had no known grave. The only official recognition of their existence was a name on a memorial to the missing.

ANDREW BOWIE

As far as Andrew was concerned, the attack on Passchendaele Ridge in October 1917 had been an unmitigated disaster. The offensive had already cost around 250,000 casualties, and in the latest attack almost everyone in Andrew's battalion had been killed or wounded, including Andrew's own Captain. Pinned down in a shell hole, Andrew and a friend survived by pretending to be stretcher bearers. However, the loss of so many men has left an indelible impression on Andrew's mind.

Walking back, we saw an old German pill box, and behind it lay a lot of our boys wounded there. The stretcher bearers were wiped out too, so the lads lay there and probably died there, and I would dare say a lot died in the mud as

The dead of a Highland Regiment cut down during an attack near Zonnebeke, 1917

well. There was nothing we could do, we had no water. It was very, very sad to walk past them and do nothing for them.

We got out, and going down the duck boards we thought we would straighten up our kilts because they were heavy with mud. So we took them off but we couldn't get the things on again. We folded them up and slung them across our shoulders and walked down in our shirt tails. We got as far as Poperinge, and we were going down the main street when a big horse charged up to us, with a very efficient officer aboard, and he said, "Why haven't you got your kilts on? You are a disgrace to your regiment." I swore at him, I think I told him to go to hell. It just about knocked him off his horse. I was beyond caring. I said, "As far as I know, we are the only two left of the battalion." He said, "Oh, all right boys, go on." I must have looked a mess because the top of my tunic was cut clean off by a piece of shrapnel, and was hanging loose. You would have thought it was cut by a razor, and it missed my throat by a fraction of an inch. I used to hear bullets fizz past, but this was the closest I came to death in the war and I didn't even know it had happened.

We found the remains of the battalion with the details, those are the cooks and tailors. We heard afterwards that when the roll call was taken, there were only 39 remained of those who had gone into action, and there wasn't a company officer left. The rest were killed or wounded. It was the worst experience I had in the war.

WALTER GREEN, born 26th November 1897, died 5th March 1998, 20th Durham Light Infantry.

The number of close shaves Walter survived on the Western Front was marginally fewer than those he gave as a barber, the profession he took up for the rest of his working life. Joining up in 1916, Walter received just thirteen weeks' training before he was sent abroad into the chaos of the fighting in France and Belgium. He served at Messines and Third Ypres, before being taken prisoner of war the following year. He died peacefully in his sleep shortly after his hundredth birthday.

Walter Green 1916

Walter Green 1998

One of the best times for the Jerry trench mortars to bombard our trenches was as one regiment left the line and another took its place. For a short time, instead of one regiment in the line there are two, squeezing past each other in the communication trenches, and therefore more damage is likely to be done.

Very often we would have a senior NCO standing in the trench, so as a mortar would burst, and before another could be loaded, he'd say "Go!" and two of us would run out of the front line trench into the communication trench and then run down the line. On this occasion this fellow, Fred Fowler, and I had been told to "Go", to run down a trench called Fleet Street, when there was an explosion just behind the parapet. I caught the blast and found myself lying on my back, wondering where I was. I started to feel round to see if I was hit and wasn't, so

I jumped up and started running. I got ten or fifteen yards when I realised Fred wasn't behind me. I looked round but couldn't see him, so I went back and found him laid on his back, apparently dead. That was a big shock for me, that was. I checked him to make sure he was dead but struggled to find where he'd been hit, so I shouted for stretcher bearers. Fortunately, two were not far away and they came and picked him up and quickly got him out of the line of fire. When they examined him they found that a piece of shrapnel had gone right through his pack and coat and hit him at the base of the spine. There was hardly any blood at all.

I followed the stretcher bearers until we came to Brigade Headquarters, when one of the stretcher bearers said to me, "Can you take over because I think we'll be needed up the line again straight away?" I agreed, and went into the Brigade office and asked to see the Orderly Officer. The officer wasn't there, so I was asked what I wanted and I explained what had happened. "Well," said one man, "the padre's here, he'll perhaps help you." The padre followed me out and satisfied himself that the man was dead and he just turned to me and he asked "Are you going to help me bury him?" Just like that. I replied that I would do but that he'd have to verify that I was helping because I'd left my unit and I did not want to be charged with being absent. He agreed, and we went into this temporary cemetery, just near Headquarters, and started digging. We hadn't been digging very long when Jerry started shelling the cemetery and we had to run for cover. "Look, I'll get somebody to help me when it cools down a bit," the

The dead gathered from the battlefield await burial. TAYLOR LIBRARY

padre said, "you get away." I watched for an opportunity to get out and caught up with my unit.

About eight days later, we were going back into the line when I asked an unusual thing. This cemetery was close to the road along which we were to march, so I took the opportunity to ask a sergeant, "By the way, sergeant, that pal that was killed when I was coming out last time, I would like to go see what they've done, do you think I might slip off quick?" He said "You've got to let no one see you." However, when we got near the place he said "Go on, nip across there quick." I ran off and found the grave. Two pieces of wood had been nailed together to form a cross and pressed into the ground with the dead man's identification disc attached.

I was satisfied he was temporarily buried. I suppose it wasn't important, it was just I wanted to see the grave because I was there and I was involved, curiosity to know, really. It was a shock when you lost one of your pals, and Fred was a nice lad, although I didn't know him well. I mean if someone came along and said Jimmy Stanley has just been killed, well, unless Jimmy Stanley was very close to you, then you just accepted it as another casualty. It was a funny experience, how often you went up the line with a pal and came back with another one.

Men were very touchy for a day or two afterwards when a mate was killed, and it was nothing to see a man in a quiet part of the trench having a little weep. If a man did not cry, then often his voice broke down and he would not want to talk to anybody else, then he would perhaps take a quiet five minutes to pull himself together. You got over the upset by getting back to the job. Even if three or four chaps had been killed, you would still have to carry on.

GEORGE LITTLEFAIR

The most poignant of all battlefield deaths were those of close friends. George Littlefair lost his mate Joe Coates when a piece of shrapnel struck Joe down in a moment of carelessness. It is a death that continues to pain George eighty years on.

It was the shrapnel wounds that were damned rough, you know. A bullet was often straight in and out, but shrapnel was ragged and it made a nasty wound. If it was your leg or your arm, the wound could be bound up but if it was your body you often had to lie there bleeding until the stretcher bearers got on to you. It was shrapnel which got poor Joe.

Joe Coates, he was a good friend. We had our ups and downs between us but still we were always good pals, we helped one another. If I was coming home on leave - "Call and tell our lot I'm all right", or I'd say the same to him and he would call on my family as well as Jenny, my girlfriend. He'd come back and say he'd seen her, "She's all right, I think I'll hang on to her instead of you". I said "You bugger, I'll shoot you if you do!" We were a pair of good pals. We shared everything down to the paper and pen we needed to write home with and the blacking to polish our buttons, we were like that.

It was long distance shelling that got him. Joe had one fault, he was too careless, he stood up instead of keeping down in the trench, he stood up and a lump of shrapnel got him. Poor Joe. He moaned. I wanted to attend to him but I couldn't. I just said that the stretcher bearers were coming, they'd take him away. He'd already gone over when they came. I never touched anything he had, you know, to remember him by, I let it all go with him. That was me pal gone and I was too full to speak to anybody after that. I never palled up with anybody else, not after you got that feeling.

I've thought many a time about it. It might have been me instead of him. When you're sat by yourself, things come and go through your mind. All this, and it was for no bloody purpose after all's said and done. After the war I never went to see his parents again because I didn't want to upset them. They knew where I was if they wanted to talk to me. I finally saw his grave in 1997 and all the memories came back. And I'm not afraid to tell you, when I was looking at his grave the tears was running down my face. I'm not afraid to say it 'cos we were bosom pals and we never even said "so long" to one another. The last time I saw all the graves, they were little wooden crosses and now they are all nice white marble headstones and I thought what a big improvement, aye, it's there, age and everything. I was pleased.

George Littlefair (standing) and his pal Joe Coates, who was killed next to him in the trenches.

A cemetery just behind the lines with the first makeshift crosses. TAYLOR LIBRARY

NORMAN COLLINS

After any attack, men would be detailed to bury the dead. For those of the 51st Highland Division who had taken part in the successful assault on Beaumont Hamel, it meant burying close mates and even relatives. Norman Collins was designated the burial officer. It was, perhaps, the most harrowing time of his life.

After the attack on Beaumont Hamel, I was told to collect the newly-killed and I took stretcher bearers, quite a number of whom were related to the ones who were dead, brothers, cousins, and they of course were very upset, very, very upset. We took the dead back to Mailly-Maillet Wood and dug a long trench and put the dead in there, wrapped in an army blanket, neatly packed in like sardines. We covered them up and we gave them a proper funeral with reversed arms; all the ceremonial of a proper funeral, blowing the Last Post and so on. As an officer you needn't stand aloof, but the best way of comforting the living would be to give them a stroke on the head or a pat on the back or some gesture like that, without words, comfort them without words. But it was a horrible thing to do, to have to bury your own cousin or brother.

Afterwards, I was told to go back into what had been No Man's Land and bury the old dead of the Newfoundland Regiment, killed on 1st July. The flesh had gone mainly from the face but the hair had still grown, the beard to some extent. They looked very ragged, very ragged and the rats were running out of their chests. The rats were getting out of the rain, of course, because the cloth over the rib cage made quite a nice nest and when you touched a body the rats just poured out of the front. A dozen bodies would be touched simultaneously and there were rats tumbling everywhere. To a rat it was just a nest, but to think that a human being provided a nest for a rat was a pretty dreadful feeling. And when the flesh goes from under a puttee, there is just a bone and if you stand on it, it just squashes. For a young fellow like myself, nineteen, all I had to look forward to at the time was a similar fate. It still has an effect on me now, you never forget it. Nobody knew what to do, we were all fresh, all newcomers to the job. All we could do was remove the paybooks and leave one identity disc on so they could be identified later and put the personal items in a clean sandbag. Then, we shovelled the dead into shell holes, most half-filled with water, about thirty to a shell hole. There was no emotion then. There comes a time when emotion becomes a strange sort of word, you get so much of it that you become deadened to it, you're bound to. You didn't know men that had been dead for four and a half months and were strangers to you, you only knew them as young soldiers and officers who'd gone to war just as you had, and they'd died. You felt in a way horrified to think that there you had, in my case, probably nine hundred or so young men - they must have been an average age of nineteen or twenty, who had all come over to France to do what they thought no doubt would be a wonderful job of work and in one day - one day - they were destroyed. You thought then and you saw what happened and you realised what their aspirations and their ambitions were and what they were going to do to put the world right, and they were going to do this and that and all they did was to die in really a few minutes. Yet you couldn't weep for them any more than you could for any of the other 20,000 who died on 1st July, but it seemed to me to be such a terrible waste of life.

I took the sandbags down to Brigade Headquarters and handed them over in a deep dugout in the chalk, where I was amazed by the luxury of the officers who were down there. I was asked to have a cup of tea, which I did and in front of me was a box of cakes labelled Fortnum and Mason, Piccadilly. I've never forgotten that. The officers down there all had red tabs on and they were all spick and span, and I was very pleased to get out and get back to my men in the trenches. I was more at home with them. I didn't like the idea of leaving my survivors of my own men - they depended on me for things that other people couldn't give them.

*Florence
Billington
1998*

FLORENCE BILLINGTON née Dillon, born 3rd December 1898, died 16th August 1998. Girlfriend of Edward Felton, 4th Kings Liverpool Regiment, killed in action 16th May 1915, Ypres.

Florence Billington was only 16 years old when she met Edward Felton, a handsome local boy two years her senior. When war broke out, Edward joined the Kings Liverpool Regiment, and went to France in early 1915. He was killed in action during the 2nd Battle of Ypres, leaving Florence to grieve alone. Without a photograph of her lost love, Florence has had to rely on the accuracy of her mind's eye and the clarity of her memory, to recall the image and personality of the boy whom she had hoped to marry, over eighty years ago.

*Florence
Billington
1915*

I was with a group of friends when I met Ted Felton. We met in a shop doorway in West Derby Road and I was introduced to him and he seemed to take a fancy to me straight away, and I liked him. We met again, started to see each other, and very quickly became very fond of each other. We had not been going out very long when war broke out. He'd been called up, being a territorial, so he had to go. But there was a rumour that the war would be over by Christmas, so we got in with the idea that as soon as it was over we would get engaged, it was like a promise.

We were entranced by each other, I should say, and I know that when he went to the Front I kept thinking of him all the time and he thought of me. He was very worried about going abroad and I tried to comfort him. I knew nothing about the war, so all I could say was for him to look on the bright side, that there were better days in store. I told him we would write regularly, which I did. Yet he was quite convinced he was going to be killed, that he knew in his heart he would not come back. I told him to shake off the depression by thinking of me, and that as soon as the war was over we would make a life together, but he took some convincing.

His regiment, the Kings Liverpools, were pushed over to France quite suddenly. On the morning they were sailing, I went all sort of haywire, hysterical. I had to do something, to get rid of the feeling of depression, so I went to a friend's house and we danced and danced, to try and get rid of the gloom.

I was ever so sad and I missed him terribly, but I couldn't show too much to mother because she was so down to earth, she'd only think I was love-sick. The letters I got from Ted told me how preoccupied they were, marching from one place to another. I would reply telling him that I missed him, missed him an awful lot, and I wished that he was a bit nearer so I could see more of him. I would promise him I would look at no one else while he was away, that I'd wait for him to eternity. I would have done, but I didn't get the chance, did I?

When I heard Ted had been killed, I was at work. I was working as a housemaid at the Palace Hotel, Buxton, when one of the porters came up with a letter from the War Office, a long envelope, official-looking, and when I saw it my heart sank. I opened it and read that they regretted to tell me that Edward Felton had been killed. I told the other girls and they were sorry, but they were getting used to hearing that relatives and friends had been killed, so much was happening, including the sinking of the Lusitania, that had only just gone down. I went away from them, just to grieve quietly on my own.

I received a letter about the same time from one of Edward's officers. The officer told me that Ted had been hit in the back and that he'd been wounded and had died. This officer wrote because some of my letters to Ted had been found on his body. They didn't have my home address, just the one where I had written the letters from, the hotel address. I sat down and wrote a letter to his relatives. What could I say? Only that I was awfully sorry. I couldn't even say I'd come and see them because I didn't know their exact address. I knew the road name, but it was a long road.

I couldn't really imagine him not being around. I thought maybe one day the army would find out they had made a mistake and perhaps he might turn up. And over the years when missing soldiers did turn up, I thought wouldn't it be wonderful if it was Ted. I just wanted to go away and hide somewhere where it was quiet and not bother to talk to anybody. I cried a lot, and my life increasingly became a roller-coaster after Ted's death. I wasn't sure what I wanted to do, I was always chopping and changing. I would get a job, then I would want to go home. I'd get homesick and I would go home and my parents thought, that's Flo, yeah, couldn't settle down. But I was thinking of him, that's what it was.

After the war, when I lived in Leeds, I met a man who was a spiritualist. He came to lunch with his wife, and while we were having a cup of tea, this man told me that he could see a very young boy in khaki standing behind me. "He says he was killed in the war - have you any idea who that is?" I said, "Yes, I know who it is." He said "Well, this young man is showing an awful lot of love towards you." I told him it was a boy I had been courting, who had been killed at Ypres. He told me, "He's here for you and he wants me to tell you that he loved you with all his heart and soul and had hoped to make his life with you, if he could have done." On occasions since, I have felt his spirit visit me, that he was thinking of me and was somewhere near.

Parting company.

*Ellen Elston
1998*

ELLEN ELSTON née TANNER, born 14th August 1908, daughter of Sergeant John Tanner, 9th Royal East Surreys, killed in action at Ypres, 6th August 1917.

When Ellen Elston was not quite nine years old, her father was killed in action at the Front. Ellen was the eldest of six children, and her childhood was effectively terminated at that moment. She took on the role of housewife, while her mother went to work to bring in enough money to feed the family. "I think when you are young, you don't know the depth of sorrow, but in a way, I think, to grow up without a dad, more so for girls, I think it's a sad life actually."

I remember going with my mother and brother on a visit to see my father at Dover Castle. As Company Sergeant Major, dad had to drill the men and it was exciting to see all the soldiers lined up and our own dad taking them through their paces. We thought that was marvellous, we were very proud of him. Afterwards all the men clustered round him and us: these were the sergeant major's kids. Dad was to me, of course, very nice-looking, fair curly hair, not too tall, a happy-looking man. That would have been 1915, when I was about eight years old.

In 1916 he was wounded on the Somme, not too badly. I remember him coming home on leave; we were delighted to see him and he spoiled us all. I remember him getting me on his knee and giving me a cuddle and singing a song "They'll Never Believe Me", very popular in those days. We had a big gramophone with a great big blue horn and he put the record on and sang to me, "They'll never believe me, and when I tell them how beautiful you are, they'll never believe me, they'll never believe me, that from this great big world you've chosen me". He ruffled my hair. I can remember that as plain as anything, and that song, it's still played today, and so of course I'm back on his knee, aren't I? Always.

A few days before my birthday he was killed at Ypres. He was 43 years old. Dad had had to go back to the war and I nearly forgot that I had a dad, until that morning in August, 6th August I think it was. The telegram boy, he rode on a red bicycle, with a pill box hat on, he notified us with a telegram. It was Sunday morning and my mother was getting the dinner ready. I can remember her hands being all floury, and all she could do was to sit down and we all gathered round. We didn't understand. All we knew was that the telegram boy had been, which was exciting to children, a message from dad.

It may sound funny, but my father's death meant a new dress to me. In no time at all, mother had made black and white check dresses with a black belt for all the girls, and I can see us now, all walking down the street together and people looking at us because father was well-known in the community. I don't think dad's death registered, somehow, as there was no funeral or anything like that because he was buried out there. The only thing that registered were the commiserations of everybody around us, the neighbours, then a letter from one of the regiment's officers. I do remember my father's brother coming round. He was a monk in a monastery and I can recall him coming to visit my mother, you know, to see her after father's death, and my mother ordered him out of the house, I can remember that quite plainly. She said "Please don't come telling me there's a God because I don't believe in him any more."

You are upset for your mother, really, you are upset because your mother is upset. We had a beautiful picture on the wall that mums used to have in those days, in a gold frame, you know, a head and shoulders shot of dad. She turned it around the other way because when she went into that room she could not bear to look at it. I can hear her wandering around the house crying, although she tried to put a brave face on it in front of the children. I cried when I went to bed but I never cried in front of other people. You are too proud to let people see that things reach you. Yes, I can remember crying and crying – for my mother – not because my father was killed.

I was the eldest, nine years old then, and life changed. Mother was working at the nearby NAAFI, packing and sending food to the troops, to help make ends meet. I had to become the head of the family, cooking the dinner, great pots of stew and rice, making dresses for my younger sisters, bathing the kids, black leading the fire grate, running errands, making cups of tea, ironing, all sorts of things. My little brother used to cry when I made him scrub his knees; we often laughed about it later as we got older. I suppose being the eldest child, the others looked up to me, they come to you for everything and I just took it that it was part of my job. You learn from experience, I mean at nine or ten years old you have to cook, and you can only go by what your mother did, and copy. So I would go to the butchers and get sixpenny-worth of bones which I just put in a pot and threw all the vegetables in and thickened it up with barley - there's a meal!

My brother and I were wandering out on Christmas Eve. Mother was indoors making mince pies, but she wasn't looking forward to Christmas because dad had been killed only months before. We wandered down the road to where there was a big toy shop, and we stopped. We were looking in the shop window, which was dripping with condensation, admiring all the things we would like but which we knew we couldn't have. I can remember looking at a lovely doll all dressed in pale blue silk, when a lady came and started looking in the window as well and said "Now why don't you go inside and look, it's cold out here". We just looked up at her. We went inside and she followed us in, and all the different things we liked she bought me and my brother. She had the assistant put them all in a bag, one big bag each for my brother and me, then she said "Now you go straight home and you tell your mother that you met Mrs Christmas". She knew my father, her husband had been in the army with dad, but all my life I never forgot that woman's gesture on Christmas Eve. Although I was ninety this year, I still feel the thrill of that kindness.

Lucy Walter
1998

LUCY WALTER née NEALE, born 4th April 1907. Daughter of Sergeant Harold Neale, 2/3rd Kings African Rifles, died of dysentery, 15th October 1917.

It is often said that the real victims of war are less those who are killed than those who are left behind. At ten years old, Lucy Neale loved her father deeply and was profoundly traumatised by his death. An only child, she quickly became a lonely child, endlessly recalling the time she saw her father on leave for the last time. Lucy slowly came to terms with her loss and has lived a full life, although even now, aged 91, the recollection of bereavement is both painful and remarkably detailed.

When war broke out on 4th August 1914, I remember my father coming into our little house in Cookleigh and saying he was going to enlist at once. I think my mother and he had a little argument about that, but anyway, the next day he didn't go to work at the carpet factory, instead he went off to Kidderminster, about two and a half miles away and enlisted, as quickly as that. I was sorry he'd joined up, I didn't want him to go. I missed him so much, I didn't think of anyone but myself, I suppose.

He must have had at least one leave before the last visit. He didn't know where he was going when he came that last day to say goodbye. I was in school, and I suppose it was about ten o'clock in the morning and there was a knock at the door. We couldn't see who was on the other side, as the teacher, Mrs Beeston, went to answer it. I heard her say "Oh Mr Neale, how lovely to see you, you're on leave then?" And then she closed the door, much to my annoyance, and I couldn't hear a thing. Then she opened the door and beckoned me and she said, "Come along, Lucy, you can go home now, you don't want to be in school any longer today, it's your father come for you." It was my tenth birthday and we walked to the village, back to where we lived, and I was so proud, he was very handsome for one thing, my dad, and he looked lovely in the khaki uniform. We met one or two folk on the road going home and they shook hands with him and chatted and wished him well and then we went home to mother. I don't remember much about my birthday, really, it was April 4th and a nice sunny day and when the other girls came home from school I went out to play with them. I remember he bought me, for my birthday present, a lovely hymn and prayer book with a little case and a handle. I'd never seen one like it before, it was lovely. I was pleased with it, in a way, but I must say, to be truthful, I was disappointed also because I'd never had a doll and I was hoping somebody would give me a doll, but nobody ever did.

At about six o'clock in the evening, my father called me in and said he'd got to go back to Kidderminster, back to barracks. "Will you walk with me a little way, just up the hill, will you come with me?" Of course I would. He said goodbye to my mother, who was crying, and we went off down the road and then up this long hill. It was a ten-minute walk, I suppose, but we didn't hurry, we just walked slowly up the hill and I really can't remember what we talked about, we must have talked, I think, but I really can't remember. I held on to his hand so tight, and when we got to the top, he said "I won't take you any further,

135

you must go back now and I'll stand here and watch you until you're out of sight", and he put his arms round me and held me so close to him I remember feeling how rough that khaki uniform was, and he said "Now I want you to promise me three things. You'll look after your mother, and I want you to go to church because I bought you that nice new prayer book and I would like to think you were going to use it and go to church, and then the last thing I want you to promise me is that you'll grow up to be a good girl." He said "You won't know what I mean now but you will as you grow older, and I do want you to be a good girl, will you promise?" and I said "Yes".

He picked me up against him and put his arms round me and held me tight to him and he kissed my cheeks and put me down and he said "You must go now, wave to me at the bottom, won't you?" And I went, I left him standing there and I went down the hill and I kept looking back and waving and he was still there, just standing there. I got to the bottom and then I'd got to turn off to go to where we lived, so I stopped and waved to him and he gestured as much as to say "Go on, you must go home now", sort of thing, ever so gently gestured, and then he waved and he was still waving when I went, and that was the last I ever saw of him.

He went back to Kidderminster and the next thing we heard he was sent off to German East Africa, Tanzania as it's now called. He wrote to me frequently from Africa, he wrote from Durban, he liked Durban, then he wrote from the loveliest place in all the world, he said, Dar-es-Salaam. I used to take his letters to school and Miss Bywater, the teacher, used to read them all to the class, I don't suppose the other girls were very interested.

I was getting ready for school one morning in October when the postman came and I picked up this registered letter. My mother opened it and it was from the Army and she just sat there and she said "Oh, he's dead", and I can't begin to tell you how I felt. I couldn't take it in for a while, but she began to cry. I felt numb, absolutely numb, and my mother said "You are not going to school today, you'll have to stay at home with me".

My mother said, you'd better take this letter up to your grandmother, because she was not on good terms with my Gran, and show her. My Gran was sitting there with one of my aunts who'd come to stay from Leamington, Jessie, her eldest daughter and my father's favourite sister. So I put the letter on the table and Gran, my grandmother, said "You open it, Jess," and she opened it and said "Oh no, he's dead, Harry's dead". My poor Gran, she could only say "Oh, not another one," because she had already lost two sons in the war. Gran didn't cry, she sat there like someone made of stone, she didn't say anything, but Auntie Jess began to cry terribly. I seem to remember my aunt making a pot of tea and then I said something like "I'd better go back home now", and left.

Back home, my mother and I went to see another aunt, Auntie Fanny, who lived on a nearby farm. Auntie Fanny cried and of course my mother cried again, but I don't remember crying. I was so stunned, I couldn't believe it – I'd never see him again. It is hard to realise tragedies when you're only ten years old.

"Gran" sitting with her four sons before they went to war. Three were not to return, including Lucy's father, Harry Neale, rear left.

Lucy Walter's father Harry Neale and his grave in a cemetery in East Africa.

I went back to school the next day and had to tell Miss Bywater, the headmistress, why I had not attended the previous day. School started, because we said prayers, all three classes together in one room and she said "Before we have our prayers, I just want to tell you that Lucy has lost her father, so I think we ought to pray this morning for Lucy and her mother", but I couldn't take it in, I was in a dream. The Lord's Prayer was said, and the usual prayers and a little hymn we used to sing, but I just couldn't, or I wouldn't, perhaps, face the fact that I would never see him again. That day, that was the worst day, and then a day or two later another girl, she lost her father, and we said prayers again for her.

Every week our local paper, *The Kidderminster Shuttle* – being a carpet manufacturing town – every week, there was some boy, some son, some husband killed. And there was a lot of wounded, they used to come home on leave and you'd see them with their arms in slings or walking on two sticks in their khaki about town or wherever. I think for a long time I felt resentful, I did, I felt very resentful – I mean why my dad – and then in time of course common sense takes over, and you realise you were not the only one, there were many more in Kidderminster, let alone the country.

My father's acting officer sent a little parcel with my father's diary and odds and ends, you know, little things from Africa, including a little picture of his grave, and I remember thinking that one day I'd go to Africa and find my dad's grave, of course I never have. My father had been sent from Dar-es-Salaam down country to fight. He'd been wounded and taken to hospital and while he was there he'd caught dysentery and died. Those field hospitals in East Africa must have been pretty awful. Of course I didn't know what dysentery was, but it killed a terrific lot of men in the war.

I missed my father terribly, for years I missed him. I never cried when my mother read that telegram, I couldn't cry when I was with my grandmother nor when I went to see Aunt Fanny the same day, but oh dear, I did cry at night when I got into bed because it was my father who used to tuck me into bed. We would go up by candle light and kneel by the bed. It was my dad who taught me my prayers. We never hurried through them, and then he'd kiss me on my forehead, and say "Goodnight Lulu, God bless you", every night, he never failed. So for years afterwards I'd got to say my prayers because my father asked me to, we'd said our prayers together and then I did the same when I was alone, when he'd gone.

Kathleen Barron
1998

KATHLEEN BARRON, born 7th March 1902, sister of Dick Barron

Longevity appears to run in families, and Dick and Kathleen Barron are just one example of the living proof. Sharing nearly 200 years between them, 103 and 96 respectively, both brother and sister live remarkably independent lives. Both retain cogent memories of the First World War, Dick as a soldier, Kathleen as an adoring sister worried, as all families were, that war might take a loved one away for ever.

Kathleen Barron
1922

Dick was a good bit older than me, and naturally, as a little girl I worshipped him. I looked up to him for everything. To think that he was going to war and might be killed was to me the most dreadful thing and it affected me very badly. It was terrible to see him go, heartbreaking. I sometimes lay awake at night thinking about him, and of course at school he came into my mind.

The headmaster, Mr Garside, would announce that such and such a boy, one of our old boys, had been killed. And do you know he actually cried, the tears rolled down his face. The sight amazed me really, yet it made me like him more, because of how he felt about the old boys. We would have a hymn and then there would be silence, and that would affect us all. Of course I was always afraid that Mr Garside might one day read out Dick's name.

At home we just waited and hoped Dick would be all right. In those days the postman knocked on the door when he delivered some letters, and my mother would say, "Go and fetch the letters"; she couldn't open them. And then one day there was a buff-coloured envelope, a long envelope, and it had OHMS on the outside, On His Majesty's Service, and this would mean that Dick had been killed, or wounded, or taken prisoner. It could only be bad news, and it was my business to open the letter. I looked at mother and saw her face absolutely ashen white. I didn't wait to get any paper knife, I just opened it and read it to her. Dick was in hospital, very ill with dysentery, and we would be informed as soon as he came back to England.

The letter was very businesslike, there was a sorry and all that, and we would be kept informed, but that is about all, I remember. I think in a way mother was a little relieved, because he wasn't killed. There was hope, wasn't there?

I was delighted to see Dick again, to have him back with us, but he looked very ill and very thin – as though he'd suffered a lot. He was rather a short man and he'd lost so much weight, I couldn't help feeling it was funny to see his great big pith helmet on his head. I noticed mum, too, and I've never seen her looking so beautiful as she did when she saw her son. She was a good-looking woman but she looked extra special that day.

Kathleen and Dick Barron in 1912

Dick wasn't quite the happy-go-lucky person that he had been. He'd altered, I mean he'd suffered a lot, nearly died, and that alters people, doesn't it? He didn't talk about Gallipoli much, no, he tried to forget it I think. He was still far from well, really, but there you are, we had him back, we had him home.

HARRY PATCH, born 17th June 1898, 7th Duke of Cornwall's Light Infantry.

Conscripted into the army, Harry turned out to be a crack shot in training and was sent to join a Lewis Gun team. He served four months in the Ypres Salient in 1917 before being wounded by shellfire and evacuated back to England. It was when he was receiving treatment that Harry discovered that three of the five-man team had been killed in the same explosion. Their deaths deeply affected him and for eighty-one years he avoided speaking about the war. A quiet, unassuming man, Harry lives in a residential home in Wells in Somerset.

Harry Patch 1998

140

You talked to your mates in the Lewis Gun team. There was always a certain amount of emotional chatter, nerves. Shall we get through tomorrow, or shall we get a packet? I am going up the line tonight and am I coming back? It's getting dark, okay, everything may be quiet, but are you going to see the sun come up in the morning? And when the sun comes up in the morning, wonder if I shall see it set at night. Sooner or later you showed your emotions. That was why the comradeship was so important because I know I was scared more or less the whole time I was out there.

There were five of them in the Lewis Gun team and we lost three of them. The battalion had been relieved at ten o' clock at night and we were going through to the support line, over a piece of open ground, when a whizz bang burst just behind me. Heavy shells made a whump sound but the light shells, the whizz bangs, they used to come over quickly with a Zupppppp, bang, flash, and that was it. The force of the explosion threw me to the floor but I didn't know that I'd been hit for two or three minutes; burning metal knocks the pain out of you at first. I saw blood, so I took a field dressing out and put it on the wound. Then the pain came.

I don't know how long I lay there, it may have been ten minutes, it may have been half an hour, but a stretcher came along and I was picked up and taken to the dressing station. There were a lot of seriously wounded there, so I had to wait. I lay there that night and all the next day and the next evening a doctor came and had a look at the wound. He could see shrapnel buried inside and said "Would you like me to take it out?" I said "Well, yes, it's very painful, sir." He said "Got no anaesthetic. All that was used in the battle and we haven't been able to replace it. I shall have to take it out as you are." I thought for a minute and said "How long will you be?" He said "Two minutes." So I thought, well, two minutes of agony and I shall get rid of all the pain, so I said "Okay, go on, take it out". Two orderlies got hold, one on each arm, and two got hold of my legs, and the doctor got busy.

In those two minutes I could have damn well killed him, the pain was terrific. I take it he must have cut his way around the metal and got hold of the shrapnel with his tweezers, so that he could drag it out. Anyway, he got it and asked "Do you want it as a souvenir?" The shrapnel was about two inches long, broad at one end, and about half-an-inch thick with a sharp edge. I said "I've had the bloody stuff too long already." The doctor went over to the next table and the fellow in the next bed said to me "If he writes anything in the green book you're for Blighty". Anyway, sure enough he wrote in the book and I thought well, that's it then. I was lucky, very lucky indeed, for the word Blighty meant everything to a soldier.

I didn't know what had happened to the others at first. But I was told afterwards that I had lost three good mates. The Lewis Gun team was a little team together and the last three who were the ammunition carriers were blown to pieces. My reaction was terrible, it was like losing a part of my life. Simply blown to pieces, there you are, but it upset me more than anything.

I'd taken an absolute liking to the men in the team, you could say almost love.

You could talk to them about anything and everything. I mean these boys were with you night and day, you shared everything with them and you talked about everything. We each knew where the others came from and what their lives had been, where they were educated. You were one of them, we belonged to each other if you understand. It's a difficult thing to describe, the friendship between us. I never met any of their people or any of their parents but I knew all about them and they knew all about me. There was nothing that cropped up, don't matter what it was, that you couldn't discuss with them in one way or another. If you had anything pinched you could talk to them, and if you had anything scrounged, you always shared it with them. You could confide everything to them. They would understand. Letters from home, when we got them, any trouble in them, they would discuss it with you.

That day, 22nd September 1917 – that is my Remembrance Day, not Armistice Day. The cenotaph service is all right – the rest of it is simply a military show to me. I'm always very, very quiet on that day and I don't want anybody talking to me really. Eighty years after and I always remember it. I shall never forget the three I lost.

CHAPTER EIGHT

Long-Term Recovery

WOUND STRIPES were small gold-coloured bars worn on the left tunic sleeve, added to the uniform every time a soldier was wounded at the Front. It is very common to see photos of soldiers with one or two stripes, and not infrequent to see men with three or four. They give the largely correct impression that to survive any length of time near the front line invariably meant being wounded.

Artillery and mortars caused the greatest number of casualties during the First World War, around 60%, while machine guns and rifles were responsible for 40% of deaths and injuries. With the increasing industrialisation of warfare, the number of shells supplied to the artillery was, by 1916, on a scale unheard of in 1914. Guns were able to lay down bombardments not only of greater intensity and accuracy, but also of almost unendurable length. With the Army Service Corps supplying the guns around the clock, bombardments, such as that which preceded the Battle of the Somme, could last many days.

Shells pulverised the front line and support trenches, catching troops as they marched up to the line. As men went into action, shrapnel burst overhead, and slivers of shell casing rained down, inflicting horrific injuries. The effect of such heavy shelling took a toll not just of the physical but also of the mental health of the soldier. Shellshock, a medical ailment not recognised at the start of the war, increasingly incapacitated men as their mental faculties became scrambled. In 1914, 1,906 cases of behavioural disorder were admitted to hospital, but by the end of 1915 this had grown to 20,327, or 9% of all battle casualties.

Officially, the army showed little sympathy towards shellshocked soldiers, and some men shot for cowardice were clearly suffering from extreme battle fatigue. However, doctors increasingly accepted shellshock as a condition of battle, and specialist hospitals or wards were set aside, such as those at Craiglockhart and Netley, for the treatment of officers and men with shellshock. By the end of the war, 30,000 cases of mental illness had been evacuated to Britain, and their treatment continued throughout the 1920s. By 1922, 50,000 pensions had been awarded to men on mental grounds alone. Recovery was often slow. In 1929 there were still some 65,000 soldiers of the First World War in mental hospitals. The official tally of all those who died during the war inevitably leaves out the thousands of traumatised former soldiers who committed suicide in the twenty years after the war.

Men who had lost arms and legs in the war were, for all to see, partially or completely invalided for life, receiving long term physical treatment and a small lifetime pension. Those who were wounded by poison gas were often less fortunate. Victims of mustard and chlorine gas often returned to the fight even though physically their lives had been blighted. Unless they were badly gassed, most men stood a very good chance of recovering, for counter measures against gas attacks quickly improved after the first attacks in 1915. Only 3% of casualties died and 2% were invalided, so although 113,764 men were gassed in 1918, only 2,673 died. However, while many men could and did return to the line and survive, their long term physical well-being was not guaranteed. Many men suffered relapses after appearing to recover, others suffered from chronic bronchial problems and the permanent loss of smell. Doctors routinely gave gas victims five to ten years to live after the war, yet despite the dire prognosis, many men had their paltry pensions reduced within six months of leaving the services. Owing to the depressed economic outlook, the Government's financial stringency meant some men lost their pensions altogether.

For those who were badly injured during the war, there would be many months or even years of interminable operations, convalescence, further operations, and physiotherapy. The Armistice spelt the end of the fighting, but the last of the stationary hospitals, at Abbeville and Boulogne, did not close until 1920. In the same year there were over 18,500 beds still carrying the most seriously wounded from the war and 48 special mental hospitals in Britain. Hospitals such as The Royal Herbert at Woolwich continued to have wards full of soldiers recovering from their wounds until 1921 and 1922. Even as late as 1928 there were 5,205 first issues of artificial limbs to soldiers.

The long term mental and physical fallout from the war was enormous. Even today, on the eightieth anniversary of the Armistice, there are hundreds of soldiers who continue to suffer significant pain and discomfort from injuries received not just on the Western Front, but also further afield in Gallipoli, Mesopotamia, Palestine, and Salonika.

Those who were badly injured during the war would experience many months or even years of operations, convalescence and further operations. TAYLOR LIBRARY

HORACE `JOCK' GAFFRON, born 20th October 1896, 1/4th Gordon Highlanders.

*Horace Gaffron
1997*

*Horace Gaffron
1916*

Jock was 19 years old when he embarked for France in May 1916, a private in the 4th Gordon Highlanders. He had served just two months on the Somme when a shell finished his military career, and he returned to England in July. Now 102 years old, he recalls the day war changed, but failed to blight, his long life. Recovering from wounds, Jock became an artist for Life Magazine, living in America for many years.

All my life I have had hunches that something was going to happen. I had no idea how or why, but I had that feeling, something was in the offing. We were going up Mametz Valley – known as Death Valley – towards the line near High Wood, and I became quite fidgety. I turned to my friend next to me and said "What a nice morning for a cushy blighty and home", a cushy one being a nice wound that would get me back to England. The next thing I heard was one stiffening bang and I went down and when I came to, I was lying on my back with both legs in the air. I couldn't move but I looked and saw that my right foot had gone. Shrapnel had hit behind the heel and took the sole clean away leaving my big toe dangling round and round. When the RAMC men came up, they just casually cut the toe away and threw it on the roadside.

An ambulance came down, and then by stages I was taken to the base hospital at Camiers, where they put me on the operating table. There were a dozen tables in the theatre and all of them were occupied. I said to the surgeon, "I don't want to lose my foot if I can manage it", and he replied "We'll do what we can." They amputated my foot through the ankle. It was hopeless. The foot had to go and that was that, but I can assure you it was no easy job, it was extremely painful and if I ever cried in my life, I cried then, I'm not ashamed to say so.

I was nineteen years old and I had just received this injury which would finish me throughout my life from quite a few things. At my age, to have that injury was quite a shock. It meant I would have to adapt my life in many ways; luckily I was never much of a sportsman apart from fishing, but even so I had to make the best of it. I had been lucky, though, because the shell had wiped out a good part of my company.

I did not look at the dressings. I know there were bandages and there were tourniquets and tightenings and things like that, but I wasn't too happy about looking at the rawness so I just let them do what was necessary. I was back in England at the Rowntrees' Convalescent Hospital in York, and the nurses there were very gentle, and seemed to take their work in their stride. The sights they saw, I could never get over that, yet we got nothing but the best treatment. I had to have further amputations higher and higher up the leg; the second one took my leg off to within four inches of the knees and that was very, very sore, I can assure you. A spot of gangrene had apparently set in, a "spot", that was the word I overheard and it frightened me, but they worked on it right away and did a wonderful job. Once again there was a lot more crying, good hefty blubbering, for it was more than I could stand. The hot poultices were incredibly painful and then there were the dressings. These used to terrify me in every way because the nurse had to pull off the blood soaked bandages and they stuck to the wound and tugging on them only took away some more of the flesh. You could hear other men having their bandages done too, and you could hear them yell and moan. Aye, it was a rotten job, that, an ordeal I dreaded.

One nurse, Mary Sutherland, had a great effect on my life. She was my nurse and she certainly looked after me in every way. She sat with me day and night until I came round after the second amputation, speaking only words of comfort as the pain subsided, helping me through this traumatic state of affairs. Later on, she used to wheel me to the shops in the bath chair and we'd go for a coffee. It wasn't a case of attraction, not at all, I was an apprentice printer and I'd come

'She sat with me day and night until I came round after the second amputation, speaking only words of comfort as the pain subsided.' Horace Gaffron and nurse Mary Sutherland, who helped Horace through his amputations.

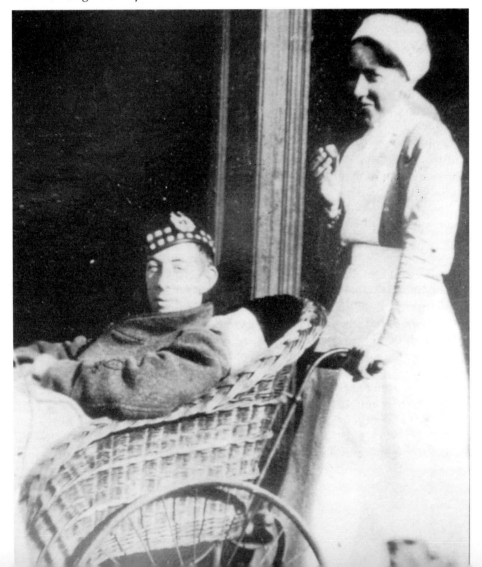

from a different walk of life. The question of any feelings didn't enter it at all, it was just that she was very good at her job. I missed her very much when I went south to hospital in London. Many years after the war, I made contact again. She had retired to Dorset and I arranged to visit, but she died about a week before I was due to go.

Of course, you felt that most of the nurses came from what we would call then a better class. They were most of them ladies of good breeding, they came from good families and we treated them with very great respect. Later, I was transferred to Nunthorn Hall, in Scotland, the home of Lord and Lady Hulme. They had given over part of their house for convalescent soldiers, and the nurses there used to take us out shooting. We would be wheeled out in bathchairs to shoot pheasants with double barrel shotguns, feathers flying everywhere, with the nurses standing behind us with their fingers in their ears.

The nurses were very proud of their uniforms and loved the occasion of taking us out, a dozen of us wounded boys, on a trip to the cinema, and of course we got in for nothing. Being a wounded soldier, you were a bit of an eye-catcher. Crowds would watch soldiers being moved, and the nurses felt very much appreciated. The uniforms were very important, it gave them a sense of purpose, a challenge. People would stop you in the street, or come up and talk to you, get you a packet of cigarettes or chocolate. If you went to the theatre for the afternoon performance, if you were in a wheelchair like me, you were always wheeled down the gangway until you got almost to the stage. If the show hadn't started, you could often see the curtain move and the girls looking at you, oh, you were quite an eyeful. It was nice to be in a wheelchair and being the wounded soldier, but the thoughts were there about having to live with it when the war was finished and that was a bit of a worry.

After the amputation came the fitting of an artificial leg, when I was sent down to Roehampton, the limbless hospital in London. You always got blisters on the stump and they could be very awkward, but you can gradually get used to them with treatment. The blisters came while you were walking, if you had something out of place or a fold or a little crumple in your trousers. If the blister broke, you couldn't use ointment because the more ointment you used, the more pain, and the more the sore spread. It could be a very small sore, but then it could turn into one the size of a halfcrown, in which case you had to take your leg off and go into a wheelchair until it dried up and healed.

There was no hard and fast rule to treat blisters. The nurses were as ignorant as we were, and we all learned the tricks of the trade as time passed. The nurses knew nothing about artificial limbs either, that was the fitters' job, the men who made the leg and fitted it. If there were any blisters, the fitters noted it, then marked the stump, replacing the stump into the artificial leg which transferred the mark onto the inside of the leg bucket. The fitter knew then where to cut a little wood out to make the adjustments.

As well as blisters, stump pains were a regular problem and I can assure you they could be very, very trying. They were also called phantom pains because they were something that the medical profession knew very little about, let

The fitters became skilled in customising their products for each amputee, then making small adjustments as the wearer required. IWM Q33687

alone the nurses. The pain was pretty much like toothache on a grand scale. The nurses knew there was plenty of pain there and they were very sympathetic, and gave us pain killers, but they didn't know just how bad they were.

I remember I was coming out of Lloyds Bank on the corner of Shaftesbury Avenue and Piccadilly Circus when I managed to step badly on my artificial foot, and there was a crack. Well, I was on sticks and when I walked away, my foot and my sock came out of my trousers and fell onto the pavement. I managed to pick up my leg but was left with my foot in my hand, hopping around. Now if you want to collect a crowd in Piccadilly Circus at one o'clock, do something like that and you'll collect one pretty quick. I was taken back into the bank and the under-manager put me in his car and took me back to Putney, to my home. I was a wounded soldier, you see, that counted for a lot.

GUY BOTWRIGHT

Guy Botwright had never wanted to serve at the Front, but out of a sense of duty he had gone to France in 1917. The horror he saw inflicted deep psychological wounds, and he was returned to England with shellshock after an explosion close by knocked him unconscious.

My job was to organise all the transport of food and ammunition to the front

148

line. The company would go to the railhead and the ammunition would be unloaded and then taken to a dump. From there it was taken up the line, and I would ensure it was going to the right place by going up the road with a column. The Germans would often shell the dumps and the roads – the biggest fire I ever saw was a dump of cordite in flames. And there were horrible sights, too. I remember once, a battery had been hit and the mules pulling it were splattered all over the place, the fire power of artillery and machine gun fire, you can't imagine. By far the worst were the wounded; when a man was badly wounded, we'd cheer him up and tell him it's all over for you old chappie, you'll go home. It is difficult to describe my feelings so many years on, but you live day to day, when you know your life at any minute could be carved to bits. I can say that I suffered fear from my toe to the tip of my head but I had a job to do. Out of the line, in rest, there were times when suddenly I thought "God, I can't go back to it", but you did go back to it, you had to go back to it. I was an officer, I had to, so I would get ready, put my jacket on and I would fall into line, as best I could.

I rarely had to go into the line, but I know I was in part of a trench that was being dug when suddenly everything went black. A shell had landed very close to me, although I don't remember feeling any pain of any kind whatever. The next thing, well, I just came round and to my utter amazement I was in bed in hospital in England. How I got there I haven't got the foggiest, nor how long it was from the time I felt nothing to waking up and finding myself in bed, days, I feel pretty certain. I can only imagine I was unconscious all that time, I have no idea, the whole thing took time to sink in – I had shellshock you see.

Well, I didn't care what happened. Any desire to continue did not exist, I went to bits. It would have been far better if I hadn't known, you see, but of course they couldn't keep me in hospital without letting me know that was what it was, I mean if I hadn't realised that it was shellshock, or hadn't been told so, I don't quite know what I would have imagined had happened, because my only physical injury was the very top of one finger gone.

I didn't care whether I lived or not. In the first stages, you're much more likely to shed a tear, to feel the depression, oh yes, the depression, I would put that down as depression. If I got a sudden depression, well, it would depend on my state at the time, I might be able to throw it off. The nurses were wonderful, they'd ask a question and by what sort of answer they got, they'd know exactly what was in the air. They were well-trained but then the hospital staff had dozens of people in exactly the same condition.

Each day I thought, "Oh dear, another day, oh Lord." It was self-pity, even knowing how lucky I was could make me burst into tears, I had to help myself but I also had to be helped out of the situation. What was to be done God only knows, was the sort of idea that one had. You lived hour to hour, I don't say day to day for the simple reason that Tuesday or Wednesday didn't exist as such. You didn't know where you were, you would, if you had only shellshock, have no pain as such. It would simply be that the mind would not work, you didn't know day from night and you didn't know about eating, whether it was lunch

Officially, the army showed little sympathy towards shellshocked soldiers. By the end of the war, 30,000 cases of mental illness had been evacuated to Britain, and their treatment continued throughout the 1920s.
IWM Q24046

time or tea time. It's a shocking state to get into, being mentally wounded, I wouldn't recommend it.

I did not venture from my bed for anything, good gracious, no fear, not until things began to settle down, then I might be told to get up for 10 minutes and somebody would come and help me out of bed to a chair. They would force you to do it and rightly, too. They'd stay there and help because my legs would flop, your legs would let you down, you never quite knew when they were going to let you down. Luckily I was never in one room alone, thank goodness, because it helped to be in a ward with other people even if they are ill too, it is a help, you know that you are not on your own. I was not embarrassed by my condition. You never thought yourself an officer, you thought you were you. I don't think being in the army came into my life until I was much better, rank did not come into it at all, we were all officers but we were pals together under those circumstances.

There was very little shakiness, my hands did not shake, on the contrary, for a while I had no real movement: it was the mind, that was the real shock. I never had nightmares, I never dreaded the night coming on, but I did get flash-backs for many years. They could happen at any time, if I was in a street, if there was something interesting I would forget myself then I would be all right, but then I might think "Well, it isn't raining but it might do", or I might sneeze and think that I had a cold coming on and that would start things off, you would feel a depression coming on. If something reminded me of incidents in France, if I had made a botch up of anything, that would come back at odd times to depress me.

I was still an officer when I was called to a board meeting at Chichester to be discharged. There was a table of seven officers and the chairman said "What are you going to do when you are discharged?" and I remember saying "I have not the slightest idea, but I want an open air existence". I decided on forestry. It was the end of the war and it was the beginning of recovery in a sense. I made up my mind, "The war has now ceased and I'm going back into civilian life". The war had so broken up my future, it had been such a shock, I decided I would never talk about it or write or read anything about it and I never did.

150

Frederick Tayler
1997

FREDERICK TAYLER, born 12th May 1898, 13th Battery, 29th Division Royal Field Artillery.

The question "what if?" has had a lifetime's significance for former artilleryman Fred Tayler. What if Fred had walked away from a shell explosion in the last weeks of the war? How radically different would the course of his life have been? As it was, the shell smashed Fred's left leg, making an amputation inevitable. His future uncertain, Fred returned to England and a hospital bed in Carlisle. However, his injury guaranteed one thing: he would meet Beattie O'Neill, a nurse and fellow Londoner. She devotedly looked after Fred as he recovered, care soon turning into romance, which turned into very happy sixty-two year marriage.

I had been attached to Headquarters for quite a time during the latter months of 1918. The war had more or less become open warfare again, and the infantry were moving steadily forward, but at headquarters we thought we were a long way behind any action. I remember there were eight of us in an empty house, when someone came in and said "Come and look, you can see the fighting". We all rushed out of the door and up the path that led to the road, and sure enough, up on a hill you could see them bayonet fighting, the glints of sun shining on the steel. The troops we had seen marching up past us a little earlier had come back over the hill with the Germans behind. We were lined up on this path and didn't realise that we could naturally be seen as well, when suddenly over come two shells. The first one fell just in front of the house and as we went to get up from ducking, the second landed on our side. I heard the first but not the second shell. Unfortunately, I was the nearest to it when it burst, about six feet away. Down we all went, but when the smoke cleared, the others got up and ran into the house. I tried, but found I couldn't. I was in no pain, but as fast as I stood up, I fell down again, so I crawled into the house and went to lay against a wall which I thought would be the safest place if any more shells came. Then I rolled over on my back and looked down at my leg and to my surprise I was looking at the sole of my foot.

The others were in the cellar when somebody called "Who's up there, anybody?" I said "Yes, Tayler". They told me to come down but I replied that I couldn't move so they came up to see what was wrong. There happened to be a doctor in our group, but there was little he could do. He asked me whether I felt any pain, but there was no pain – it didn't hurt, and there was no blood, except a little on my shoulder, but not on my leg although my leg was the wrong way round. They were trying to get the front door off to use it as a stretcher when some German prisoners were coming down the road and were ordered to carry me back to a first aid post.

When I arrived, there was a padre I knew standing just inside and he looked round and spotted me. "Hello, Tayler, what are you doing here?" I said I thought I'd got in the way of a shell and we laughed. He told me not to worry, he would get in touch with my parents and said he'd write and let them know I'd been wounded and that I'd be writing. At the aid post, they dress what they can dress. They took my jacket off and got the bit of shrapnel that was sticking out, but they couldn't do anything for my leg because the leg was intact, the skin wasn't broken.

I wasn't capable of thinking about much, about what might happen to me. If there'd been any blood, I think it would have made me wonder more, but there was no blood. I suppose not being able to understand what had happened, or how serious it was, perhaps it didn't affect me quite so much. I was placed in an ambulance with a corporal of the RAMC. He seemed to be lightly wounded and had walked down to the dressing station. He was moaning and groaning a bit. He told me he could look after other people's wounds, but he was terrified of being wounded himself. Unfortunately when we got to the operating theatre, the poor chap was dead.

At the hospital, I tried to look around 'cos it seemed there were so many operations taking place at once. Someone came to examine me. I don't remember passing out, but I came too when they put me on the table to be operated on. I remember seeing this man and I tried to raise myself up, to look around, but I was pushed back down again on my shoulders, and somebody put their hand on my head. I hit out, I hit the poor chap in the face, there was no reason to it, it was just that something was stopping me lifting my head up, so I hit them, then I was off.

I had an operation but I didn't know what they had done. I was taken to a ward and the next day a train arrived to take the wounded down to the base. They didn't seem to want to take me at first, but they were shouting "Any more for the train?" The chap looking after me said "I've got one here, but he won't be long", and I thought he meant I was going to die. I don't know if that's what he thought, but I said "I'm all right, I'm all right, I want to go". Whoever was in charge of the ward said "Oh, take him out, take him out". I got to a little window with a girl sitting behind it and she wanted to know my name, address and army number, but I couldn't remember a thing. This poor girl was asking me questions which I couldn't answer. I thought I was going to be left behind, the others were gradually moving on, getting in the train, and then I suddenly remembered, it came to me who I was and my number and everything, and I called out.

My particulars were taken and I was wheeled out to the ambulance train, no seats, just three racks on each side of the carriage. As they lifted me up, a corporal receiving the patients said "What's this one?" and a chap looked at a label on me and the answer came "Amputation". Well, that was the first I knew that my leg was off, it was quite a shock. I didn't realise because there was no sensation that it was off and I wasn't in pain. I just wondered how long it would be before my mother got to know and how it would affect her. That was my first thought when I was injured, what would my mother think, then you suddenly realise that you're going to be a different person. My leg was intact but smashed. I was hit half-way down the calf, half-way down the leg itself, but the damage was so severe that the actual knee was shattered, so that was why they had to take my leg off above the knee.

I was taken across the Channel but because they didn't like you to be too near home, the inconvenience of so many visitors, they sent me up to Carlisle which is a long way from London and my home, there was no chance of visiting me there. I was the only Londoner there, so there were all sorts of different brogues. One day, the matron came in with a nurse and said, this is a new nurse on this ward and she comes from London, it might be a bit of a help for you. I thought that was very nice. So she came and had a chat, after she'd been round all the patients she came back to me and we had our little chat, and our friendship just grew and grew.

Her name was Beattie O'Neill, a lovely girl. When I got onto crutches, we started going to the cinema in Carlisle, but we had to go out of the hospital separately. We daren't be seen because the rules were that patients and nurses don't mix. We couldn't meet until we got to the cinema, same with going for a meal, we would not meet until we both got to the restaurant. We started going out and when I left hospital we married, married for sixty-two years we were.

HARRY WELLS, born 1st January 1900, died 19th July 1998, 17th Royal Fusiliers.

Harry Wells was as old as the century, literally. Over-exertion by his mother at a New Year's Eve party brought Harry into the world as the new century dawned. Eighteen years later, Harry was in the trenches in France, one of the thousands of soldiers just old enough to train and still see action in the First World War. Yet his short sojourn at the Front nearly ended his life, when, badly gassed, he fought for over two years in hospital to regain his health. He was finally released from hospital in October 1920.

We'd been in the line for over a week and all the boys were saying how quiet it was. There hadn't been any shells for a couple of days, and in all the time we had been in the trenches there had just been the occasional shell to let us know Jerry was still around. At the time, an attack was being prepared and a lot of reinforcements were coming into the line. The idea was for these new troops to go over the top at first light, followed by the Fusiliers of my battalion.

We could hear the troops as they filtered up the line, and the guns and limbers further back, the steel wheels on the French roads. The Germans must have heard the same thing and guessed what was happening, because all of a sudden they started blasting with everything they'd got. High explosive and gas shells were raining down and the trenches were being blown to pieces of course, so instructions came round to go down into a gas-proof dugout big enough to hold up to a hundred men, I would guess. We'd been down there about an hour when a few wounded men began to be brought down, one I remember with his arm off. Unfortunately, no one thought, but some of these men had had liquid gas splashed on their uniforms and down below in the warm air given off by our

Harry Wells 1998

Harry Wells 1918

153

bodies, the liquid gas began to evaporate. We had begun grovelling about before anyone realised what was happening. We were told to put our gas masks on, but by this time we'd more or less gassed ourselves.

After a couple of hours, we were ordered out into the trench. It was a little after dawn, but we found it bright daylight and we simply could not keep our eyes open. I knew I had been gassed but I was hoping in my mind that it was only just a whiff of gas and perhaps a bit of fresh air might blow it away. However, the longer we stayed out in the open air, the worse the effects got until we couldn't open our eyes at all. There were dead bodies in the trench mixed up with the earth and we walked over them as we had to feel our way around. Somebody gave me someone's shoulder to hang onto and we were led out of the broken trenches some three or four kilometres to a first aid post, where we were sorted out into badly amd less badly wounded, and those playing up. I couldn't see what it was, but from the noise, it sounded like the floor of a warehouse. I got the impression there were about 200 men or more, myself included, lying on the floor on stretchers waiting to be taken down the line.

Just lying there had quite a nasty effect, because I was only a lad, and to hear

A line of men blinded by tear gas during the Battle of Estaires in April 1918. The effects, painful and debilitating as they were, usually wore off. IWM Q11586

these men crying out with the pain, crying like children, not so much from wounds but from the flesh burnt by mustard gas on the skin, was awful. Mustard gas used to attack the warmest parts of the body and would take the skin off as if you had scalded yourself, so you can imagine what that was like under the armpits, the crotch, that sort of area.

Some trucks were provided which took us down to an American hospital at Le Treport, the 16th Philadelphia General, I was later to find out. Our eyes were covered, but as we entered, I always remember an American nurse's voice saying "Good God, they're sending babies now to fight their war." I looked very young in those days. I was very fair and very fresh-looking, eighteen years old. We knew we were in good hands, and that was a relief. I knew I stood a good chance of living. Having no experience of being gassed or wounded, you didn't know what was going to happen but they got down to the treatment of my eyes straightaway. After a couple of days, I was able to open them and see a little, but I had to have a shade over my eyes all the time for the next year. The only treatment that I can recall was we were given something called Mistexpect. This was a sort of mixture which helped break up the phlegm which we brought up, as well as easing the coughing caused by the gas.

After about two weeks, what they called the walking wounded were cleared out to the trains, onto the ships and over to England. Now in those days they put you on a Red Cross train and the train went straight onto the ferry and off again at Dover and on towards, in our case, London. We actually stopped at Clapham Junction for a few minutes to get clearance to carry on up north. This was where I was born and my mother still lived there, so I hurriedly borrowed a pencil and wrote a postcard saying that I was home in Blighty and that I would drop her a line later. I threw it out of the window and somebody picked the card up from the platform and took it to my mother.

While I had gradually got my sight back, the gas which I had inhaled had meanwhile done near-fatal damage to my chest, affecting one lung which they told me had collapsed. The gas itself began burning its way out of my chest, forcing bits of rib through the skin. It made an open wound which the doctors could only hope to syringe, hoping to kill the germs and cure the gas poisoning inside. It was lysol they used all the time, I think. They would syringe me out every morning and then use something called a Silver Stick, a whitish substance which caused very severe tingling as it burnt off the dead flesh but importantly kept the wound open. They would then bandage me up again from top to bottom using what they called a butterfly bandage, then the job was repeated again later that day.

My open wound was, if anything, getting worse, and slivers of the rib were coming out. I had a high temperature and I was going in and out of consciousness and was seriously ill. Eventually I slipped into a coma and my mother was sent for, to see me for the last time. She received two telegrams that day, one to come and see me, the other to see my brother who was in Carshalton Hospital. He was just fourteen and he was ill with peritonitis. I was in a coma for about a fortnight, although when I awoke I assumed I had only had a long night's sleep. My brother died at that time, unfortunately, they couldn't save him.

Nurse Blake, a Welsh girl, she was the one who really pulled me round. I think it was the motherly instinct, because I looked so young at eighteen, very fresh, clean shaven, almost babyish. She tended to me the whole time, talking to me. You are inclined to go off into a stupor and give up, you know, say "why worry"? You are so ill you let go, as it were. This nurse kept on at me and saved my life by just being there, talking, holding my hand, keeping me occupied. "Do you want anything? Can we get you anything? Would you like a cup of tea?" Just like this until the day you suddenly sit up in bed. This did not mean I was better; the process of bandaging and cleaning the wound continued for many months. It was only when the last surgeon decided to have a go at carving out the entire infection, that I made permanent improvements. He cut away the infection like pieces of cheese, and used the Silver Stick to burn away any further dead flesh. The wound gradually healed up.

Looking back, I wonder how I put up with the whole ordeal. I suppose part of it was the stiff upper lip. The pain was bad, but it was recognised that it was for a man to be a man and not to show pain – and when you are eighteen you so want to be a man. We found by experience that the harder the nurse was, the better she did her job. We didn't much care for these nurses, but if she took no notice of whether she hurt you or not, she was generally much more efficient than the nervous girl who feared hurting you.

The efficient nurses were the Queen Alexandra nurses, the military nurses who were fully trained and knew what they were doing. They would tell you not to be a baby, or I would hear them say to other patients "that's nothing much", that sort of thing. The others were volunteers, the VADs, and of course they were unsure because they were not qualified nurses. But there were thousands of boys who had come home injured, and these nurses were doing jobs they ordinarily wouldn't. On one occasion, an inexperienced nurse had syringed me but she got a bit close to the lung, because I found lysol was coming up my throat. It frightened me almost as much as it frightened this girl, because she knew she wasn't doing it right and she was nervous. There was a bit of bleeding and I ended up swallowing much of the liquid, but it was one of those things, and it wouldn't have been fair to blame her. I say you can never speak too highly of the work both the VAD girls and the army nurses did, and the hours they spent looking after us.

CHAPTER NINE

Women and the Home Front

IN DECEMBER 1914, German battle cruisers shelled Hartlepool, Scarborough and Whitby, on the north east coast of England, leaving 230 dead and 500 injured. Early the next year, the capital was attacked by Zeppelins, enormous gas-filled airships, and bomb-laden aeroplanes, which together would kill almost 2,000 Londoners by the end of the war. These raids were in military terms a failure. Civilians weren't frightened into submission and no prized targets were hit. But they signalled an important change in the nature of warfare. Women and children were among the targets and victims of these attacks – the horror of war was no longer restricted to men. This was total war, in which everyone on the home front was in danger and everyone had a vital role to play in achieving victory – especially the women.

When the war began, the predominant image of women in Britain was essentially Victorian. They were widely seen as frail and vulnerable, in need of protection from the harsh realities of the world. The most common job for women was domestic service – there were one and a quarter million domestic servants. Most physically demanding, skilled and professional jobs were

A German daylight bombing raid on London, July 1917. Two victims are being taken home from hospital with an accompanying nurse. Civilians were not frightened into submission and no prized targets were hit – however, women and children had become legitimate targets.
TAYLOR LIBRARY

generally restricted to men, and women were not considered responsible enough to have the vote. During the pre-war years, the suffragettes had campaigned passionately for a recognition of women's rights, but it was the war itself that provided the greatest impetus for change. With so many men away at the Front, there was a desperate shortage of labour at home.

The greatest need was for women to work in the munitions factories. In 1915, there was a serious lack of arms for the troops, including an acute shell shortage. The government intervened, converting hundreds of factories to supplying munitions and by 1918, several hundred thousand women had been recruited to work in them. But the working conditions were arduous and extremely dangerous. The task of filling the shells with TNT turned hands and faces bright yellow, as a result of which the workers were nicknamed the "canary girls". Small explosions and fatal accidents were commonplace in munitions work. There were catastrophic explosions at Chilwell in Nottinghamshire, which killed

Women bagging TNT, a job which turned the girls' faces and hands a bright yellow, giving rise to the nickname "canary girls". TAYLOR LIBRARY

250, and at Silvertown in London's East End, which cost 300 lives.

The other jobs that women were called upon to do were less dangerous, but often equally demanding. They helped to run the trains and the trams, they kept the country fed by joining the Women's Land Army, new women police maintained law and order on the streets, and women kept the wheels of heavy industry turning. One of the most popular and prestigious wartime jobs was nursing. Nursing had, since the days of Florence Nightingale, been deemed a respectable occupation for a woman, but now thousands more were needed to help nurse the injured back to health. There was an upsurge in women choosing nursing as a career. With the mass of war-wounded soldiers needing urgent treatment, military and general hospitals became so overstretched that nurses, assisted by VADs, often took over the running of the wards.

When the war ended, however, most women had to give up their jobs to the returning soldiers. Most offered little resistance. The conditions had been so harsh that many young women were now looking forward to the pleasure of marriage, and bringing up their children at home. Nevertheless, women had enjoyed a vital moment of freedom and independence. Many new areas of employment had opened up to them, and they had proved that they could do a wide range of jobs as well as, if not better than, the men. The old prejudiced ideas about men and women would never be the same again – as was signalled when women (over thirty) received the vote for the first time in 1918.

CORA TUCKER, born 13th January 1904. Resident of Colwyn Road, Hartlepool, 16th December 1914.

The attack on Hartlepool was as sudden as it was unexpected. The idea that German ships could bombard a sleepy coastal town was beyond the comprehension of children. Cora Tucker was ten years old when the shells rained down on the town. Eighty-four years on, she lives only minutes away from where she stood that day, watching as panic-stricken civilians streamed out of the old town.

You heard little bits about the war at the Front, but we thought it was a war that would happen abroad, that it would never touch us. We never dreamt we would be attacked.

My mother was ill in bed when we heard the bangs in the distance, and we thought, "Oh, it's our ships practising". We didn't realise the war had started. We were looking over the garden wall, and across the Byrne Valley we saw all these people going up the road and out into the country, taking their possessions with them. We didn't know why it was, until it got to nearly tea-time, and we were told the place had been bombed and people had been killed. Of course we were horrified, although we couldn't go anywhere, with my mother ill in bed. We lived away from the main destruction, in Colwyn Road, and right opposite us was Thurmier Street. A lady there was cooking

Cora Tucker
1998

Cora Tucker
1917

breakfast, and a piece of shrapnel came through the window and killed her. That was fairly close to us. But the main damage was in the old town, nearer to where the shipyards and the aerodrome were.

I was only ten years old and I couldn't understand why the Germans were killing civilians, it didn't make any sense. On the Friday there was another scare. We were on our way to school when we were stopped. "Go back again, the Germans are coming." Who put that about I don't know, but it was a false alarm. But at the time I had some little pet Bantam hens, I was so scared, I said to my father "If we go away and I leave my little pet Bantams, the Germans will come and eat them". I was so upset. That Friday, during the scare, my aunt decided she would come round to our house. She had her baby in one hand and the Christmas cake in the other. She met a woman on the way over, and she was carrying candles in one hand and her Christmas cake in the other, and they looked at one another and laughed. The women had all made their lovely Christmas cakes and were saving them from the Germans, if nothing else.

West Hartlepool Baptist Chapel received a direct hit from a shell fired by the German North Sea Raiders, December 1914.

On the Sunday after the bombardment, my father took me up to the old town to see the damage. I couldn't believe it, it was horrifying. All these houses were down, rubble lying everywhere. Later in the war, we went to Wales on holiday, and people didn't believe the attack had happened. Were we sure that it had happened? Hadn't we dreamt it?

EMMA CUSSONS née HARRISON, born 25th July 1908. Living in Hartlepool, 16th December 1914.

For those who lived in the old town, the attack on Hartlepool was devastating. Six-year-old Emma Harrison was still in bed when the enemy shells struck her house. Grabbed out of her bed by a neighbour, she was taken downstairs to find her mother badly injured by shrapnel. Now ninety years old, Emma's memory of that day remains remarkably vivid.

My mother was doing the washing when she heard what she thought was someone beating a carpet. She went to the door with my little sister and met a lady who lived opposite who had come out into the street looking for her sister. She said to my mother "Oh my God, the Germans are here." My mother told the

Emma Cussons 1998

lady "My three bairns are still in bed." Well, this lady said "Go into my house and see to my mother, and I'll get your children up." My mum went to see her, but the old lady was ill and was apparently going berserk with the shelling. Mum told me later there was nothing she could do for her. Every minute seemed like an hour for mum, as she left the house to cross the road home again, but when she got to the front door, this shell exploded, shrapnel hitting her in the shoulder.

I had heard what I thought was thunder, after which this neighbour came into my bedroom to get us all out of bed. We were half-asleep, but I remember this lady saying "Come on, come on, you've got to come downstairs with me." We were literally dragged out of bed. Mum was losing so much blood, she must have felt herself getting faint because she said "I can't stay in here or I'll bleed to death. Come on." We walked down the street, well, it was just a little cul-de-sac, and as we got to the end of the street there wasn't a sound, everything was dead quiet. Everybody had gone, they'd left the houses, leaving all the doors wide open as they went. Mum told us to keep behind her, and she looked around; I think she was looking to see if there were any Germans. We followed her to my aunt's house where mother told me "Get all the drawers open, and get some shawls out," because we kids were still in our night things. We wrapped the shawls around us and came out again just in time for mum to see a man go back into a house, so we followed him in to get help.

I think there was a young lad there who was in bed getting over pneumonia. Anyway, he was turfed out of bed and my mother was put in, and the bed was pushed nearer the fire. We were there for a while because there was more or less a crowd outside the house, I guess they'd heard what had happened. I was more excited than anything. I mean, when you are seven years old, you just think "Oh, I won't have to go to school today." I knew my mam had been hurt, but we were being fussed over, so I don't think I realised the danger we had all been in. At one point I had to push my way through to get to my mam, and people were saying "hey, hey", as if to say don't push, and I said "It's my mother!"

We kids were put in front of the fire with her, because it was bitterly cold and we were freezing. My mam had lost an awful lot of blood, she had bits of shrapnel all over her body. We were also covered in mum's blood, because I remember these people looking at us to see if we'd been hurt. A long time afterwards, mum told me that as she lay there, she kept going into a faint, and each one was a bit longer than the last, and that was when she was given brandy and hot tea. She said she could feel the glow going right through her body, and mum said that saved her life.

There were no ambulances around, so a man who used to sell fish, door to door, brought his cart round to take my mother to hospital. She was just wrapped in blankets and taken away, and we were taken to my grandmother's, until my dad managed to get home from work.

While mum was in hospital, she was in a bed next to a girl who had worked for a German family, owners of a pork butcher's shop in West Hartlepool. The German men had been interned when war broke out, but after the shelling the

CLEVELAND RD. HARTLEPOOL. DEC. 1914

Cleveland Road, Hartlepool, and serious damage to private houses caused during the German bombardment. People in other parts of the country found it difficult to believe that the attack had really happened.

rest of the family sent this girl a bunch of flowers and a pork pie. She said to my mother "I don't think I'll eat that pork pie, 'cos they're Germans and they could have put poison in it." The food in the hospital wasn't very good, so mum told the girl "I'll tell you what. Cut it in half and we'll share it and, if it is poisoned, we'll both die together". She said it was delicious.

My mum was in hospital for about six months, as beside the injury to her shoulder, they also thought they might have to take her leg off. Even when she came home, she still had a bad scab on her head, but the doctor did not seem worried about it and told her that it would drop off. Well, it did drop off, but it would fester again and that went on for nine months. She went to my granny's and my gran said "Don't you think it should be better by now? Do you think there is anything in it?" Mum said "No, there can't be." But my gran said "I'll put a bread poultice on." This was made by laying strips of bread in linen after which boiling water was poured onto the bread and then the linen twisted and slapped onto the wound. It was very painful but it worked. She put the poultice on my mother's head and when she took it off, she looked, and there was a piece of shell. It was the size of a sixpence and it was as shiny as anything.

There was an awful lot of damage to our street. My mother had a picture and there was a piece of shell embedded in it, and there was a chest of drawers and a bookshelf, and a piece of shell had gone through them. All the windows were out, and the chimneys were down, and there were bits of shrapnel in the walls. One piece of glass in the bookcase had a hole through it but the glass hadn't shattered. Dad didn't want to have it mended, you know, to keep it as a souvenir, but mum said "No, if you want to look at any scars, look at me," because she had plenty. She received eight pounds compensation for the trauma and the damage they'd gone through.

The effect of the bombardment was terrible on the town. There was one woman who lived close to us, and she had lost three of her children, and lost a leg herself, it was blown off. Her name was Dixon, and I saw her after the war walking around on crutches with her one leg. She had another three children after, and she named them all the same as the three she had lost.

I was nine when they brought the Zeppelin down. We'd heard it come over, and so dad got us all out of bed and said "If we have got to be killed, we'll all go together." We sat round the fire, when all of a sudden there were terrible screams went up, and he said to my mother "My God, I think they've hit something." Mum said "Don't go out," but he opened the back kitchen door, and it was all lit up red. He said "They've hit something." It was the Zeppelin, and he said "Come on, kids, come out and have a look at this." All us kids went out and there were pieces of this Zeppelin dropping off, and dad said to my mum "Come and have a look at this". But she said "No, I couldn't, they're somebody's lads aren't they?"

The Zeppelin had come down into the sea close to the rocks, because dad went down to the rock one day and brought a piece of the airship back. My mum told him to get rid of it. "I don't want that in my house, it smells of death." She had sympathy for the crew. I mean, these lads were just doing their duty, same as our lads were.

MARY JOLLIE, née Clarke, born 1st April 1894, died 5th May 1998. General Nurse.

Although the outbreak of war provided the catalyst for Mary Jollie to nurse, caring for the sick and wounded had always appealed to her since she was a child. Mary nursed soldiers and civilians throughout the war, but in 1918, she was given charge of a ward containing shellshocked soldiers. For Mary, it was a traumatic but rewarding time, caring for men shattered by their war experiences. She continued nursing throughout her working life, and lived in Glasgow until her death earlier this year, aged 104.

Mary Jolie
1997

Mary Jollie
1918

When I was eight years old, I remember visiting an aunt who was unwell with pleurisy. She had the district nurse in, and I remember how flattered I was when she asked me to pass the kettle from the hob, when she wanted a basin of hot water or to make a poultice. I made up my mind then that I was going to be a nurse and never swayed from that thought.

In 1914, my brother came in one day and said "You're always talking about going to be a nurse, well, there's an advertisement in the Labour Exchange window" – people who were interested in nursing should apply for a form to so and so, at a particular hospital. I answered the appeal, and that was the start of my nursing career.

I went for an interview in July and was accepted for training, starting 1st September, which pleased me very much. That day I went to the Matron's office to see about my uniform. I was on duty next morning and people were calling me nurse, which was ridiculous since I'd been a dogsbody the day before.

Strict discipline was enforced in the wards by the Ward Sister. All beds had to line up and even the castors had to be positioned the same way. The ward depicted was at Redlands War Hospital, Reading; the room is a school classroom today.

REDLANDS WAR HOSPITAL, READING
(WARD 2. A BLOCK.)

I had a high opinion of myself, but when I arrived that first morning I was given the lowliest position in the ward – that was taking the night report up to the Matron's office. The office was in a big house where there was a very imposing front door, while at the back there were two small doors. I had delivered the report and was coming down the steps feeling very grand in my uniform, when I saw Matron coming in the distance. She was a very imposing person and I thought she was obviously going to speak to me, so I readied myself and she said "Have you been to my office, nurse?" I said "Yes." She said "In future when you go to my office, in at the back door, and out at the back door." I was put firmly in my place!

The ward routine was very strict. The Sister would come onto the ward and look down all her beds, and each bed had to be precisely in line with the others. She would take out of her pocket a handkerchief to measure the distance the beds came out from the wall, and then ensured that all the castors at the bottom of the bed pointed the same way, not higgledey piggledey, one pushed back, one forward. The Sisters were very particular, and a Sister's ward was a Sister's territory. I felt it was all so unnecessary and nothing to do with treatment.

There were so many rules attached to the giving of medicine, too. A nurse did not just lift a bottle and pour it out, there were half-a-dozen specific movements to be gone though. You lifted the bottle so that the label was in the palm of your hand and your forefinger touching the cork. You read the label, shook the bottle and poured out the required dose. The routine had to be gone through. It was the same with bandaging, so many rules. And you had to know them all. I dressed the soldiers' wounds, although as they were convalescent, there was less to do. But there were leg wounds, arm wounds, neck wounds, head wounds, less often back wounds because that would mean they had been running away, wouldn't it? The men were very stoical, and we were very impressed, and it was moving for us as well; some of them were very, very brave. There would be a man having his wound dressed under only a part-anaesthetic and it was very painful, and it was painful for me. You tried hard to control yourself because my suffering was imaginary – what they had suffered was very real. Some of the nurses were very near tears, all the time. I was one of them, but you had a job to do, you couldn't let yourself go and think of your own feelings at all, you were part of a team.

For all the heroism shown by the wounded, now and again we would have malingerers, men who pretended they were more ill than they were. Often the other men spotted them first, and would advise us about something they had seen, but spotting malingers was part of your training, to be observant in every way, and most were easy to detect over a short period. There was a man called Ian, a Company Sergeant Major in the army, who had a history of not being able to keep food down. He would take his dinner like everybody else and then he would vomit it all back again, yet nobody could understand why he didn't lose weight. He was weighed religiously until one day when he was seen by one of the VADs to go up to the hospital fence and receive a parcel of food from his wife, secreting it somewhere about his person. That was how he was getting his food. Well, of course there was an interview with the Surgeon General and he was told to go back to his regiment the next day, and that was the last I heard of him.

The VADs did a lot of very good work in the wards but some of them thought, because they were unpaid and the staff – the Sisters and the nurses – were paid, that we were beneath them and they acted accordingly. We were playing a game of cricket with some of the convalescent soldiers at Grangemouth. I was a staff nurse and was the official scorer for the teams. The game finished early, and they were going to play another when the Sister came to me, a charming lady, and said that one of us would have to go back to the ward. I said I would go back, and as I went in there was a VAD, a very nice girl, older than I was and I said to her "Will you give me the keys and I'll give out the medicines." She said "Miss Clarke, I'll give the medicines out if you'll go and check the dirty laundry." I said "No, Miss Brown, I'll give out the medicine and you will go and check the laundry and do you mind doing it now!" That was just one episode, a VAD trying it on, bossing a staff nurse around. But these VADs did very valuable work out in the field, in France, doing work that trained

Helping wounded soldiers recover involved some recreational activities – here, a group enjoys a game of cricket away from the clinical smell of the wards.

General Nurses never had a chance to do. The military nurses went abroad, with the VADs, while our work was at home. Of course there was a bit of jealousy on our part, too, or resentment in my case, undoubtedly.

In 1918, I was made a Sister to the Notts County War Hospital and appointed to a shellshock ward of forty-five beds. These men were nearly all convalescent and they could go out as much as they liked. Many suffered from nightmares, and I would read about them from the nightly report. A lot of them feared sleeping at night because of the nightmares and some could get quite violent. There was only one orderly at night on each ward, but he had a bell that he could ring to summon help to control the patient, to physically control him so that he did not hurt himself.

Some of the dreams were very terrible and there were tearful moments when the patients woke up, shaking with fear at what they had seen in their mind's eye. Some wanted to get what was troubling them off their chests and were glad to talk to you, although they knew they were upsetting you. Many were not conscious of what they had dreamed, although there was one soldier who would talk about his nightmares. He was afraid of going to sleep – of course it wasn't my business to go into that, it was the medical officer's business, but I couldn't help trying to ease his situation and I said "What did you see?" And he said, "Well, I saw wounded men on the ground and our tanks coming along and just mowing through them." He said it was very terrible. That was one of the worst ones. It hurt me very much hearing that story, but it had to be, our tanks were going forward and the wounded were in the way.

I did see it as part of my job, sitting talking with them, trying to make them forget, but they couldn't forget. They were all shellshocked to various degrees, many were apparently better and waiting to be boarded out from my ward, but they were finished with the army. Many years afterwards, I was visiting a psychiatric hospital and some men came in carrying milk cans which had obviously been delivered to the Centre. Suddenly, I heard a man call "Oh, Sister Clarke". I looked up and I saw among these men one called Waterhouse who had been at the War Hospital years before, so I suppose many of these patients of mine landed up in a mental hospital after all.

Many of the shellshocked men weren't any different to any other convalescent soldier. Occasionally a man would have facial tremors, hands trembling. Sometimes they would be asked to help in putting out dinners, and in the middle they would just have a shaking fit that they couldn't control. The tremors would come on quite quickly, with nothing to cause them, nothing that you could link the tremor with. They would just start shaking and not only lost control of their speech but slavering, you know, not being able to control their saliva, and it was a very terrible thing to see. I would call for an orderly and of course the man would be helped back to his bed to rest. Tremors needed to be controlled and I could use drugs at my discretion, but in the meantime I would probably have sent for the Medical Officer. We had no specific training in dealing with shellshocked soldiers; you had to use what you had here – in your head – to deal with problems, it was common sense.

NORAH CLAYE, born 11th July 1895. General Nurse.

With the rapid expansion of wartime nursing services, thousands of young women were drawn into a profession that few had hitherto considered entering. One such recruit was Norah Claye, a nineteen-year-old girl from Macclesfield. While her brother and father were serving at the Front, Norah tended the wounded at a hospital in Leeds, routinely treating horrific injuries. Despite the terrible suffering, Norah adored her job, and continued nursing long after the First World War. Now aged 103, she lives quietly with her 99-year-old sister in Cheltenham.

*Norah Claye
1997*

My father was out in the Middle East and my brother was in the Dardanelles, when mother spoke to me one day. "You know, Norah, we had hoped you would be able to stay with us in the home until you got married, but with your father away, you'll have to do something to earn your living. What would you like to do?" I said "What could I do?" I couldn't be a governess which was the only thing I seemed to think you did. I'd no idea about nursing.

I'd taken my first aid and home nursing certificates before the war, and lapped it up. "Well, you've enjoyed the nursing. Wouldn't you like to train as a nurse?" mother said. "Could I?" Inquiries were made and I was taken on at a General Hospital in Leeds in 1915. Beforehand, mother and I had to attend an interview with the Matron of the hospital. We had a delightful time, the Matron gave us tea in her office, and mother made all the arrangements. Later, I was put on a train for Leeds and I quite expected this very nice Matron, who had a 1400-bed hospital to run, to meet me at the station! Luckily I had sufficient nous to take a cab to the hospital.

So there I was, a very unsophisticated little twenty-year-old in Leeds, soon to get my first introduction to wounded soldiers. I was met by the Home Sister who called me Nurse Claye and I thought she was a bit in advance, I was hardly Nurse Claye yet. She took me and showed me how to put my uniform on, introduced me to the other girls.

It was just before Christmas. Two Sisters, about six months senior to me, had rather taken me in hand and were mothering me, telling me what I ought to do and not do, and they said "You'll come and sing carols." "Oh, yes," I said, so we went in a little group. One Sister we met asked the first Sister "What do you sing?" – mezzo-soprano – "and you?" mezzo-soprano. Then she turned to me. "And what do you sing?" I'd no idea what mezzo-soprano meant but I wasn't being separated, so I said "Mezzo-soprano", and so we sang carols in our red cloaks round the wards.

I hadn't felt apprehensive about working at the hospital. There was a little anxiety, not that I'd meet things I couldn't do, but that I might fail to do the things I ought to do. I felt under command and didn't wish to fail. In the event, I loved the job. I liked the discipline and I enjoyed the companionship of the other probationer nurses. I had only had a rather simple education in a private school and I don't think my capacity for learning was really stretched at all, so I loved the lectures we had at hospital.

The work was very hard and the hours were very long. We were called by a bell ringing on the corridors at 6.30am and we went to breakfast at 7am and were on the wards by 7.30am. We were allowed half-an-hour about 10 o'clock to go and get a drink and put clean aprons on ready for the doctors' visits, and we got two further hours off during the day. We came off duty at nine at night, and we were then expected to go to chapel for prayers before going to supper. Lights out at ten. We used to be very tired at night, we'd flop into bed and sleep soundly until the bell in the morning. Some of the nurses thought they worked too hard and lots of them had trouble with their feet, dropped arches, that sort of thing.

We wore a pretty uniform, mauve and white check with a very attractive net cap that fitted on our heads with a tail that hung down the back. It took ages to make up – one a week – so you took great care of it – that it didn't get crumpled up or crushed during the week. Everything was very regulated: we were made to wear low-heeled laced shoes, while our skirts had to be exactly eight inches from the ground. We didn't wear belts but white linen aprons that just fastened at the back with a button. The assistant Matron would cast her eye over you – "Nurse, your apron is not sitting very well" – that sort of comment. She had been in the hospital a very long time, and how we all behaved mattered to her a lot. That said, I found the uniform fascinating. I'd enjoyed the Red Cross uniform but this was what I called a very pretty uniform.

The discipline was very strict. They would have probably five nurses in ascending rank in a ward, one or two probationers like myself, and a Sister. The probationers never scrubbed the floors but you had to keep them tidy, be sure to pick up any bits that fell. The beds had to be immaculate, and even the patients had to be disciplined; they weren't allowed to spread their beds with books or paper. You were expected to be able to report on any patient on the ward at any time. We had two very old Sisters who spent a lot of time in the ward office. They would call you in. "Nurse, who is that coughing in the ward?" And you had to think quickly who she might mean, and if you said, "Well, it's Mr. so and so in bed number so and so", the Sister would say "Well, you mustn't let him. Give him a drink and see if that will improve it." She knew what was happening all the time and we were terrified of her. I had a cousin in the RAMC who'd been out in the Middle East. He came to see me at the hospital while he was home, and we had a conversation outside the ward door. But when I got back in – "Nurse, Nurse Claye, who were you talking to?" "My cousin, he's just come back." "Well, you must not talk to your cousin on duty." I mean, nothing was hidden from these people.

When the doctors came onto the ward, you were expected to stop what you were doing and stand to attention by a bed. The doctors were treated like gods and would walk around with probably a train of students and a Sister. Nobody was allowed to talk and the patients knew they had to sit up and look intelligent. A nurse would not address a doctor at all. That was part of the discipline. If he asked a question, well, you answered it to the best of your ability.

We treated soldiers who had been very seriously wounded in the trenches.

They came in with terribly septic, deep gangrenous wounds and one of my vivid recollections was a man with a gaping wound about fourteen inches long, right down to the bones of his lower leg. In the depth of that wound there were patches of gangrene, and they found that by introducing maggots into the wound, the maggots ate the gangrene and then they could start to heal the leg up. That was a shock for me, to see all these nasty little things crawling about in the man's leg.

We would talk to the soldiers about all sorts of things, about their homes, about what we had done. You know, a lot of young nurses and a lot of soldiers who had been deprived of women's association for a long time, they were anxious to keep you in conversation, although I never experienced any ungentlemanly behaviour. One or two would talk about their experiences in the trenches or make a joke. Anything you did for them, they would be so grateful and would say "This is a lot better than being up to the knees in water and mud." They were so grateful to be out of that terrible trench warfare. It was such a relief for them to be clean and comfortable and their wounds cared for. Of course occasionally they'd have to lose a limb and we would go with them to the theatre, and if you were on theatre duty you might perhaps see limbs amputated. If I was on the theatre staff, I would help to cover the man with sterile towels, just exposing the leg that was going to be amputated. I can't remember that I was ever what you call deeply affected by the sight of the

It was discovered that when maggots were introduced into a gangrenous wound they consumed the gangrene and the wound would start to heal. IWM Q33467

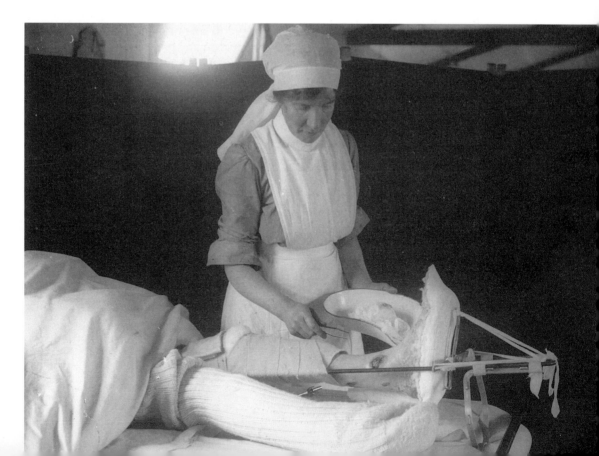

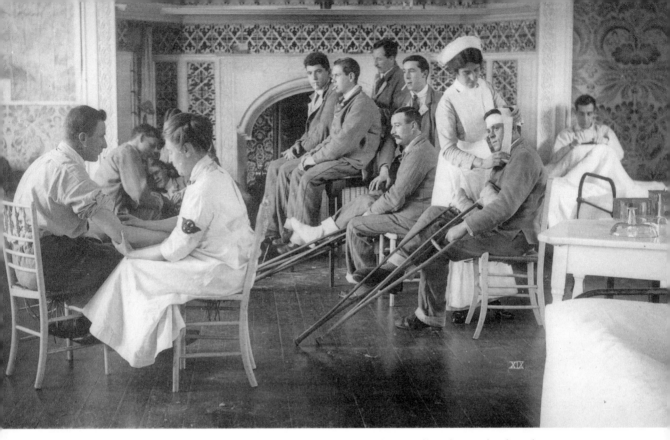

'You felt that you wanted to do anything you could to get them well and to make them happy – that you were responsible for their happiness.' IWM Q108081

tissues being divided and the bone either being cut through or disjointed and the limb carried away. It may sound heartless, but it's all part of the training. The real horror was not seeing the blood, rather the thought of the handicap to the man of losing a leg or an arm.

When the man returned to the wards, if he was in my care, then I would do my best to make him comfortable, to make him realise what had happened. When someone has an amputation, it's a long time before they know that the limb has gone. I would try and get him to accept what had happened and tell him how good artificial limbs were. The reaction to the loss depended very much on the particular man. Some were prepared to accept – they were so glad to get rid of a limb that had been painful and difficult to cure. Then there were those who bemoaned the loss. I think a leg was more important to a man than his arms. I tried to put the best side, the fact that he wouldn't get that pain once the stump had settled down, and how the artificial limb would fit comfortably. Gradually, the man would come round to himself again. He usually accepted what had happened, just as he'd accepted the fearful privation of life in the trenches.

We didn't have anything to do with the fitting of the artificial leg, that would happen after they left hospital. When we were able to get them up, we would get them used to their crutches, to get them accustomed to the balance. We would be near to help if necessary, if they looked like falling over. The wards were long, a row of 18 beds on each side, and the men would walk up and down, rather proud I think, of the fact that they'd got through the operation and were amongst their fellows in bed. They would be careful hopping with the one leg, but they very soon got used to the crutches.

Naturally, the nurses knew how bad it had been in the line, the difficulties of getting them out of the trenches down to the Clearing Stations, and the possibility that even then they weren't free from being shelled. One felt sympathetic towards them, and I think a nurse develops a certain amount of what I call motherliness towards them. My brother had been through the Dardanelles, came back to Gaza and was killed by the Turks in 1917. That was a fearful blow to me. His death did rather alter my feeling towards these men. You felt that you wanted to do anything you could to get them well and to make them happy – that you were responsible for their happiness.

DAISY COLLINGWOOD née Major, born 11th August 1897, Munitions Worker, Kynocks Munitions Factory, Shellhaven.

Daisy Collingwood 1917

Daisy Collingwood 1998

Conscious of the fact that she had no brothers to serve at the Front, seventeen-year-old Daisy Collingwood felt compelled to do her bit in the war, working for two years in the blending and reeling rooms of Kynocks Munitions Factory at Shellhaven. Now 101 years old, Daisy remembers with clarity and no little affection her twelve hour shifts making cordite for the guns. For although war work was always exhausting and often dangerous, she never forgot the new–found sense of responsibility and liberation it gave her, away from the insular and mundane life she had lived at home.

I had no brothers to go to the war and fight for us, so I asked dad if I might go and work on munitions. He said no, but dad was always my favourite so I set about wheedling him round, to let me at least go to the Labour Exchange to see if I could get work on the munitions. Dad admitted afterwards that he only let me go because he never thought I would get taken on. It was the middle of 1915 and I wasn't quite eighteen, the minimum age to work, but they wanted workers so badly I was given a job.

I went to work at Kynocks munitions factory at a place called Shellhaven. There had always been an old munitions factory there making gun cotton but, with the war, the premises had been expanded to make cordite of all different shapes and sizes. The expanded factory was built on the local marshes for safety's sake, each workroom being built up on brick pillars, and reached by means of cinder paths built to a height of six feet above the marshland.

During the week, I slept at a girls' hostel in Corringham, two girls to each cubicle. To get to work, we had a twenty minute walk to the railway, which was

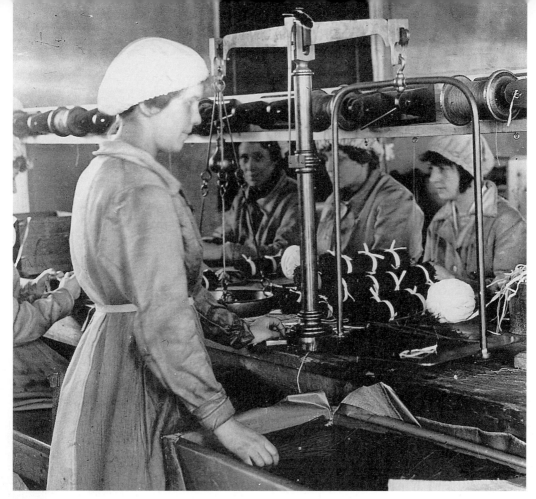

Munitions workers cut up and weigh cordite. IWM Q27892

Working with munitions was highly dangerous and explosions were not infrequent. The worst at Silvertown in 1917, devastated one square mile of London's East End, killing 69 women and injuring another 72. IWM Q30014

built for the workers by the factory. Fifteen minutes, train ride, then another mile to walk to the dressing room. Here we all changed into danger clothes, which consisted of a khaki and scarlet dress, hat and a hooded cloak, and a pair of brown canvas shoes, which were worn only in the workroom. Everybody was searched in the dressing room, to make certain they carried no metal of any kind, or matches.

I loved the job. I'd lived such a sheltered life in the countryside that for me to get up and work with a lot of other people was just heaven. I didn't mind the danger, because I was given responsibility. I started on the night shift, a novelty in itself because I'd never stayed up all night in my life. Each shift was twelve hours long and alternated with a day shift of equal length. You worked one week on nights and then the next on days, so you came off at 6.20am on Sunday morning and began again on the day shift at the same time on Monday, week in, week out. When I finished work on a Sunday morning, a bus used to come down and take us home, in my case to my parents' place at Grays in Essex. I used to have a meal and go to bed and sleep and sleep and sleep. Several times mum and dad tried to get me to leave, but I refused because for the first time I was living my own life.

The cordite was a paste before it was made into pliable strands and then baked. Well, in the reeling room there used to be this stand with nine aluminium reels on it and you just wound the strands of cordite from these reels onto one larger wheel, the strands passing through a brass guide which tested to make sure there wasn't any fault in any of the strands. We were very proud of how fast we could work. Our shift turned out the biggest work load, and we used to leave notes for the other shift coming in, you know "beat that one" sort of thing, all very catty! Working as fast as I could was a source of great pride, and I was always looking for ways to improve my rate of work. I wanted to be the best reeler and I discovered, for example, that if I let the strands of cordite go through my hands instead of the clip, I could feel for a break quicker and so we could work even faster.

The speed I was working at aroused some suspicion because one night, while I was on the machines, the forewoman and two gentlemen came in and walked over to me. They said "Now we're going to put the light out and we're going to ask you to reel. Get your reel set up ready and we're going to ask you to do it just the same as you do every time." I nearly died. In the dark I could see that the friction of the cordite going through my hand caused a flame to shoot out, three inches long. I just couldn't speak because this had been happening for weeks and weeks and I could have blown the whole building up sky high and everybody in it. I felt terrible and learnt my lesson, although I wasn't punished. They

Daisy Collingwood 1915

174

could see I was only trying to do my very best, and they understood that. However, even now, eighty-three years later, it still make me feel a little shaky when I think about what I could have done.

The stove for cooking the cordite was in a big building next to ours. It was like a concert hall, no windows and a flat roof, and the cordite used to be taken in on trolleys and put into the stove and slowly cooked by steam. The work there was quite close to our workroom and one day the stove exploded. It was a terrific explosion, which I can hardly describe, but it was as though the whole world had been shaken. The explosion must have been caused when one of the men was putting a load of raw cordite into the stove. Anyway, a sudden blast of air shot me head first out of the workroom door down the stairs and into the ice-cold gooey mud and slush of the marsh beneath. I faintly remember seeing a body flying through the air, but I didn't know whose it was, of course. There had been a terrible bang followed by two smaller explosions as two of the loaded trolleys which were waiting to go into the stove also blew up. I was lying in the marshes by this time, nearly suffocated, because I didn't realise what had happened for a few minutes. I pulled myself out and began to clear the mud from my eyes and ears, and when I looked up I saw the place was a shambles.

It was a very frightening ordeal. The medical team which was based at the old factory came up and shifted all the wounded down on the bogeys to the hospital. I don't know what the casualties were exactly. At least one person was killed near the stove itself and there were a lot of people with cuts, and several suffered minor burns from flying debris. I was soaking wet, from head to foot, and was taken to hospital with fright and one or two bruises, but nothing serious.

I came out in a terrible rash afterwards, scabby sores which lasted a long time, apparently fright does that and I was frightened, I'm not afraid to admit it. Even a slamming door used to set me trembling. The doctor advised me against returning, but my father wouldn't let me go back to the factory anyway after that. I still felt I wanted to do something, though, so I said I was going to join the WAACS. I went down again to the Labour Exchange and was given a ticket to London. I was drafted to the Canadian Convalescent Camp at Epsom where I worked in the cookhouse, cooking potatoes and milk puddings. When I wasn't doing that, I was more or less our officers' batwoman. I used to go everywhere in a car with two lady officers, sitting in the car waiting for them to come back and opening and shutting doors and things like that. It doesn't sound much but it was all so fresh to me, compared to the life that I'd been used to.

We were allowed one late pass a week, and once a month I used to take it to go and see my parents in Essex. I arrived home on one of these visits to find my brother-in-law on leave from France and my family having a little party. My pass meant I would have to leave home at 6pm to get back to camp by 10pm, but I threw caution to the wind and said to mum "I'm not going back yet, I'm going to stay tonight, they can't kill me for it".

Of course I didn't realise I was a soldier and I'd got to play by soldiers' rules. I went back first thing in the morning, arriving in camp at 8.15am and was promptly put in the guardroom. I stayed there for about three or four hours, all by myself, not a drink, nobody to talk to, and I wondered what the dickens was happening to me. Afterwards I was taken to my room where I was kept for three days until I received what was an Open Court Martial.

Two soldiers came to my room and, walking on either side of me, took me right up the wide main road past all the nissen huts filled with convalescent soldiers, all whistling marching songs. Well, in the end I just couldn't help laughing until I got a poke in the ribs from the chap beside me. I was taken to a table behind which the Camp Commandant and five other officers including our own QMAAC Commandant were sitting taking notes. The word "HALT" boomed out and the charge was read to me, but every time they read out about me breaking my leave, I couldn't help laughing, it was really funny. To me, I hadn't done anything very bad and I couldn't see what all the fuss was about. They kept reading out "And the accused this," and "the accused that," but when I was asked if I had anything to say, I stated the facts, saying "I'm not accused of anything – I was home with my parents and I can prove I was". Well, if I had thrown a brick at the C.O., he couldn't have looked more surprised. Poor man, I don't suppose he had ever been spoken to like that in all his career. He looked absolutely dumbfounded. The sentence was passed and I was confined to camp for 28 days and fined one week's pay.

Looking back on the war years, I can honestly say that I always gave of my best. I couldn't fight, so I was doing the next best thing and because I was a conscientious kind of person, I felt I was making up for the fact that I hadn't got any brothers to go and fight. I felt very proud. And when the news from the Front was bad, I used to go out and work as hard as ever I could. I did put other people in danger once or twice while working on munitions, innocently, and I was sorry when I knew, of course. But I really and truly enjoyed the job, relying on each other, knowing one slip can just be goodbye. I knew the danger I was in, but when you're young, you don't think about that. Looking back now, I think it was the most exciting time of my life, I really felt I was living.

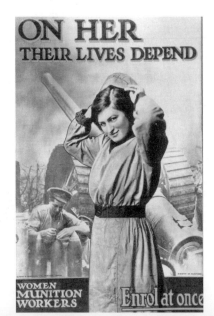

IWM Q79989

CHAPTER TEN

Prisoners of War

FEW OF THE SOLDIERS who went to France gave the subject of surrender much thought. The waving of a white flag or the raising of hands were usually deemed sufficient and were probably the only tactics of surrender known to soldiers at the Front.

If any soldier had anything appreciably white to wave in the muddy battlefields of northern France and Belgium, then it was in no way thanks to the army. In August 1914, all white handkerchiefs were handed in, to be replaced by red spotted alternatives. Whether this was solely an attempt to avoid a soldier unwittingly giving a position away whilst wiping his nose is not clear.

Over 190,000 British soldiers were taken prisoner during the First World War, one in sixteen of all battlefield losses. The vast majority were captured when they were cut off and surrounded by the enemy. Unable or unwilling to fight on, they surrendered in the hope that the enemy would choose to interpret their

British prisoners marched off the battlefield after being taken during the German Spring Offensive of 1918. Their lives spared in the heat of battle, they would spend the next eight months on food rations which deteriorated daily, as the Allied blockade of sea ports gripped Germany.   IWM Q 24052

dropping of weapons and raising of hands as a clear sign that they had indeed decided to give up.

In the heat of battle, however, there was no guarantee that a soldier pumped up with adrenalin would necessarily understand an enemy's attempt at surrender, or indeed would choose to do so. The killing of prisoners was against all international law but frequently occurred. In action it was up to the individual, often on the spur of the moment, to decide whether to take a man prisoner. An enemy soldier might have his hands in the air, but a look in his eye or an apparently furtive movement could easily be misinterpreted as renewed defiance and might well lead to his death.

Despite the efforts of the Geneva Convention to safeguard prisoners' rights, there were unwritten commands that the taking of prisoners was undesirable in a specific attack and indeed might jeopardise the successful outcome of operations. On other occasions, rumours were spread, unfounded or not, that the enemy had opened fire while waving a white flag and therefore could not be trusted. Soldiers were occasionally reminded that every prisoner taken had to be fed, which meant less food on the table for loved ones back home.

It is hardly surprising, then, that soldiers were extremely nervous and usually very co-operative when first taken prisoner. There were tricks of the trade that soldiers taught each other to aid survival. Certain troops, particularly machine gunners, bombers, or snipers, removed all unit badges in combat, for these men could inflict grievous casualties amongst enemy ranks and consequently

More British prisoners were taken during the German offensive of 1918 than all the rest of the war. On 21st March 1918, the first day of the offensive, it is estimated that 21,000 British troops became PoWs. TAYLOR LIBRARY

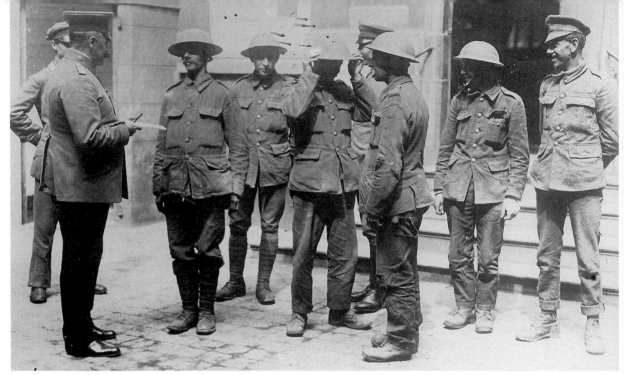

Some prisoners were selected for interrogation by an English-speaking German officer. Most would stick loyally to the required 'name, rank and serial number'; a few, with some persuasion, could be encouraged to reveal a little extra. TAYLOR LIBRARY

received short shrift if captured. Another ploy was to hold up photographs of loved ones, in the hope of winning the compassion of enemy soldiers, in effect asking the capturer to see the captive as he saw himself, a family man with young children to support.

For those prisoners taken back behind the lines to makeshift cages, there was the expectation that at least they might now survive the war. It was a prospect which had seemed gloomy while they remained soldiers in the trenches. Now they would be fed, clothed and watered until the end of the conflict. The reality was somewhat different for British prisoners. At the end of the war, these troops were often found to be grossly undernourished and in a parlous state of health.

During the war, many British POWs were routinely reported by the Red Cross as having died of wounds or illness. However, in January 1919 when Britain demanded the overdue release of one final group of 35,000 men registered as having been taken prisoner of war, the Germans replied that only 22,000 remained in their hands. The difference, some 13,000 POWs, had in fact died in Germany owing to the many and varied privations they lived under.

There was no central organisation responsible for prisoners of war in Germany. Owing to the federal nature of the state, POWs were sent to prisons right across Germany, where commandants were left to rule camps as though they were personal fiefdoms. Discipline was often iron, and punishment harsh for indiscretions. But the real problem was the desperate lack of food and resources allocated for prisoners, a crisis that deepened as the war dragged on. Ironically, the Allied naval blockade of Germany, introduced to cripple industry and weaken the enemy's fighting capability, also drastically reduced the country's ability to feed the POWs. Not surprisingly, the Germans blamed the Allies for the POWs' predicament – the half-starved soldiers having to work for any edible scraps once the army and the civil population had received first call on all foodstuffs and raw materials. With most fit German men away at the Front, British, Russian and French prisoners were typically sent down salt mines, stone quarries and coal mines to dig out the raw materials to keep German industry working. Unknown thousands died.

JACK ROGERS

For the troops in the front line on 21st March 1918, the launch of the German offensive was akin to all hell being let loose. Jack Rogers was lucky, as his trench did not suffer the intense bombardment felt elsewhere, but even so, he found himself quickly surrounded as the German troops poured forward.

One day in Amiens was the only leave I had had in all the time I'd been in France. Headquarters were aware that I had not been home, so I was given leave the day before my 24th birthday, so I could be home on the day, 21st March 1918. Well, of course this was the launch of the great German offensive. The military authorities didn't know it was going to be that day, but from prisoners we'd taken, they knew a big attack was due any time. I'd written to my mother telling her not to send a cake or anything like that because I was on my way home, when, on the 19th, the army cancelled all leave.

Out in front of our line, working parties had been sent with engineers in charge to dig a small extra trench. This was being prepared for the expected attack and would be occupied solely by a few snipers, eight I believe, including me. On the night of 20th March, a group of us were sent in there. We took all our equipment, everything we'd got and we was told to hold out as long as possible. We waited there all night until at five in the morning the Germans opened up as anticipated, the big barrage.

The Germans did not bombard the whole front, they left sections, shelling to the left and right of us, very, very heavily too, but not directly on us. The next thing we knew, German troops were pouring through but we were still there holding this bit of trench, hanging on, just trying to have a pot here and there. Eventually we looked round to the back and we could see Germans galore in every direction. Mopping up parties were being sent out to clear up little pockets of resistance, working their way round to us. They got nearer and nearer and they were sort of shouting – we weren't shooting. Then they began to throw in some of these potato mashers, as we called them, handgrenades, and one of our chaps was badly wounded in the legs. I looked at my mate Charlie Shaw and said "What do we do?" He says, "It's no good, Jack, throw your hands up." We realised it was hopeless, so we all just threw our guns at either end of the trench. There was nothing else to do, we just looked around and saw these blinkin' Prussian Guards come tearing down the trench.

I didn't know what to think. One guard came straight for me, fixed bayonet. He came rushing up and from that moment I said goodbye – there was to be no more of me. I expected the bayonet to go directly into me, but it didn't. Strangely enough, when he got right up to me he stopped, and said "Cigarette, Kamarad?" I nearly dropped to the ground in surprise. He wants a cigarette! Of all the things that anybody would ask for at that stage. So I felt in my tunic where I carried a little tin of ready-made cigarettes and I said "Yes" and he took some and put them in his pocket, then pointed to my equipment and said "Los". Any equipment had to be taken off and left with our kit bags and sandbags on the trench floor, while we climbed out on top of the parapet.

I forget the name of the fellow who was wounded, but he couldn't walk very well, so he put his arms round our neck and we dragged him away up a slope. The three of us hadn't got far when a young German officer came up to us – I can see him as plain as if it were now – and said in English better than I could speak, "Where are you from?" pointing at me. I didn't know what to say, but said "London". "Oh, London," he said "So am I. I was at college there but they brought me home, and now I'm in this lot. Anyway, you're lucky, the war's over for you, get on your way." Off he went and off we went, to walk back as prisoners of war: my 24th birthday!

We reached a great big field and just stopped there all night with a lot of other prisoners, nothing to eat, nothing to drink. In the morning, we were marched to a railway line to await a long line of cattle trucks, forty men to a truck. They packed us in as fast as they could, no windows, all blacked out, with just a little

British prisoners being herded into cattle trucks for their journey to the camps in Germany.
IWM Q24056

ventilator at the top to give us air. We travelled in this truck for two days, still with no water or food, and the only place we could use as a toilet was one corner of the wagon chosen amongst ourselves for us all to use.

We got into Germany, to a place called Münster. There were three laagers or prisoner of war camps, numbers one, two and three. We were for number one camp, and when we got out of these trucks they brought round dixies full of some sort of ersatz coffee and a slice of brown bread. In the huts were bunk beds made out of chicken wire with one blanket per man, however, the blankets were outside the hut when we first arrived and it was raining, so that first night we slept on chicken wire and under wet blankets.

During the war, the British and the Germans had come to an agreement to exchange prisoners who had been badly wounded and could not fight again. The commandant at our camp was one of these, a tall man who had been partially blinded and wore black glasses. He hated the British like poison, and never missed a chance to vent his spite on us. For example, we used to try and keep our huts fairly clean, whereas the Russians had the reputation of being some of the dirtiest people in the camp, filthy, using the corner of their huts as toilets instead of going to the latrines. So every now and again, perhaps once a month, this German would parade everybody on a Saturday and swapped you all round, and we were always made to change with the Russians, so we had to occupy their dirty hut and they went to our clean one.

My first job was on what they called the sanitary police. Behind the camp latrines were troughs, well, everything that was dropped, all the sewage, went into these trenches covered over by two big doors. My job, along with five others, was to go to the trenches with a great big barrel on four wheels. Two of us would open these troughs, one each, and we used to have a big long piece of wood, like a big oar, with which to keep stirring up the sewage until you made it into a very fine liquid. The third member of the party would lower a bucket on a chain into the sewage and pull it up and hand it to a man standing on a ladder alongside the barrel. He'd take it up and empty his bucket until the barrel was practically filled. When it was full, we took the barrel to an allotment just outside the camp and with a tap on the barrel slowly deposited the muck all over, spreading it out.

The food was terrible. The Germans themselves had little to eat and used to boil great big mangel wurzels for themselves, and give us the cooking water in tins to drink, as it was supposed to be nourishing. That was our mid-day meal, with bread and ersatz coffee, that was our ration for the day. We were in a pretty bad state, I can assure you. You can imagine the relief when the first parcels from the Red Cross started to come through. A friend of mine at home, Mrs Addis, discovered through the Danish Red Cross that I was a prisoner at the camp. She got me onto the official prisoners of war list at home, and so I began to receive Red Cross parcels. We used to get two or three parcels every two or three weeks, or were supposed to receive them. They got as far as the railway station, when some Germans would go down and collect a few occasionally, bring them to the camp and call out the names and numbers on them. These parcels might have articles of clothing in them or they might have food. One of the pictures I have, we are all dressed in black, well, that's what we received from home.

The Danish Red Cross were allowed to pay a visit to our camp on one occasion. They were to visit all the huts and have a look at what we were being fed, so of course the Germans laid on everything they possibly could. We had diced and baked potatoes and a dixie fill of stuff they called Reisgries, semolina we call it. Anyway, we had a dish each of these which was quite a big meal, all designed to impress the Red Cross that Jerry was doing all he could for us.

The Commandant had the habit of calling us schweinehunde, he never addressed us in any other way. He used to have his spite on us every now and again, having us march round and round the square for an hour or so. Well, on this occasion he was smoking what looked like a small cheroot, little cigar, and he would stand there puffing away. Presumably he must have put it down on one of the window sills, and of course we're marching round and someone couldn't resist the temptation to pick it up. He found it was gone, so he kept us there for another two hours, marching round just because he'd lost the end of his cigar.

On one particular morning, we were all brought out on parade and the commandant spoke to his interpreter and the first word this little man said was "Gentlemen". You can just imagine the roar that went up when he said that, cheering, shouting, he couldn't keep us quiet. After a bit everything settled and he said the war was over for us. All we had to do was to wait until they could bring a train to evacuate us.

Jack Rogers (5th left, sitting) with fellow prisoners, all of whom were given the task of making wooden shoes, Jack's pre-war trade.

At Münster railway station, there had accumulated hundreds of these small Red Cross parcels which were supposed to have been delivered to the prisoners. They were no good to us and we did not want German soldiers to have them, so we had a chat among ourselves and said that if the authorities could arrange for all the poor people in the village to come to the station, we prisoners would be there and we'd hand them each a parcel.

To be going home, it was marvellous. I thought what's it going to be like to be home – just to see my people again, you know, to be free, oh, I couldn't believe it.

We travelled home via Rotterdam to Hull, and as we sailed into Hull all the sirens of the ships were sounded. There were great crowds of people, as we were the first prisoners to arrive there, about 150 in all. There was a long train waiting for us. We climbed aboard, and as we looked out of the windows these poor mothers were walking up and down the platform, each of them carrying a picture of a missing son or husband. They came up and showed you the picture and asked "Did you know him?" Was he in your regiment?" And so forth, all up and down the train. Finally we were taken off to the repatriation centre at Ripon in Yorkshire. Before we were allowed to go home, we had to drop everything and have a series of showers to make sure you did not take home any disease or any lice, that sort of thing. Then we were given either a new uniform or suit and that was it, the war for me was over.

WILLIAM EASTON

William Easton
1918

For most prisoners of war, capture meant swift relocation to a barbed wire cage and shortly afterwards to a POW camp. For stretcher bearer Bill Easton, the route to imprisonment took a remarkable and unexpected detour.

One night in late November 1917, my unit was withdrawn from the Ypres front. There were not many of us left, and we no longer had enough men to make up an ambulance unit, so we were told to wait for reinforcements. I was on supply, which meant I could be sent anywhere to fill a gap, so eventually I was sent by truck to join another unit. I had no idea what was going on, but I was supposed to meet an officer of the Norfolk Regiment. I arrived in the line on 20th March 1918, and I met a sergeant who knew nothing about this officer I was supposed to meet. He was new out to the Front and was with about forty conscripts, all of whom had been in the army only about three months.

They were in this trench as if they were expecting an attack, and were frightened out of their lives. Well, in the morning the Germans came over in their thousands, as far as you could see across the fields, singing and shouting. As it got lighter, this sergeant said "Shall we fire on them?" but I said "No". We could see these Germans but they never came towards us. I said "They're bypassing you." He said "What does that mean?" "It means they'll go so far and then stop and when they're ready, they'll come back and pick us up," which they did not long afterwards.

Well, one man, he'd gone to try and get back to our troops but after wandering around for a while, he came into our trench. He'd still got his weapon, and I said to him "It's hopeless, we're surrounded, and there are hundreds of the brutes nearby, so you'd better get rid of the rifle." I noticed that several of these young chaps had kept their blinkin' guns and I said to the sergeant "You'd better tell them to dump them." The sergeant said "Oh, they've only just got them." "Well, if they have them much longer there'll be a few rifles without men," I replied.

I don't know who the lad was who'd kept his rifle, but he didn't seem to understand that we were already prisoners. Of course he'd still got his rifle knocking about when the Germans surrounded us, and they promptly shot him. I thought it was such a pity, but it was his own fault, he ought to have known when to give his weapon up.

We were formed up when all of a sudden a young German caught me such a bang in the back with his rifle butt, I nearly fell down. I swore at him. These Germans, they never spoke to you, if they wanted anything it was the rifle butt, and my goodness that hurt you. He said to me, "Cavalry." He had two or three goes at me before I was hauled away in front of an officer. He was about the same age and he was yelling at me, banging on the wall, stamping, shouting out "Cavalry, Cavalry" and I said "No!" then he said "Artillery." Again I said "No", but I knew what he was getting at. I had come from the 25th Division and its Divisional sign was a red horse shoe. It was a sign I wore on my back, whereas all the men from the Norfolks had yellow oblong and square patches sewn on their backs. I told him I was in the RAMC, when there was a calm voice behind me, honestly it was like a comedy, somebody said "He doesn't like you". I said "I don't like him a lot either," and this voice said "He can't speak English, what's the problem?" The voice then spoke German to the officer, I don't know what he said. I looked round and saw a high-ranking officer like you see in a caricature, he was dressed up to the nines, he'd got a monocle, a stick and a cigar. I said "He thinks I'm cavalry." "I know you're not cavalry, you're 25th Division. What are you doing down here? You are about the only one of your lot. I've been all the way down this front these last two or three days, and I haven't seen any from your Division. Where are they now?" I told him I did not know. "I was sent here and I don't know why." "Oh well, it's quiet out there now," he said, and I replied "It wants to be!"

A minute or two later this man spoke again. "I'll tell you what, I'll get my man up here and I'll show this officer a chart." This high-ranking officer then produced a chart on which there was every divisional sign of the British army. "Here you are," he said. I looked at it and agreed. "Now his lordship will kick up a row, he's going to be very annoyed, and he's going to take it out on you," this German told me. I thought to myself "Yes, he'll bring a rifle and give me the butt two or three times." I wasn't looking forward to it, so he said "Come here a minute." He spoke to the other officer and then told me in English, "While I show him this chart, you had better slide off, now you have the chance," so I left the dugout and rejoined the other prisoners.

We were taken back to a field, where barbed wire was put around us, and as we would stop there until next day, so we should lie down. The ground was as wet as anything, but they told us anyone who got up would be shot.

At about four in the morning, a voice came. "Any Field Ambulance men who would like to do their comrades a good turn, come to the wire." I went, and this German said "We have got a lot of wounded in the church and we can't look after them because we haven't got enough men." There were about twenty ambulance men in the cage, but none of them volunteered. I thought "That's a good advert for the RAMC", so I said that I would go. I was taken by a friendly

British prisoners help to carry wounded men away from the firing line. Both sides employed prisoners in this way. TAYLOR LIBRARY

sergeant who could speak English. He took me to a big church and there were a few candles, and he said "You'll find a good supply of water here, and I'll see you in the morning". I went round and found that a lot of these chaps were dead, but gave a drink to those I found alive. Funny thing, the wounded weren't concerned with their drink so much, those wounded chaps who had blood on their hands were most keen to get their hands washed. I'd never had that happen before. I'd got buckets of water there and I spent my time going round, I don't know how many men, trying to clean them up. In the morning, a German sergeant came in and after a lot of ritual stamping about, he saluted me. I thought, that's a funny thing, saluting a prisoner. Then he said "I'm to thank you very much from my commanding officer." He told me that there were quite a lot of supplies coming up in lorries and that the lorries were going back empty. There was a railhead about ten miles behind the lines, and would I be in charge of getting those wounded who could move onto the lorries. I said "I'm sure I can manage it", and over the course of the next day I helped to evacuate these British soldiers down the line. I was given permission to accompany the last of the wounded down to the railhead, but when I got there and the wounded were unloaded, I was ignored, everyone just carried on and I was left standing there until a German came up and I was taken to a canteen for some food. After a while, I was approached by a German sergeant who said "I have a request. If you agree, we are allowed to keep POWs close to the front to help with the wounded." The German medical service's motto was "The wounded always come first", they used to quote it to me, and they needed as much help as they could get. There was a hospital being opened about four miles from the line, and I consented to stop and help, and wrote in this sergeant's diary on 25th March the following: "This is to certify that I, William Easton, do, quite voluntarily, proceed within thirty kilometres of the front with the 625th Sanitäts Komp."

I was nicknamed the Kleiner Engländer, the small Engländer, and I worked at this hospital under a German sergeant called Charley Feldner. He was very good to me and called me William and spoke to me in beautiful English. I had been working there a while when this sergeant, he seemed to run the show, came up to me and said "I have an invitation for you. It's not right that you should be here giving orders to men and you're not a sergeant, so while you're with us you'll be an acting sergeant". This meant I could ask one of these German orderlies to do something and they'd do it, and I thought to myself, well, what a thing.

Honestly, we were friends and I worked among the Germans quite willingly, helping the wounded. On one occasion, Charley said to me "As a mark of respect, you'll be the guest of honour at our party." The Germans had managed to get together free casks of beer, and I was asked along where this whole blooming company toasted my health, they were shouting and cheering and I don't know what. I was offered a beer but I never drank, because I was a teetotaller, but they said "Well, you'll have to have a photo taken". They made a real fuss of me and I had to sing a song for them.

I worked like a free man. I went into the Mess as a sergeant, and slept in the

An extraordinary, and probably unique, photograph. William Easton is seen with cigar and beer in his hand being toasted by men of the 625th Sanitäts Kompany. William willingly stayed within the battle area to help remove the wounded and was made honourary sergeant in the process.

same room as them. By that time I'd come to respect the Germans, individually I mean, because they were so friendly. Eventually I got dysentery and that put an end to my work near the front line. I was sent to a camp with other British POWs where I spent the rest of the war repairing roads and that sort of thing, but it was an experience I've never forgotten.

PERCY WILLIAMS

So powerful were the sustained attacks made on the British lines during March, April and May 1918, that many new recruits were thrust into the fighting with only minimum training. Percy Williams was one eighteen-year-old among many, who found the horror of the Western Front almost too much to bear.

We were sent into a quiet sector which we had taken over from the French near Rheims, a place called Fismes. We were just manning the lines, we didn't do anything. There was a bit of shellfire and a man called Sutton, a chap from Wakefield, was killed. He was the first of our young boys to die, then next a lad from Accrington was killed. But Sutton was a friend of mine, I'd met him in Doncaster when we were in the KOYLIs, then we were transferred to the Northumberland Fusiliers together. We were in C Company, and he was in my platoon; when a shell fell only fifty yards away and they told me "poor old

Sutton's had it", I was very upset and depressed.

On 27th May, I was in a dugout in the third line trenches when an officer came round and said that there might be action tonight. I'd not been under bad shellfire before and I was almost sick with fright as we waited, just waited until all hell broke loose. When the guns opened up, the shells were falling, causing tremendous explosions and destroying not only the trenches above our heads but the stairs leading down to us. We were told to leave the dugout and we scrambled up. Gas shells had been falling all night and saturated everything, covering our masks with a film. You couldn't see. I felt faint and sick and had to spew up, forcing me to take the gas mask off and vomit as best I could. I was absolutely terrified for hours. I'd never experienced anything so terrible in my life and after only a month in France!

Casualties were being suffered and we could hear them shouting for stretcher bearers. I thought "Oh my God, I'm going to die, I'm going to die!" Then Corporal Collins came along. He was panicking and said that the Germans had broken through and we were surrounded. "Every man for himself, everything has collapsed," he said, "there's no chance, we must get out of it, otherwise we shall get captured." As I stumbled from the trench I dropped my rifle, it was panic, you didn't know what was happening fifty yards on either side of you, the noise was terrible. I was weighed down by my pack, by ammunition, by my entrenching tool, the earth was all blown up all around and I couldn't see. Then a shell burst close by and I was suddenly wounded in the leg. It wasn't bad, we had puttees on, but I saw my leg was bleeding and I remember having a towel to staunch it. I couldn't walk, so another chap said we'd better crawl for it, to try and get away.

I could see the Germans running across, scores of them, I was so confused, and turned and saw this German with his fixed bayonet standing over me; I thought he was going to kill me, I thought he was going to bayonet me. He shouted at me "Halt, halt, halt!" and then he motioned, "or else", and then he grabbed me. I was petrified, I put my hands up. We were told in the newspapers a few months before, that the Germans weren't taking any more prisoners, so you can imagine what I thought. He grabbed me and ripped my spare ammunition off.

There had been absolute panic. We could see the Germans in their grey uniforms, with their rifles and fixed bayonets; I had never seen a German before. I never saw an British officer, there was no command of any sort, we had to act on our own. A lot of the boys ran away to get out of it. You must remember that we were nearly all boys of eighteen and we were up against seasoned veterans, and when you see a lot of Germans coming with rifles and bayonets, well, I think you'd be a very brave man to wait until you were bayonetted, and they were big chaps, they looked so formidable in those big grey helmets. We were lads of eighteen, just boys.

I had to remove all my equipment and take off my gas mask and steel helmet, then, after about a quarter of an hour, they came along with some ground sheets and those who were not wounded carried us back to the German lines. We were not out of danger, as one of our own shells burst only fifty yards away at one point. I could hear it whizzing and saw the explosion, but thankfully nobody was hit, but it made me think that our own bombardment was nothing to deter the Germans. When we stopped, a German asked us if we were American or English, then he said "Don't worry, we are not going to kill you, but if you show any resistance or try and run away, you'll be shot," and that put our minds at rest. I was carried to a little dressing station about half a mile behind the lines where they put a bandage on my leg. We were all dazed, sort of shellshocked, the drum in my ear had been affected and I had difficulty hearing anything, it took a while to collect myself. I felt awful because we had been running away, but there was no alternative, the lines of communication had been cut, there was no command. For a couple of days we slept out in the open, and then they took us to a village called Abbey Fontaine, not far from Laon, and put some barbed wire around us and eventually an electric light was rigged up to see that we did not try and escape at night.

We had no food, and we couldn't speak German. After a few weeks my leg was getting better, so I was put to work carrying water in billy cans and digging latrines. Each morning we simply had a bit of black bread and then a few potatoes with their jackets on – well, fair enough – only glad to have them, but we were always hungry and always filthy dirty. One day in seven we were given off, when we were able to take our shirts and pants off to kill the lice in our clothes, but we stayed in our khaki for months, not until I was in a camp at Bremerhaven were we given clothes.

For weeks, my parents had no idea what had happened to me and this worried me. The Germans did not take our details until July, so all the information my parents received was that I had been reported missing. Not until I was in a German POW camp at Limberg was I allowed to write on a special card to send through Switzerland that Private Williams 757273, 5th Northumberland Fusiliers, was a prisoner of war in Germany and that I was alive and only slightly wounded. We were kept in France for at least two months, so my parents knew nothing until at least August and of course they feared the worst.

The Germans never hit us, there were never any physical attacks, but they used to curse us "bloody schweinehunde". The Germans used to smoke Turkish cigars, horrible things they were – and then they'd throw their stub ends over the wire, these Jerries, these bloody square heads, they used to think it very funny that these poor buggers would scramble for a fag, for a cigar end. The lads who smoked were so desperate for a fag they used to gather up the leaves in the autumn, cut them up, and with a bit of newspaper make them into a cigarette and have a smoke.

The Germans used to tell us through their interpreter, the Dolmetscher, they called him, they said it was our fault we had no clothes or proper food. "You schweinehund, it's your fault, you're not allowing any food to come into the country, we are hard up, we're starving, the children are hungry, you are the aggressors, therefore you deserve what you get." They said there were no

The lot of captured officers was sometimes better than that of enlisted men. Here British officer prisoners talk to members of the Red Cross at the camp at Heidelberg, Germany. TAYLOR LIBRARY

clothes in the country, there was no leather, soap, or fats to be had because of the blockade. The Germans told us they were fighting a righteous war, that God was on their side.

I was sent to work at the shipyards at Bremerhaven, at a place called Diestermunde at the mouth of the Weser. I was what was known as a catcherboy. Red hot rivets were thrown up to the side of the ship, and my job was to get hold of these rivets with some tongs and take them to be bolted down, helping to fix the plates on the side of the ship. You had to be careful, these rivets were thrown up in twos and threes and landed on the floor, you'd go and pick them up but you had to be careful not to tread on one and I've had to jump out of the road to avoid them. Mind, you were under their thumb so you had to damn well do as you were told.

By October it was very, very cold. We were living in an old warehouse and there was no heating. We had little underclothing, we just wore a shirt, underpants, trousers, socks and sabots – clogs – on our feet. On Sunday we used to have to wash our clothes in cold water, no soap, and try and get them dry otherwise our clothes would be wet for the next day. I thought if we could get some wood, we would be able to warm ourselves and we could get dry. Myself and a friend, a man called Hughes, managed to steal some wood on a couple of occasions but we were caught in the end and given two days' solitary confinement as a punishment.

On 11th November we had no idea it was Armistice Day. I was in a little hospital in Bremen. I had gone down from twelve to six or seven stone, my leg was giving me trouble, and my head was covered in sores from malnutrition. One night I heard some noise, it sounded like rifle firing and I asked a German guard what was going on but was told it was nothing, "nichts, nichts". It wasn't until three or four days later that a doctor was coming round and I noticed he was no longer in his army uniform but in civilian clothes. I asked him and he said "There's an Armistice, but it's only for a few days, it'll start again, you'll see." We didn't know anything else for a fortnight because we were so isolated. We had no newspapers, there was no radio in those days. I was sent under armed guard back to Bremen and carried on working for a few more days before we were told that we weren't to work any more, the war was over.

We couldn't believe our luck that after all this time the war had finished and we should go back to England. But so many of the men were ill, a lot of them were dying from the Spanish flu epidemic. The clothes used to hang off them and their faces were thin. Their arms were thin, their legs were thin, they were not in a position to work, they could hardly stand, some of them. There were men of all nationalities in the camp – French, Belgians, there were some Russians, great big fellows who were now all skin and bones, scores and scores died and we had to dig the graves. In Bremen there was an Australian called Wheatley, he was an engine driver from Sydney, and he was in the next bed to mine. He died and that upset me terribly. He'd been a prisoner for a couple of years and was as thin as a rake, he looked desperately ill – no resistance. It was very sad.

CHAPTER ELEVEN

Road to Victory

THE final collapse of the German war machine in October and November 1918 brought about an Armistice that few expected. For victory came less than nine months after the Allies had appeared in mortal danger of defeat, as they reeled from the Germans' massive March Offensive. This was made possible when Russia sued for peace in November 1917. Peace on the Eastern Front allowed the German army to transfer a million men to the Western Front for a last major onslaught to break the resistance of the Allied armies in France. For the cracks in the German army were already beginning to show: up to 10% of soldiers deserted while being transferred from east to west. The German High Command was also well aware of the increasing number of American soldiers arriving on the Western Front.

The launch of the German offensive on 21st March resulted initially in a great but not a decisive success, and so further efforts were made at different parts of the line in April and finally in May. The casualty figures for both sides were enormous, but while offensive action always stretches the lines of communication and supply for the attacker, the opposite is generally true for the defender. German forces inevitably thinned as they pushed deeper into Allied territory, with physical and mental exhaustion increasingly evident. Poorly fed, ill-equipped and low in morale, German troops over-ran British canteens and supply depots, discovering how much better supplied the Allied troops were. The offensive stalled, and while June and July saw a stalemate on the Western Front, the tide of the war was decisively turning in favour of the Allies. German defeat was inevitable, and was secretly acknowledged by the German High

The German offensive finally ground to a halt in May 1918. The Allies took the initiative in August and began to push the Germans back, with spectacular results. By October the trenches, which had so characterised the Western Front, were abandoned as open warfare resumed.

IWM Q 11757

Command from August onwards.

As the Allies launched renewed attacks in August and September, the Germans were pushed back, no longer by hundreds of yards but by miles. The German retreat was in general orderly, but large numbers of prisoners, many little more than boys of fifteen or sixteen years old, were taken. They were cold and hungry and, according to the British soldiers who were there, usually glad to be out of the war. During the last 100 days of the war nearly a quarter of the German army in the field was taken prisoner, and half of its guns were captured.

Trench warfare was left behind by late September and the war took to the roads, British troops liberating towns and villages that had been under German occupation for four years, undamaged by war. The civilians were often jubilant, although many of them complained bitterly that the retreating Germans had stripped them of all remaining foodstuffs, particularly cattle, horses, and even dogs. German rations were meagre and made of ersatz ingredients, ground acorns used in coffee, fine sawdust in bread. As the British troops pushed on, they discovered the carcasses of dead horses alongside the roads, sometimes with great hunks of meat taken out of them, at other times almost stripped bare.

The similarities between the German retreat of 1918 and that of the British in 1914 were increasingly clear. By October, warfare was being conducted in the open countryside. Determined and often courageous German rearguard actions held up the Allied advance, with carefully positioned machine guns at cross-roads and the blowing up of bridges – reminiscent of actions taken by the British after the Battle of Mons. Even the cavalry, not really seen since September and October 1914, made a belated and final battlefield reappearance in the corresponding months of 1918, harassing the retreating Germans and disrupting communications.

ROYCE McKENZIE

Royce McKenzie
1917

Despite being on the Western Front since 1916, Royce McKenzie remained one of the few perenially lucky soldiers. From March 1918 until the end of the war, a period which saw the largest number of casualties, Royce was never hit. He finished the war at Mons, where it had all started.

The Germans broke through the Portuguese in March 1918 and we had to retire out of line, all together. I says to Bill Nielson "Come on, Bill, we've got to make us way back now." We'd no sooner got on road than we came across a group of Canadian soldiers, I think they'd got lost and got mixed up with us. They were just to our right, going up a track, when all at once these machine guns started out right into these Canadians, ripped 'em all up, killed them all. Bill was just in front of me, and I managed to knock him into a hole that had been used as a cesspit, with me on top. Anyway the gun stopped firing and I looked up and could see this 'ere bloke top side of me, and I could see where bullet had gone in his brain, aye and he was just twitching. The whole lot of them were dead bar this one, he was still alive, but you could see it wasn't long before he'd be gone. I said to Bill "I'm not going to be taken prisoner. If I can get out I'm going to walk out there and you do the same." I said "Don't duck and dive, just keep walking." If we'd run, they'd have fired, I'm sure of it. I think by walking it surprised them that we got out of that bunch, eight or nine dead there were, anyway they never fired a shot at us.

We walked into a little copse and who should be there but a high-ranking officer sitting on a horse. He said "Who are you?" I said "Drake Battalion, Naval Division." He said "Oh, where's all the battalion?" I said "They've gone back, sir, we had to retire out of line because Jerry had broke through," and I thought to myself, if you don't get out soon you'll be captured an' all.

We walked back. It was a hot day and we'd had nothing to eat or drink so when we came across a shell hole with water in, we wet our mouths despite the water being tinged red with blood. Soon after, we came to a small river where there was a bridge and who should be there but the Adjutant. He says "No wonder they call you Lucky Mac! Are there are more of you? I've got about 150 out of the company and there might be some more further on." He says "Can you do me a favour, can you find transport for me?" The transport was about two miles back and they had a shock when they saw us. I had a shock too. Two chaps I knew were looking through kit bags belonging to troops. I said "What are you doing?" He says "I were just looking in bags." I said "You what! How do you know they're dead? I've got a good mind to bloody shoot you, you are doing something that's not right. These blokes might still be alive and you're

German prisoners watching Canadian Highlanders during the advance of August 1918.

raiding their bags." Anyway, I told him I'd been sent back to get transport up to lads. "They've had three days and three nights without a wink of sleep and nowt to eat, no drinks either." I said "The Adjutant is waiting, so you'd better get something down for those lads as soon as possible."

Jerry was eventually held, and for a time we remained where we were, being made up with reinforcements, getting quietly ready to push him back. Then it started, we pushed forward towards Bapaume. We began taking lots of prisoners, at one point we came across twenty down an old dugout in a former German trench. We motioned for them to come out after letting Jerry see a Mills bomb, and except for one who was a bit awkward, they put their hands up. The Germans were retreating now, and we were coming across some of our prisoners who had been held behind the lines. These lads were just walking back, and one of the first I saw was Dickie Westfield, a lad from Bristol. He'd been a runner like me but had been taken prisoner. He was only a little fellow and when he saw me, tears rolled down his cheeks, in relief I suppose at seeing a few of our lads, and he says "Mac, you're still at it", and cried his heart out. I asked him where his boots were and he said "The buggers has took me boots off me." It was a bit rough walking without anything on your feet, shell splinters

The Mons Gate at the Belgian town of Maubeuge. The town, liberated from German occupation, was close to where the fighting had begun back in August 1914. TAYLOR LIBRARY

and barbed wire, so I took my puttees off and wrapped 'em around his feet. I says "That'll help ye on until you can get some boots, Dick." "I'll see you after, sometime, I hope," he said, but I never saw him again. It gives you that feeling when I saw that, that you hated the Germans for what they'd done.

We were waiting to go over the Canal du Nord but was held up because the Germans were still in the gatehouse. I could see an officer of B Company, he was hit, and a petty officer of the same company, he was dead and laid in the dry canal. There were about twenty of us in a bit of trench, when this here shell come right in middle of us, killing three and wounding another seven. I was unhurt. I was helping to bandage the survivors when up came the Adjutant and he says "What the hell's going on here?" Then he saw me, "You again, McKenzie!"

The Lewis gun was turned on the gatehouse and we could see the Germans running out and away, they weren't bothering about fighting or anything like that. We saw what they were eating, we came across some of their black bread and how they managed on that we just didn't know.

We were at Mons when the war ended, we were back on the battlefield where it had all started. Soon after, the C.O. rode up on his horse and said everything's stopped, and that was it, we moved to a little village called Dour, a mining village, and were billeted on the local people. I was billeted with an old couple who were very relieved that the Jerry had been kicked out. They had very little at all, Jerry had taken everything from them. The lads brought up blankets for the troops but some were dished out to the local people, and by the following morning these ladies were walking about in overcoats, they'd spent the night converting them.

Because I was a miner I was demobilised quickly. I do remember playing the Engineers in a cup-tie in Mons, which we lost 1-0, and soon after that I was sent back to England. They were all in bed when I got home, it was the middle of the night, so I got down on the front door step and went to sleep. My mum came to the door in the morning and got a shock. She said "How long have you been here?" I says "About two or three hours." Oh, they made a right fuss then, when I got home.

ANDREW BOWIE

During the last two months of the war, the trenches that had been such a part of life on the Western Front were left behind forever. Open warfare resumed, and the fighting resulted in the last casualties of the conflict, as Andrew Bowie poignantly remembers.

On the 3rd of October, I went over the top on my 21st birthday, and they were the last trenches I left. After that it was open warfare, and by the middle of October the Germans were certainly going back. We were confined to roads more than cross country, and it was a treat to be a soldier then after being in the trenches. Behind the

*Andrew Bowie
1917*

197

German lines we found that the French inhabitants had still been using the fields for agriculture. Our advances were during the day, held up at night by the German rearguard who fired their machine guns down the main roads. Mines, or rather shells, were wired up together to blow up a crossroads, to impede us, to slow us up. The Germans pulled back so quickly, and their retreat was one of the most orderly you could wish for. They hardly left a tin can when they pulled out; you would have thought they would have left equipment, guns, all sorts. As we passed through villages which had just been liberated, the flags would come out, and the civilians would cheer us by the roadside, especially when we had the band going and the pipers were playing.

We took a young prisoner. The Germans had pulled back and had had to leave him. I was assisting the intelligence officer, and they brought this boy to the officer; he was only about sixteen and the area just above his hip had been shot away by shrapnel. Oh, it was a bad wound, it was bleeding a lot at the back. This poor child could speak a little English and he said his mother had told him that at the first opportunity he was to give himself up to the English, they would look after him. He was a nice-looking boy, a healthy-looking lad with a big face. The fellows came in to look at him, about a dozen of us, and they were giving him chocolate. He could eat a little. They felt he was their own brother, there was an atmosphere of love, he wasn't the enemy then, he was a mother's son. The stretcher bearers put him in a blanket and carried him. The poor little soul, he died on the way down. You felt so sorry, he was the enemy really, but you couldn't help but feel for a little kid being killed like that. It was all fruitless.

A very young German soldier lies dead on the battlefield. Such sights often engendered great sympathy from enemy soldiers. IWM Q1284

HAL KERRIDGE

As each new Allied thrust was made, fewer and fewer Germans had the stomach to stand and fight. A veneer of resistance was often broken within a couple of hours before a retreat. Hal Kerridge took part in one of the last offensives of the war, when crack German troops made a concerted effort to fight.

Not long after I got back, my Battalion was ordered to take part in a major attack. Most attacks on enemy trenches were made at dawn. However, in late summer 1918 I was to take part in a night attack across the La Bassée Canal. It was a big attack, about two or three miles width. The first thing we had to do was get across, to dig what we called posts on the German side of the canal, not true trenches but holes about thirty yards apart for cover whilst the attacking force assembled for the big do which was to come. We knew where the enemy trenches were, otherwise there wasn't much to guide us, all we could hope for was to see silhouettes, a line of trees that looked like lamp posts with their branches missing, that sort of thing.

If you knew what a barrage was, and thank God you don't, you'd realise that the noise was terrific. Guns were going, heavy guns at the rear, field guns in front of them. In front of the field guns there are lines of machine guns and infantry fire. And on the other side there are the Germans doing the same thing because when they are being fired at, they will fire back. The whole atmosphere was one chaotic mess of shrapnel and bullets, of metal flying about, screams and wallops. And there

Hal Kerridge 1918

you are crouched in the front line waiting to go. The feeling was always "Oh for God's sake let's get it over." You knew you would have to go, so the longer you delayed the worse you felt, just like waiting for the dentist's chair. You sit and wait, all waiting to go together, waiting until you hear either a whistle or a signal to go to be part of what we called the PBI, the Poor Bloody Infantry.

Over we went. Some of us got knocked out straightaway, most of us didn't. I was trying to keep a straight line, hoping to see the outline of things I'd seen in daylight. I reckon I was somewhere about twenty yards from the German trenches when I got hit and I went down immediately. I was hit in the back, shrapnel or bullet, whatever it was had gone through the upper part of my kilt into me. I couldn't apply a bandage, and I had no way of knowing how bad the wound was. I couldn't do anything but lie in No Man's Land in the dark and I began to panic. I didn't know if I could get back to our own lines. If our attack was repulsed, the Jerries would come over the top and we who were lying there, well, the wounded had an even chance of being shot, bayonetted, or taken prisoner and I didn't want any of those.

I was within hearing distance of the German trenches and there was an awful lot of noise, shouting and bawling and instructions being given, Germans shouting, British shouting, hand to hand fighting I suppose; hell's panic loose. Guns firing, the clatter of machine guns everywhere. I could hear other men calling out "Stretcher bearers!" but you could call stretcher bearers for ever, there were not that many about. I was capable of crawling back and got within ten yards of our barbed wire when I got up and ran. In front of the barbed wire there's what we call the trip wire, well, I hit the trip wire and went head first into the barbs, cutting myself to pieces on our own bloomin' wire – bare limbs with a kilt too! Oh it's vicious stuff, all in coils, you release yourself from one barb and find you're caught somewhere else. It had been out there for months, years on end, and was rusty as hell so if you got torn up on it the chances are you'd get blood poisoning straightaway.

I could feel blood running down my arms and legs. You're hurt and you're being hurt by the barbed wire and you struggle, you struggle mighty hard and you get out of it, somehow.... I got back into our lines, it all happened so quickly. I was glad to be out of it – temporarily anyway.

FREDERICK HODGES

Fred Hodges had been drafted over to France only months earlier to help halt the enemy offensive. By June, when the German push petered out, Fred had seen enough action to qualify as a seasoned soldier, and had survived many close scrapes. He remained on the Western Front until the last day of the war.

A German field gun seized towards the end of the war. Artillery pieces were prized battlefield gain, and capturers usually chalked their unit name along the barrel. IWM Q 11243

Younger and younger German boys were being captured at the end of the war. These three look no older than fourteen or fifteen. IWM Q6133

We got down to this place where the Australians had made an attack. We were mopping up any remaining Jerries, sending them back as prisoners, when we came to some German guns which had been written on in chalk. The words said "Captured by the 1st AIF", in other words, the Australian Imperial Force. We cheered out loud, we were ecstatic. The Australians were making such quick progress because the Germans were pulling back, leaving their field guns behind, something we never thought possible. In all those battles of the Somme and Ypres, we had advanced such a little way really, and, as for capturing guns, well, we never got anywhere near them. But a victory that went all through the lines of infantry and reached the guns, to be able to chalk on them, it was like winning the pools.

We were exhilarated, moving forward, it was something to cheer about, like scoring a goal. We came to what had been the rear of the German line and we went down into several dugouts and slept there, a place where the Germans had lived safe from any danger. We could still smell cigar smoke and we joked that this must have belonged to a millionaires' battalion.

Then we pushed on, and came to the place where the Germans had had a gun shelling Paris. It was a huge gun on a railway track and this too had been captured. At another place we were able to bathe in a river: imagine the satisfaction and laughter to think we could have a bathe in a river. I then heard that a train load of Germans had been captured because they thought they were going up to the Front, only to find the Front was in our hands.

'Prisoners were docile and were thankful they were prisoners. I didn't feel any anger towards them, rather, I just thought what an untidy-looking lot they were.' TAYLOR LIBRARY

I felt that the war was near the end because we were capturing men who were not infantry, old men with long tail coats with buttons on, cavalry probably, and boys of sixteen. Neuville was the last place where Jerry fought like the Germans can fight, and they defied us for eight days and inflicted heavy casualties.

We were liberating villages which had been untouched during the war. Civilians could be seen coming back with hand carts and luggage on them, surveying their devastated property. The Germans were intent on saving their lives, and prisoners were docile and were thankful they were prisoners. I didn't feel any anger towards them, rather, I just thought what an untidy-looking lot they were.

The last village we entered was on the night of 10th November. It was eerily quiet until two women opened their door to see who we were, and when they saw our uniforms they screamed "Les Anglais, les Anglais!" The Germans, they told us, had left earlier that evening and had posted a machine gun at the far end of the village, but, when we looked, it was gone. We returned to the house and found that the women had wasted little time in opening an old oak chest and producing the French Tricolour and some hot coffee.

CHAPTER TWELVE

Armistice and Aftermath

WHILE all the evidence showed that the Germans were in full flight back to the Rhine, most men had become so immune to the possibility of peace that news of its arrival was more often met with silence and disbelief, than with cheering and excitement.

Ironically, the war finished where it had all started some 1559 days earlier, at the small Belgian town of Mons. A few men of the original British Expeditionary Force of 1914, who had contrived to survive four years of war, found themselves only a couple of miles from the place where they had stood during the battle of Mons in August 1914. Indeed, at the moment of peace one contingent of Allied troops actually arrived on the Mons-Brussels road at the very spot where the first action by the British Expeditionary Force had taken place. The fight then had involved British mounted cavalry with their swords against German mounted cavalry with their lances, a far cry from the mechanised war machines used by the combatants in 1918.

The face of war had completely changed. Machine guns, heavy artillery and aeroplanes had come into their own, while the war had in effect seen the advent of poison gas, flame throwers, handgrenades, mortars, and tanks on the battlefield. The casualty rates of 1914 bore no comparison to those of 1918, in fact, those of the last year of the war numerically outweighed those of any other year of the conflict. It was the prolonged and sustained nature of industrialised warfare which had been different. No troops had ever been expected to remain in the battle zone for so long, and in such appalling physical conditions, as they had on the Western Front. Little surprise, then, that when despatch riders toured the battlefield distributing the news that the war was due to end at 11am, they were often met with bemusement and disbelief. The overwhelming impression given by most soldiers on the battlefield that day was that the Armistice was the cause of depression rather than of happiness. Many soldiers talked of feeling lacklustre and aimless; the end of the war, rather than providing an emotional uplift, was more akin to an anticlimax.

The public outpouring of relief and happiness at the Armistice produced scenes of great celebration throughout Great Britain, in contrast to those on the Western Front. Politicians quickly made promises that Britain would be a fit place for heroes to live in, promises they were never to keep. There was a great public clamour for retribution against Germany and resolutions were made to hang the Kaiser, to try many others as war criminals, and to make the German people pay huge reparations for their folly. The Versailles Peace Treaty of June 1919 would seek to impose many of these harsh penalties, yet for the average British Tommy who had fought the war, there was little desire to punish the Germans. Those, for example, who went to the Rhineland with the occupying forces in December 1918 often found the Germans compliant and very friendly. It left many of them wondering if the war had been worth the sacrifice.

ANDREW BOWIE

The last day of the war, of course we didn't know it was, we had fallen out by the side of the road and suddenly we heard the patter of horses' feet and round the corner came a squadron of cavalry. There they were, sitting on their horses, looking proud. And you should have heard the remarks. "Oh, they've come on their gee-gees to help us finish the war," and "Oh, they haven't brought their hobby horses with them." They had gone through about an hour or so when we got word the war was over. We were right opposite a convent and all the nuns came out and decorated us with flowers, and they stuck them in our rifles, and we moved off and were cheered along. We were happy but we remained fairly calm.

I was like a lot of fellows after the war, I was very depressed. I had been in the accountancy world as a boy, and I went to ask my firm to take me back again, but they couldn't – they were a small firm and unable to afford it. I was happy to get out of the army and get home, but the prospects were very bad. You go away as a boy and come back as a man. What are you going to do? There were so many people like that. There seemed to be no future for you. There were hundreds of thousands all in the same boat.

GEORGE LOUTH

I left the Somme Battlefield behind me in December 1916 and was invalided out of the army. I had been deafened by all the shelling so from that time until the end of the war I was sent to work on a farm near Blandford, and tried to put the fighting out of my mind. When the Armistice came it didn't interest me, I didn't take any notice of it really. I was interested in being married, bringing up kids, seven of them! I was interested in my job. All things else disappeared. I didn't want to talk about the war, I didn't want anybody to know my business at all. Nobody. No, there was nobody interested anyway, so it would have been useless telling them and if you did they would only laugh at you, say it wasn't true. It wasn't a conscious thing, nobody talked about the First War in those days, even my wife, even she never heard my story and we were married seventy years. I blanked out the war, the whole time after I got demobbed, and only once spoke about it from 1918 until 1990. It was with the woman whose husband was blown to pieces, she came to my house in Portsmouth and asked me what happened to him. I told her and she went away satisfied with the answer because she had been told he was wounded and missing. Wounded and missing! Rubbish, he was blown to bits.

George Louth
1926

204

NORMAN COLLINS

I had recovered from my wounds and I'd been given a permanent commission in the Indian Army when the Armistice came along. I was on leave and I was up a bit late that morning, I was shaving, and the sirens went. My first feeling was "It's too late – all my friends are gone – it's too late. It's no good having an Armistice now." I had a vision and I was standing in a trench and at eye level there were feet marching, marching feet going along, and these were all the men I had known who were killed in the war. And they were marching away into the distance where I would never follow. All the people I knew had gone. Except me.

Norman Collins 1917

My lance corporal was a Lewis gunner, called Meikle. We got to know each other very well because every night, every four hours, I used to go and visit him in his forward position out in No Man's Land, because he would be posted there in case of a counter attack or a raid. He was the same age as myself and he was only my height, tiny little chap, a bookmaker's runner in Glasgow. We got very close, we used to have long, long talks and he would tell me all about his life. After I was wounded in 1917, I heard that he had won the VC, Sergeant Meikle then, and he had been killed overwhelming a machine gun position on his own. He wouldn't have won it if I'd been there because I wouldn't have let him do it, I wouldn't have allowed such a silly thing, my dear old Sergeant Meikle. I went to have a look at his gravestone. I have a lovely picture and there I am, standing looking down, and Sergeant Meikle is young bones, of course, still young bones and there I am, nearly a hundred, standing on top – very old brittle bones with plenty of pain in them, but who won in the end? I mean, who had the better life? Nobody knows. Meikle died. Anyway he won't know, he has no memory and eventually I will go the same way.

GEORGE LITTLEFAIR

When the Armistice was signed, we had been moving up quickly for a while but we'd got bogged down in this ploughed field. We were near a little village when Munro, an officer from Gateshead, he came round and told us to take it easy, because an Armistice was being signed at 11 o'clock in the morning. This was Sunday night. He told us to get a bit of rest and in the morning we'd get out and go to this little village, which we did. As we got there, the church bells started ringing, and one of our lot, a man called Slater, promptly disappeared. Munro was right, it was the Armistice. The local people were coming out shoving drinks on to us, you know, happy that the war was over. Anyway we went to look for this Slater, and we finds him sitting in the church playing the organ, playing the damned organ as happy as a sandman.

JACK ROGERS

The war was a terrible thing, all those lives that were lost, thousands and thousands and thousands, for what? As to what I did, I've got nothing to be delighted about in any way. I thought it was a terrible experience and I was only grateful to think I'd come out of it alive.

I arrived home to be met at the door by my mother and sisters. I nearly had a fit, I didn't know what to say. Oh it was marvellous to see everyone, my poor father who was a cripple sitting in a chair indoors, oh it was a moving experience and was for days afterwards. To be home again with them and to be free, I couldn't believe it and then of course I had to start a new life.

ALICE McKINNON

With the Armistice, the first thing the colonel did was he invited anybody off duty for a big dance, and we danced all the dances we could think of, the Highland Fling, Polka, Waltz, Veleta, Cake Walk even, all kinds. I had long curly hair and it fell from underneath my uniform in big curls. After the dance a doctor came to me and said "Hurry up now and get back and put up your hair." It was an awful disgrace to have your hair down!

HELEN GORDON-DEAN

A lot of nurses would like to have gone to France but they didn't, or couldn't. When I came back, I found there was such a lot of jealousy, I kept as quiet as possible about having been there. I'd done things they hadn't, and that's never popular, is it? I was so young then, and of course I felt the tops. To them, I shouldn't have gone to France, but I am definitely glad I did. It was history in the making, wasn't it? And we were part of it. Small, insignificant but true.

FREDERICK HODGES

We were told by a despatch rider at dawn that the war was going to end at 11am and my first thought was "So I'm going to live." I was stunned, total disbelief, and at the same time a secret and selfish joy that I was going to have a life. For months I had lived with the idea that my life belonged to my country and they can have it at any time, and I can't stop it. I couldn't say "I've had enough, I'm going home," or "Can I have a fortnight off?" but now I knew I was going to have a life after all.

I went back to our guns and found the crews quite nonchalant, they were just cleaning up. They had begun to fire just before 11am, at what I've no idea, anyway at the allotted time they had ceased fire and were now just clearing up the gun sites. I didn't want to talk, so I carried on walking over the battlefield. I noticed some German graves that had been hastily dug, with the dead

Frederick Hodges
1919

206

man's rifle turned upside and his helmet hung on top of the butt. They stood in threes and fives and once again I thought "Their parents don't know they're dead", but it now came home to me too that these graves were also now the graves of our former enemy.

FREDERICK TAYLER

Did I feel sorry for myself? I might have done. I felt a bit miserable on Armistice Day to think that it was only four weeks ago that I got wounded. I mean, if the war had ended just a month earlier I wouldn't have lost my leg. Too true. You just wonder, you wonder what the future holds. I was twenty when I lost my leg, you can't always think straight, so you hope for the best. I thought about my future a lot, because I was an apprentice to the printing trade and I knew that I wouldn't be able to stand very long, not in the first stages of recovery. It was something all amputees thought, we couldn't tell until we tried to get jobs, to get a living.

Still, there you are. I had my luck, I mean it's a wonder I wasn't blown to pieces, when you think a shell dropped six feet away. As we won the war I suppose you can't grumble, you'd done what you thought was necessary to be done. Some poor souls gone, but you managed to come through, scarred but not scared. No, I am more of a matter of fact person, you know.

LUCY WALTER

I suppose in a way I was heartbroken. When you're young, you can't realise and take in a lot, but you can still have an aching heart, you can really. I know from experience. It was then that I would miss my father so much. He'd been such a patient man. You see I wanted to know, questions. I must have driven the poor man mad sometimes with everlasting questions, but he was always patient and answered me as best he could, and if he couldn't, he'd say "Oh well, we'll have to look that one up." He was wonderful really. He was so kind and gentle. I used to lie in bed and go over that last walk many, many times, when we walked up that hill together holding hands. I can remember it now as if it was yesterday. I've never forgotten it, I never will, and that's been a lot of comfort to me many times in my life.

HARRY PATCH

I was on the Isle of Wight, at a place called Golden Hill Fort, that was our regimental depot at the time. I was A1 and on the next draft to go back and rejoin the regiment in Belgium. We were up on the firing range and they had told us that if the armistice was signed they'd send up a rocket. We watched for the rocket and about 11 o'clock we saw it go up. There was a lot of spare ammunition which we were using on the range and the officer said "Get rid of it, fire it out to sea, we don't want to carry it back". The fellow next to me started blazing away when I noticed that his rifle was across mine and I said "What the hell are you firing at?" He said "That bloody hut up there." I said "That's where the markers are!" All the markers on the targets were inside taking refuge on the floor as this lad fired live ammunition through their hut.

HAL KERRIDGE

The First World War was an experience the like of which had never been seen before and the world will never see again. I am glad I served, I wouldn't have missed the experience, and nearly every old soldier will tell you the same; they hated it, they abhorred it, they loathed it, but they wouldn't have missed it. You were there, you learned, you were taught to take orders, whatever they might be, and you were taught to execute those orders. If you were lucky, you're given a stripe or two and then you learn to give orders, and so you creep up the tree. It's an experience that can make or mar you for life but I have no regrets, none whatsoever. I came through it, and I came through it whole and healthy, fortunately.

There are so few of us left now. The younger generation are curious and they want to know, and that's why when we are asked we will perhaps talk about that war, but otherwise we prefer to brush it aside and say nothing. It's past, it's gone, it's finished.